Helen Matthews Lewis

Helen Matthews Lewis

Living Social Justice in Appalachia

Helen M. Lewis

EDITED BY PATRICIA D. BEAVER AND JUDITH JENNINGS

UNIVERSITY PRESS OF KENTUCKY

Excerpts from *It Comes from the People: Community Development and Local Theology*, by Mary Ann Hinsdale, Helen Matthews Lewis, and Maxine Waller; "Introduction" by Helen Matthews Lewis, in *Images of the Appalachian Coalfields*, by Builder Levy. Used by permission of the Temple University Press, © 1989 by Temple University. All rights reserved.

"No Ordinary Teacher: Helen Lewis of Highlander" by Patricia A. Gozemba, in *Pockets of Hope*, ed. Patricia A. Gozemba and Eileen de los Reyes. Copyright 2001, reproduced with permission of ABC-CLIO, LLC.

Scholarly publisher for the Commonwealth,
serving Bellarmine University, Berea College, Centre College of Kentucky, Eastern Kentucky University, The Filson Historical Society, Georgetown College, Kentucky Historical Society, Kentucky State University, Morehead State University, Murray State University, Northern Kentucky University, Transylvania University, University of Kentucky, University of Louisville, and Western Kentucky University.
All rights reserved.

Editorial and Sales Offices: The University Press of Kentucky
663 South Limestone Street, Lexington, Kentucky 40508-4008
www.kentuckypress.com

Unless otherwise noted, photographs are courtesy of the Helen Matthews Lewis Papers, W. L. Eury Appalachian Collection, Special Collections, Appalachian State University.

The Library of Congress has cataloged the hardcover edition as follows:

Lewis, Helen Matthews.
  Helen Matthews Lewis : living social justice in Appalachia / Helen M. Lewis ; edited by Patricia D. Beaver and Judith Jennings.
    p.   cm.
  Includes bibliographical references and index.
  ISBN 978-0-8131-3437-6 (hardcover : alk. paper)— ISBN 978-0-8131-3454-3 (ebook)
   1. Lewis, Helen Matthews. 2. Women political activists—Appalachian Region, Southern—Biography.
3. Political activists—Appalachian Region, Southern—Biography. 4. Women college teachers—Tennessee, East—Biography. 5. Social movements—Appalachian Region, Southern—History—20th century. 6. Social justice—Appalachian Region, Southern—History—20th century. 7. Community life—Appalachian Region, Southern—History—20th century. 8. Appalachian Region, Southern—Social conditions—20th century. 9. East Tennessee State University—Faculty—Biography. 10. Appalachian Region, Southern—Study and teaching (Higher)—History—20th century. I. Title.
  HN79.A127L49 2012
  303.3'72092—dc23
  [B]
                               2011034188
  ISBN 978-0-8131-4520-4 (pbk. : alk. paper)

This book is printed on acid-free paper meeting the requirements of the American National Standard for Permanence in Paper for Printed Library Materials.

Manufactured in the United States of America.

Member of the Association of
American University Presses

Contents

Illustrations

Acknowledgments

OUR FIRST THANKS must go, of course, to Helen Matthews Lewis for her lifelong commitment to social justice. This book would not have been possible without her faith, her vision, her words, and the time, care, and patience she gave us over the last three years. Although we have managed to keep the focus on Helen here, it was no easy task. In her generosity of spirit, she constantly guides and deflects us to the important work of all those whom her life has touched. We are deeply grateful and truly humbled by working with her on this enterprise.

Gurney Norman, novelist, poet laureate of Kentucky, and Appalachian studies activist, first inspired the book by suggesting the value of a Helen Lewis reader to Laura Sutton, who was then an editor at the University Press of Kentucky. Gurney further suggested that Judith Jennings take a leading role in putting together such a reader. Judi consulted with Helen and other women friends attending the conference of the Appalachian Studies Association in Knoxville in 2007. At a gathering at the home of Mary Thom Adams, a happy band of women—including Helen, Mary Thom, Beth Bingman, Amelia Kirby, Judi, Patricia D. Beaver, and others—agreed to work together to develop a reader that would capture the range and diversity, the challenges and joys, the lessons and reflections, we all witness in Helen's life.

That same year, Pat Beaver began acquiring Helen's papers for Appalachian State University (ASU). Pat moved boxes of files, clippings, notes, and photographs from Helen's house in Georgia to the ASU campus in Boone, North Carolina. These treasures went first to Pat's office, on their way to their permanent home in the W. L. Eury Appalachian Collection archives. As an important first step, graduate assistant Zach Fulbright compiled an initial list of all the published and unpublished papers and reports in the collection.

Helen, Judi, and Pat began working together on this manuscript in brainstorming sessions at the Center for Appalachian Studies at ASU in 2008. Zach volunteered to help and enthusiastically converted the extensive written notes from a whiteboard into the first spreadsheet of texts, tracking all those preliminarily selected to be excerpted. Graduate assistant Seaton Tarrant traveled with Pat back to Georgia to gather up final items, taking notes as Helen narrated names and places from her photo albums. Seaton scanned and prepared the first full-text digital files of Helen's papers. Several cohorts of graduate student assistants then organized, cataloged, and retyped the papers selected for inclusion in this collection. Graduate assistants Brittony Fitzgerald, Tracey Jerrell, Katie Phillips, Danielle Rector, and Rachel Westrom and undergraduate students Hayley Sherman and Ashia Tabb retyped Helen's unpublished speeches and papers, proofread and cataloged material, and moved the book process forward in many other valuable ways. Graduate student Donna Corriher proofread the entire final manuscript. Office manager Debbie Bauer supervised the work of each of the students, deflected telephone calls, and applied her MLA skills to the bibliography.

During the first work session in 2008, Pat's neighbor and retired Spanish teacher Mary Boyer helped us come up with the title: *Living Social Justice.* Subsequently, Jeff Boyer, ASU anthropologist and Highlander Center board member, provided encouragement and a bibliography for chapter 2. Sandra L. Ballard, editor of the *Appalachian Journal,* offered editorial advice, friendship, and wise counsel from the beginning of the project to its completion, as well as editing the final text of the bibliography. Fred Hay, professor and librarian of the W. L. Eury Appalachian Collection at ASU, provided editorial advice, as well as sure attention to Helen's papers in his oversight of cataloging them, along with reference librarian Greta Browning.

We are grateful to the *New York Times* and Temple University Press, respectively, for permission to use the photograph of the Children's Campaign of 1946 and excerpts from *It Comes from the People.* Appreciation also goes to Sandra Ballard for permission to reprint excerpts from four articles published in the *Appalachian Journal,* which she edits. Dr. Fred Hay of ASU's University Archives and Records generously gave us permission to use a wide range of writings from the Helen Matthews Lewis materials in the W. L. Eury Appalachian Collection. Susan Williams, who oversees the library at the Highlander Research and Education Center, granted permission to use their printed materials. Dr. Patricia A. Gozemba gave us permission to reprint excerpts from her essay "No Ordinary Teacher," which appears in her book *Pockets of Hope,* coedited with Eileen de los Reyes.

Many thanks to the chapter introducers, who not only provided brilliant overviews and contextualizing information but also made sound suggestions concerning the selections of texts and additions to the bibliography. Great appreciation to Helen's friends near and far who contributed beautiful nuggets of friendship and insight interspersed throughout the book. Steve Fisher not only produced an outstanding introduction but also supported the idea and development of the book from the very beginning and through all its stages. Steve wishes to thank Larry Richman, saying the introduction is better because of him.

Cate Fosl, director of the Anne Braden Institute at the University of Louisville, always gave a willing ear and good advice to Judi and offered especially helpful suggestions about the writing of the "Final Word." Pam McMichael, executive director of the Highlander Center, made us welcome, as did Susan Williams, who also assisted with library resources for our final meeting at Highlander during the center's homecoming in 2010. Judi's sister Becky Hornbeck Hague responded with helpful technical assistance on at least two occasions when Judi needed it most.

Thanks to Laura Sutton, who helped us develop the book from an idea to a successful proposal, before leaving Kentucky for Georgia, and to Anne Dean Watkins, who cheerfully took over from Laura and helped us through the final stages. The anonymous reviewers who read the proposal and the completed manuscript offered many useful suggestions for improvement. Equally important, they encouraged us to develop a format and style that aspires to reflect Helen's creativity and verve.

Special thanks to copyeditor Carol Sickman-Garner and to Ila McEntire, editing supervisor at the University Press of Kentucky, who worked with Judi to create a format that connects and clarifies Helen's memories and reflections alongside her scholarly writings and critical analyses. With their able assistance, this format embodies what Helen names in this book as the major goals of popular education: to recover experience, reflect upon it, understand it, and improve it.

We greatly appreciate the two dozen writers and publishers who graciously gave us permission to reprint their materials in this collection. We are deeply grateful to each and every one.

Friends and colleagues throughout the region, across the country, and beyond our borders have responded to the idea of this book with deep enthusiasm. Many have expressed gratitude that Helen's work will now become more broadly accessible. We sincerely hope that each and every one of you enjoys reading this book as much as we loved working on it.

Introduction

Stephen L. Fisher

Many in the Appalachian studies community have been urging Helen Lewis for years to find the appropriate context to tell her story, to reflect upon a life that has been at "the nexus of social movements in the region calling for social, economic, and environmental justice" and in "the forefront of a new pedagogy, which envisioned student empowerment and community engagement" (see Patricia Beaver's introduction to chapter 2). At long last, Patricia Beaver and Judith Jennings, working in close collaboration with Helen, have created *Helen Matthews Lewis: Living Social Justice in Appalachia.* Using a chronological and thematic format, this book presents Helen's many accomplishments and contributions, viewing her life as a vantage point for exploring key aspects of the Appalachian movement during the second half of the twentieth century and the first decade of the twenty-first.

I am honored to have been asked to write the introduction for this important book. I have known Helen since the early 1970s, have benefited immeasurably from her spirit and mentoring, and have spent much of my political and intellectual life learning from and building upon her ideas and examples. Countless others could offer similar testimony on the various ways Helen has touched their lives, and some of them do so in brief essays throughout the book.

There are a number of ways to assess the legacy of a person's life work. The chronology and bibliography included as part of this book offer some notion of why Helen is considered by so many to be the most important public intellectual in Appalachia. She helped give birth to Appalachian studies and has taught and lectured at many of the leading educational institutions in the Appalachian region, mentored seminarians working in the mountains, and been involved in participatory research work and adult and community educational programs throughout the region and abroad. She is the author or editor of ten monographs and almost fifty articles, book chapters, and reports and is the subject of at least ten published interviews. (For a complete listing, see the bibliography.) She has served as president of the Appalachian Studies Association and in major leadership roles at two of the region's most well-known and -respected community-based institutions, the Highlander Research and Education Center and Appalshop. She has been a consultant on a wide variety of projects and an advisor to the Kellogg Foundation International Leadership Program. She has received four honorary degrees, is the recipient of more than a dozen awards, and has had three "named" awards created in her honor.

This listing underscores many of Helen's accomplishments and the respect she has earned regionally, nationally, and globally. Standing alone it makes the case for this book, but in no sense does her justice. There is far more to her story. Who are the people and what are the events that helped shape Helen's intellectual, political, and spiritual growth and led her to a life of activism and scholarship intimately connected to the major social movements of her time? In what ways have her moral courage, intellectual honesty, empathy, and faith in people enabled her to have such a profound impact on so many people and communities? What is the full nature of Helen's legacy, and what can we learn from that legacy and her life that will help us more effectively fight for social and economic justice in our communities, region, nation, and world? Answering these questions lies at the heart of this book.

Helen's story spans much of the previous century and the opening years of this one, and her impact on Appalachia is in a sense comparable to that of contemporary cranky and courageous antiracist white women, such as Lillian Smith, Virginia Durr, and Anne Braden, whose profound impact on southern history is well known. Like Helen, these unruly women were always a step ahead of their time, outside of traditional academic life and the accepted public arena, and they paid a heavy price for their vision of a just and humane world. Their stories, and others like them, have offered important new insights into the civil rights and women's movements and provided much-needed examples of women's social justice activism in the South. Comparable studies are hard to find for Appalachia, and *Helen Matthews Lewis: Living Social Justice in Appalachia* helps fill this crucial void.

Moreover, a book on Helen's life and work is especially timely at this moment in history. The Appalachian experience is highly instructive in light of the national and global economic, political, and environmental crises we currently face. Helen's story and writings underscore the systemic causes of these crises as they have played out in Appalachia during the past half century and offer examples of the ways in which Appalachians have chosen to fight back and of how one person can live a life that makes a significant difference. In addition, national election campaigns continue to bring forth many of the old stereotypes of Appalachians as ignorant, parochial, racist, and fatalistic. Helen's story offers a powerful counter to those negative images and stereotypes.

Drawing primarily from her published interviews, this book offers a narrative of Helen's life interwoven with relevant selections from her analytical writings. Each chapter begins with a brief introduction written either by one of the two editors or by a well-known scholar who worked with Helen during the time period covered in the particular chapter. Each chapter introduction is followed by Helen's recollections relating to the selected analytical texts and any needed contextualizing content by the scholar. This creative format reveals the intimate connections between her research and scholarship and her political engagement and work in communities.

The editors give Helen the "Final Word," where, looking both back and into the future, she reflects on her life and offers her take on the current state of the region and the world. Interspersed throughout the book are photographs of Helen at various stages of her life, as well as her poems, recipes, and gardening tips. Numerous essays by friends, former students, colleagues, and community activists testify to Helen's impact and influence. In sum, the editors, working with Helen, offer an innovative model that includes biography, memoir, critique, context, and testimony. Consistent with Helen's commitment to active learning and participatory research, this multifaceted format trusts you the readers, as teachers, students, and activists, to make meaning and find the lessons that apply to your own lives in Helen's life and writings.

The excerpts from Helen's academic, educational, and persuasive writings were selected based on their significance, their accessibility, and how each text advances the major theme of "living social justice" during the time period covered. The editors have included excerpts from published work that broke significant new ground in Appalachian studies but have also taken special care to include a wide variety of unpublished pieces that clearly demonstrate the broad scope of her intellectual and political work. The full texts of all excerpted selections and many of the other works listed in the bibliography are available to researchers in the Helen Matthews Lewis Papers, archived in the W. L. Eury Appalachian Collection at Appalachian State University in Boone, North Carolina.

Chapter 1 traces Helen's formative years growing up and attending college in northern Georgia and reveals how and why she began to confront rural poverty, racial segregation, economic injustice, and traditional gender roles. We see the origin of several values and beliefs that have remained consistent throughout her life: her willingness to take risks; her deep care and concern, inspired in part by a faith-based social justice message, for those who are suffering; her anger against injustice; and her increasing awareness of the interconnections among racism, sexism, and economic exploitation. We also see that Helen early on understood the importance of "subversive" research and of combining action, reflection, and writing. The major text in this chapter is an excerpt from Helen's master's thesis, written in 1949, in which she applies lessons from Gunnar Myrdal's groundbreaking critique of race relations in the United States to the struggle for women's rights. This remarkably insightful work is an early example of the comparative analytical skills and political commitment Helen would bring to her writing on Appalachian issues.

Chapter 2 focuses on Helen's initial experiences in the coalfields of southwest Virginia. As she learned from her students about the struggles of their families and communities, her impulse, as has been the case throughout her life, was to get involved in the issues around her. This led to her participation in struggles related to the severance tax on coal, strip mining, black lung, and union reform; to her insightful research on coalfield families and culture; to her adaptation of the colonialism model as a counter to prevailing mainstream notions of the causes of poverty in central Appalachia; and to the establishment at Clinch Valley College, as part of her social work curriculum, of what many believe to be the first full-blown Appalachian studies program in the region. As Patricia D. Beaver points out in her chapter introduction, the writings and speeches resulting from these activities (some of which are reprinted or excerpted here) helped to reframe for a new generation of scholars and activists (myself included) the most basic assumptions about Appalachian culture, community, and inequality. It was also during this period that the political and theoretical implications of her own unfolding analysis led Helen to adopt what was at that time a radical pedagogy that embraced local knowledge, participatory research, and popular culture and sought to empower students through engagement in the communities in which they lived and worked. Such activities did not go unnoticed by the powers-that-be. Under intense pressure from the coal industry, the college dismantled her program. This led Helen to a conclusion that has served her well throughout her life: if they want to fire you, they will find a way, so you might as well try and accomplish all that you want to do—don't ask for permission; just do it, and then ask for forgiveness.

Chapter 3 traces Helen's movement from the classroom to become, in the words of John Gaventa, a full-time public sociologist and "a *participatory* intellectual, who used her teaching and networking skills to *enable* others to learn and act for themselves." This chapter explores Helen's experience in Wales, including her ongoing research projects and the development of ex-change programs and travel seminars for American and Welsh coal miners. Through her actions and writing, she was among the first to demonstrate that an international perspective is crucial in helping combat the parochialism of Appalachian studies and strengthening political resistance in the region. The chapter also examines her role as director of a Highlander Center health proj-ect that included working with community clinics throughout the region and organizing and educating around environmental health issues. It concludes with a discussion of Helen's work as director of Appalshop's Appalachian His-tory Project, where she coordinated the work of filmmakers, researchers, and academic consultants developing a documentary film series on the history of the region. As she has done for most of her work, Helen reflected upon and wrote about what she learned from these various experiences, and selections of that writing included in this chapter reveal her ability and willingness to cross traditional boundaries; to stimulate discussion by raising crucial ques-tions for others to struggle with even when she doesn't have answers; and to question the validity of value-free education and research, while encouraging community people to become their own experts.

Chapter 4 focuses on Helen's participatory research methodology, ex-amining her work in Appalachian rural communities, especially in Jellico, Tennessee; McDowell County, West Virginia; and Ivanhoe, Virginia. In this work, Helen expanded on the theories of Paulo Freire and Myles Horton by incorporating feminist pedagogy and philosophy. She also saw how to draw on faith-based and cultural traditions and personal stories to demystify and analyze the economy. She became more fully aware of the worldwide movement of popular education and participatory research and, through her travels and research abroad, developed a more holistic approach to community development. Some of Helen's most important and insightful writing comes out of this period, including the influential *It Comes from the People: Community Development and Local Theology,* which she wrote with Maxine Waller and Mary Ann Hinsdale. Also of particular note are the excerpts from several pieces that explore the changing nature of women's work in families and communities in the coalfields and how and why rural and poor women were emerging as leaders of the most creative and progressive community-development efforts. This chapter also includes an example of Helen's ongoing critique of Appalachian studies—always a step ahead, always pushing others to look at the region and world in new ways. In sum, this chapter confirms the truth of Helen's view of herself as a catalyst—someone good at pulling together people and resources to facilitate educational encounters.

Chapter 5 describes the different ways Helen lived out and built upon the values, beliefs, and practices discussed above during the period that took her from Highlander back home to Georgia. Her work and writing became more prophetic and visionary, while remaining grounded in reality and offering concrete steps for action. She helped to mentor and train seminarians in the region, challenging them to live out a religion involving both faith and praxis in promoting justice for people and communities on the margin. She painted a picture of a moral economy while offering a twelve-step recovery program to help communities move in that direction. In an essay calling for a "clean glass of water for every Appalachian child," she helped focus attention on the next big extractive industry in Appalachia—taking the water out of the mountains. She continued to reflect on concrete ways that Appalachian studies could become a more effective resource for positive social change. She kept calling attention to the active role of women in community development. She worked with Monica Appleby to cowrite *Mountain Sisters: From Convent to Community in Appalachia,* celebrating the contributions of a group of former Glenmary Sisters in the region. A number of her writings during this period emphasize the importance of storytelling in social change. In a sense, that is what Helen spent most of her life doing: inspiring individuals and communities to reimagine and tell their stories to discover what we have in common and to construct new stories for a changing world.

Helen's story needs to be told, not simply to honor who she is and what she has done, but because of what she has to teach us. There are indeed countless lessons for readers in the pages that follow. I've chosen to comment briefly on just a few: what Helen has taught us about Appalachian studies, being a public intellectual, and how to "live social justice" in Appalachia.

Helen is quick to deflect the notion that she is the mother or grandmother of Appalachian studies, always naming other mothers and fathers. But there is little question that her program at Clinch Valley College served as the major catalyst for the current Appalachian studies movement and that no one has done more over the years to shape its direction than Helen. Just beginning an Appalachian studies program in 1969 was to make a controversial political statement and commitment, but to then ground it in student involvement in the region's major social movements was such a radical act at the time that it eventually contributed to the program's demise. But during the six years that it flourished, Helen and her students laid the foundation for what were to become and remain the defining elements of meaningful Appalachian studies curricula and programs. These include (1) following the philosophy of Paulo Freire by abandoning the traditional value-free "banking" approach to education, in which the student is simply a receptacle that receives, memorizes, repeats, and stores information, and developing instead a "problem-solving" approach based on a dialogue across disciplines in which students and teachers are jointly responsible and critical coinvestigators together; (2) focusing on the root causes of Appalachia's problems, not just their consequences; (3) helping students develop a knowledge of and pride in their communities and the region, encompassing a sensitivity to the area's problems, culture, and needs, while making a commitment to work for change; (4) using Appalachia itself as a learning laboratory so that students can acquire the skills needed to become agents of change; (5) implementing cross-cultural experiences for students to enable them to compare Appalachian problems with those of other areas; (6) broadening the notion of teachers to include those who directly experience the problems being studied; and (7) working to ensure that the resources of the region's colleges and universities are used constructively to attack the real problems of the area.

Helen became a circuit-riding Appalachian studies missionary, freely sharing her syllabi and visiting college campuses throughout the region. Many of us who benefited from her generosity and wisdom at the time have over the years implemented these principles in our courses and on our campuses and have preached the gospel to others. The fact that her principles speak to current best practices in the world of higher education, especially the emphasis on integration of knowledge and interdisciplinary thinking, service learning as community engagement, the application of research to solving local and regional problems, and the effort to encourage local to global connections, is a credit to Helen's foresight and determination.

Helen Matthews Lewis: Living Social Justice in Appalachia offers many examples of the ways that Helen's scholarship and work in communities have profoundly shaped the nature and direction of Appalachian studies. It serves little purpose to repeat them here. Suffice it to say that both her writing and her example have played a central role in ensuring that the Appalachian Studies Association (ASA) began as and has remained a place where community-based activists and Appalachian scholars can interact and inform each others' work and where scholarship designed to promote social justice in the region is encouraged and celebrated. You will read in the chapters that follow excerpts from some of Helen's analytical writings that challenged and changed major paradigms in Appalachian studies and that took the ASA to task when it showed signs of undue academicism and parochialism or of ignoring key trends and issues in the region. It is by no means a coincidence that Helen has served as the ASA's president and that it has named one of its major awards in her honor. She has served as its spirit and its conscience.

No consensus exists concerning what qualifies one to be considered a public intellectual. But whatever criteria are applied, there can be little doubt that Helen is one of the leading public intellectuals in the Appalachian region and arguably the most significant. In *American Power and the New Mandarins: Historical and Political Essays,* noted linguist and political thinker Noam Chomsky offers a simple and direct statement on what he believes is the responsibility of intellectuals: "to speak the truth and to expose lies" (325). This might seem enough of a truism to pass without comment, but Helen's experience offers a clear example of how trying to live out that responsibility in one's life is a complex, difficult, and sometimes painful endeavor.

Unlike many public intellectuals who spend their lives grounded in academic institutions and whose contributions to public life are defined primarily by what they write, Helen has pursued a different route in speaking truth to power. As noted, she most certainly has left her mark as a teacher. But she has spent most of her life outside of colleges and universities, working instead in adult learning settings, such as the Highlander Center and rural communities. Despite not being under the publish-or-perish mandate associated with university life, Helen is a prolific writer, whose analysis is almost always ahead of its time and wise and provocative enough to endure. She does not view herself as a particularly detailed researcher or creative writer, but more as a catalyst, who sees the broader picture, makes connections, and acts as an integrator who builds on other people's work and ideas and popularizes them. One of her greatest strengths is serving as a connector, building bridges locally, regionally, and globally among students, academics, cultural workers, coal miners, and community activists. She is a collaborator, both in her writing projects and in using her professional credentials to empower others, not by assuming the role of the expert, but rather by sharing information while encouraging folks to think for themselves. She has never separated her teaching and writing from her social activism or compromised her integrity, even if this meant sacrificing job security or ruffling feathers within the communities in which she worked. Helen has demonstrated what it means to live an integrated life of social engagement, described by cultural theorist Bruce Robbins as "putting together political commitment with the life of the mind" (37).

Perhaps motivated in part by the example of her grandmother, who spoke back to those in authority and wouldn't shut up, Helen Matthews Lewis has lived social justice throughout her life. She never planned to be an activist, but influenced by Clarence Jordan's "Cotton Patch Gospels" and nurtured by teachers who had been suffragettes, she became one during her college years, speaking out against economic injustice, joining the Young Women's Christian Association's national campaign against racism, and becoming involved in Georgia politics. She didn't want to leave northern Georgia, but once she arrived in southwest Virginia, she never looked back and quickly became converted by Appalachia as she witnessed the impoverishment of the coalfields and the injustices perpetuated by the coal industry. This speaks to one of Helen's many strengths as a social justice activist: her willingness and ability to respond to and shape the issues before her as she changed jobs and locations. It wasn't that Helen left behind her spiritual underpinnings and her passion for racial and economic justice and women's rights when she left Georgia; rather, she was able to channel them in ways that helped her confront what she was witnessing in Appalachia. Wherever Helen had ended up, she would have adapted. As she puts it in her "Final Word," if she had found herself living in the cotton fields, she would have been writing about and organizing around cotton.

Helen has been involved in a wide variety of social justice struggles. Indeed, her acumen for picking out important ideas or formulating issues is truly impressive. She brought no overarching ideology or strict agenda to her social justice work, but there are some common themes that reappear: connecting private troubles to public issues; the importance of culture and religion in promoting social change; a focus on the economy, the impact of capitalism, and sustainable community development; a transnational perspective; the growing strength of women as community leaders; the effectiveness of participatory research in empowering communities; and a commitment to the long haul. But from the very beginning, one overarching belief has shaped who she is and defined the nature of her work: a deep and abiding faith in the wisdom of ordinary people. As Richard Couto points out in his nomination of her for a Wonder Woman Award, excerpted in chapter 4, Helen's immersion in the lives, strengths, and struggles of ordinary people is the foundation of her achievements and creativity. Convinced that local people are best suited to solve their own community problems and create their own hopes and future, Helen, in her role as listener, researcher, challenger, and critical friend, has learned from them and then taken those lessons to the next level.

As an educator, scholar, activist, theologian, friend, and mountain sister, Helen has spent her life as a mentor helping others make hope practical and despair unconvincing. Speaking for myself, she has modeled for me the necessity of taking risks, following my passions, and embracing the unknown. She has shown me why I should not fear conflict and immoderation and demonstrated the importance of telling and constantly reinventing my story. Time and again, she has pointed the way to how I can better serve the various communities in which I live and work. She has also helped me understand that working for change means developing a sense of limits and cultivating a sense of joy—taking time to travel, make chowchow, sip an Old Fashioned, write or read poetry, take in a movie, plant a garden, dance to good music, or watch a sunset, while appreciating the beauty of the world we're trying to save. Most important, Helen teaches all of us that building relationships with others is at the core of living social justice. Doing the things that are necessary to build and maintain sustaining relationships over the long term is hard, risky, time-consuming work, but it is one of the most important things we can do as social justice activists. It is how we learn, where we get sustenance and courage, where we find hope. It is how we become connected to the joys and frustrations of people working for a better world. Helen's life story and analytical writings powerfully demonstrate that fundamental, long-term political and social change comes from the people and that working in relationship with others is what gives real meaning to individual lives.

CHAPTER 1

The Making of an Unruly Woman, 1924–1955

Judith Jennings

> I had a grandmother who loved to argue with preachers. She was Scotch Presbyterian, as she said, and she loved the Baptist preachers to come to the house so she could argue with them about predestination. And I see myself as I get older being more like this grandmother, who speaks back at things and won't shut up and says the wrong thing at the wrong time.
>
> —Helen Matthews Lewis, quoted in Lori Briscoe et al., "Unruly Woman: An Interview with Helen Lewis"

Helen Matthews Lewis grew up, attended college, became a social justice activist, and married in Georgia. She both loved and worked to change the land-based society that shaped her formative years. As she learned and developed, Georgia developed and changed, too. Urban growth and rural poverty, populism and progressivism, religious conservatism and religious radicalism, racial hatred and racial justice, traditional gender roles and new opportunities for women, galvanized her and her home state from the mid-1920s through the mid-1950s.

Helen's roots in Georgia run deep and shape many of her lifelong views and values. She grew up knowing that two of her great-grandfathers fought for the Confederacy during the Civil War. She saw how Georgia, like other southern states, enforced a rigid system of segregation, denying African American citizens their basic rights to vote, own property, and gain high-quality education. As a child, Helen recognized the power of racism. While still a young girl, she witnessed her father's kindness and respect for a Negro neighbor, but she also witnessed the effects of a memorable incidence of racially inspired community violence.

Growing up in rural Georgia meant that she understood rural poverty. Although her family was not poor, the town where she lived did not yet have a public water system or electricity. By the late 1920s, when she was a girl, the boll weevil had decimated the state's cotton economy, forcing many farmers to become tenants or sharecroppers. Many rural Georgians experienced structural poverty long before the Great Depression, which deepened, rather than caused, the economic inequality she critiqued as a young college student.

She also became keenly aware of the role of women and saw how women could claim power in a male-dominated society and how they could be punished for what were considered social transgressions. One grandmother, Mary Ida Dailey Matthews, the Scotch Presbyterian who argued with Baptist ministers, chopped down a family member's moonshine still. Another grandmother, Jane Victoria Harris, birthed a daughter without being married and lived the rest of her life in isolation and denial.

Despite, or perhaps because of, Mary Ida's argumentative Presbyterianism, Helen became more concerned with the power of religion to advance social justice rather than becoming attached to a particular denomination or doctrine. In 1941 Helen enrolled in Bessie Tift College, a private Baptist women's school in Forsyth. There, she heard Clarence Jordan preach his Cotton Patch Gospels. A homegrown social justice activist and Baptist theologian, Jordan taught economic justice and racial reconciliation by retelling New Testament scriptures in "Cotton Patch" versions, using language and settings familiar to rural listeners. Forty-seven years later, Helen vividly recalls the transformative impact Jordan's social justice gospel stories had on her.

While Helen studied at Bessie Tift, the United States entered World War II. As in other historical time periods, war accelerated the economic, social, and cultural changes already under way. Thousands of women went to work in greater numbers than ever before as men entered the armed services. Women also joined the armed services, swelling the numbers of WACs and WAVES. Although federal spending on the war effort began to end the Depression nationwide, Helen no longer had the financial resources she needed to continue her college studies and temporarily left school in 1942.

In 1943, Helen enrolled in Georgia State College for Women (GSCW), a public four-year liberal arts institution. Many of her teachers had been suffragettes, helping to win women's right to vote in 1920. At GSCW, Helen learned that women could be leaders. She worked with her classmate Mary Flannery O'Connor on the 1945 yearbook and became the yearbook editor in 1946.

Helen also became an activist, speaking out against economic injustice and joining the Young Women's Christian Association's (YWCA's) national campaign against racism. Helen's story of participation in the YWCA provides new insights into understanding the importance of this organization in the rural South.

When Georgia became the first state to allow eighteen-year-olds to vote, Helen joined the GSCW League of Women Voters. In 1946, with eighteen-year-olds going to the polls for the first time, Helen, now a graduate, moved to Atlanta to take part in the "Children's Crusade," a statewide effort mobilizing young voters to support a progressive candidate for governor. A photograph in the *New York Times* pictures her among the young leaders in the campaign. The progressive candidate lost, but Helen maintained what became a lifelong commitment to political engagement, human rights, and social justice activism.

Encouraged by GSCW faculty, she entered graduate school at Duke University. There she met Judd Lewis, a graduate student in economics. When she decided to discontinue her studies and return to Atlanta, he enrolled at Emory University there. They married in 1947, Helen envisioning "an egalitarian partnership marriage." She continued her social justice activism after her marriage. While he attended classes at Emory, she was arrested for participating in an interracial event in Atlanta sponsored by the YWCA.

When Judd accepted a job in Virginia, Helen entered a master's of arts program at the University of Virginia. In preparing her master's thesis, she analyzed Gunnar Myrdal's influential 1,500-page-book published in 1944, *An American Dilemma: The Negro Problem and Modern Democracy.* Extending Myrdal's groundbreaking work, her thesis, "The Woman Movement and the Negro Movement: Parallel Struggles for Rights," points to similar social and economic barriers facing both African Americans and women, predating the civil rights and the women's movements of the 1960s, as well as later postmodern theoretical constructs of intersectionality. Demonstrating her synthetic analytical skills and commitment to practical applications, she provides both a theoretical and a common-sense basis for alliances and cross-organizing between the two groups.

After Helen left Georgia, she did not live there again for nearly fifty years. Yet her knowledge of rural life formed during her youth in Georgia, the deep religious faith that inspired her commitment to social justice, and the conviction that she, as a woman, must take action against racism and economic exploitation shaped the rest of her life.

Family Memories

I was born in a little place out in the country from Nicholson, Georgia, which is 12 miles north of Athens in Jackson County. My father was a farmer when I was born, and he passed the test during the depression and became a rural letter carrier, which was wonderful because he had a job. So we were well off because he was a mail carrier. ("Unruly Woman: An Interview with Helen Lewis")

My grandmother on my father's side was Mary Ida Dailey. She was the daughter of James Monroe Dailey, a Confederate veteran. People always said, "he was so mean he didn't even die at Shiloh." After the war, he spent much of his time sitting around the courthouse with other veterans telling war stories. He apparently was a moonshiner and taught at least one of his sons the craft. Mary Ida Dailey married Daniel Presley Matthews, and their son Hugh Presley Matthews was my father. Mary Ida played the organ at the Presbyterian Church, and she strongly opposed drinking moonshine. The story is that she chopped up a still my [d]ad's brother was building. Mary Ida was the Scotch Presbyterian grandmother who liked to argue with the Baptist preachers.

My grandmother on my mother's side was Jane Victoria Harris, and the family called her Vicki. Vicki wasn't married when she had my mother, Maurie Harris. Maurie wasn't allowed to call Vicki her mother, and she had to pretend to be the daughter of her grandmother Martha Harris. Vicki became a sort of recluse, staying in her room and smoking Asthamador cigarettes.

After Hugh Matthews married Maurie Harris, they lived in a rural community outside Nicholson. Then they moved into town when I was probably about one or two years old. There were about 300 people in the town, and it had a post office and a train came through every day. There wasn't any electricity, paved roads, or water systems, though. (Unpublished correspondence with Judith Jennings, 2010)

I remember experiences with race relations when I was a child that made me start thinking. My father was a farmer and a rural letter carrier. He took me out to this black community in the country, which was on his mail route. He said he wanted me to meet the most educated man in the county, and it was a black schoolteacher and preacher who did calligraphy. My father got him to write my name on a card because he was intrigued with his handwriting you know, seeing it as a mail carrier. It was just a very impressive thing that here was the most educated man in the county, and my father took me to meet him. I saved that little card for years. Later that same man came to my house to see my father—I must have been seven or eight years old—and he, as black folks did, came to

Helen at age four, in 1928

the back door. My mother was in the front room with some women, quilting or something, and I ran to her and said, "Mr. Rakestraw is at the door," and the women laughed because you weren't supposed to call a black man "Mister." And I was so shamed by that. You know, as a child to be laughed at is a terrible thing. ("You've Got to Be Converted: An Interview with Helen Matthews Lewis")

But then when I was ten years old, we got transferred to Cumming, Georgia, which is in Forsyth County, the county where there were no blacks at all. They had a bad race riot in the 20s and had run out all of the African American population and had lynched several and hung them around the courthouse. I heard these stories. And I went to people's houses that had gravestones from the black cemetery—they'd dug them up and took them home and used them for flagstones. So I had grown up in a community that was just old-timey south, complete segregation and all that. But before I got to Cumming, I was not familiar with hostility. My father was very kind to everybody, blacks, whites, whatever, on his route. I'd never seen the signs of hostility that I saw when we moved to Cumming. And to hear these stories was just horrible. I had a music teacher who brought a black woman with her, who had been with her family for years, an old woman. And

Helen (*right*) with her father,
Hugh Matthews, and her sister,
JoAnn, in the 1930s

Helen (*right*) with her mother,
Maurie Harris Matthews, and her
sister, JoAnn, in the 1930s

they had lived together ever since she had grown up. A group of men came with torches and stuff and made her get up in the middle of the night, and they took that woman out of the county, wouldn't let her stay in the county, so the black woman had to be taken back to Alabama. So things like that just made me aware of real racism and real violence against blacks. ("Unruly Woman: An Interview with Helen Lewis")

Radicalization and World War II

In 1941, Helen entered Bessie Tift College for Women. Founded in 1849 as the Forsyth Female Collegiate Institute, it became Monroe Female College after the Civil War. In 1907, the school was renamed for Bessie Willingham Tift (c. 1861–1936), an alumna, community leader, and wife of businessman Henry Tift (1841–1922).

As part of the Georgia Baptist Convention, the college welcomed presentations by visiting preachers, such as Clarence Jordan. Like Helen, Georgia-born Clarence Jordan (1912–1969) grew up witnessing economic disparity and racial animosity between African Americans and whites. As a preacher, Jordan delivered his Cotton Patch Gospel sermons in small towns and rural areas across the state. In 1942, he helped establish Koinoinia, a Christian community in which members pooled their resources, treated all persons as equals regardless of race or class, and learned new farming techniques to increase production and profit and help break the cycle of poverty for local families (see Andrew S. Chancey, "Clarence Jordan [1912–1969]").

I was converted by Clarence Jordan. There is no doubt about that. I was 17 years old, a freshman at Bessie Tift College, a little Baptist school in Forsyth, Georgia, and we had required chapel. All these preachers and people would come and talk to us. One day this young preacher came, 1941 or '42—it was either the fall or the spring. He had just finished going to Baptist seminary and was starting this interracial farm in rural Georgia called Koinoinia. And he tells us about it, what he's going to do, and he retold the story of the Good Samaritan, only it was his Cotton Patch version. This man was going down the road and gets beat up by thieves and is left bloody on the side of the road. And the first car that comes by is a preacher, and he's hurrying off to church, and he sees the poor man beside the road, and he's practicing up on his sermon, to get them to come up and get saved that night. And he says, "Oh that poor fellow, but I don't have time. I've got to get to church." Then the next person is the choir leader and the person is so-and-so—you know he goes through these—and finally this old black man, he's riding down the road in his wagon and he sees him. He gets out, he bandages him up, he puts him in his wagon, and he takes him down to town and tries to put him in the hospital, and they won't let him in because this black man has brought him in. So he takes him down into "niggertown" where there's no lights and there's no pavement, and there's holes in the road, you know. And he's the Good Samaritan.

I'm sitting there listening to this man, and it's kind of like, "My God that is it, that is it! This is the story. This is it!" And there's no going back after that. I mean it just turned my mind. From then on. ("You've Got to Be Converted: An Interview with Helen Lewis")

The United States entered World War II after the bombing of Pearl Harbor in December 1941. In the spring of 1942, in the European theater of the war, Germany bombed the cathedral cities of Britain, the United States' main ally. Helen published this brief poem in the college newspaper.

The Campus Quill
Bessie Tift College
April 30, 1942

Two Stories Told in
England, sirens, signals, darkness,
Planes, terror, fright, fears,
Bombs, fire, shells, destruction.
Pain, death, silence, tears.

America, music, singing, laughter
Lights, gladness, fun, thrill,
Parties, rides, school, frolic,
Work, play, peace, good will.

In Georgia, as in other southern states, thousands of men and women joined the war effort. Federal defense money stimulated the national economy and funded new industries in Georgia and other southern states. As men entered the armed forces, large numbers of women, in Georgia and across the United States, went to work outside the home for the first time. Helen went to work, too, leaving Bessie Tift College in 1942 to become a wage earner.

Helen reentered college in 1943, enrolling in Georgia State College for Women (GSCW) in Milledgeville during a new era in Georgia politics. Before 1942, Populist Democrat Eugene Talmadge (1884–1946) dominated the state. Elected governor in 1932 and again in 1934, he declared martial law and physically removed opponents from their offices. A strong critic of the New Deal, he opposed the renomination of President Franklin D. Roosevelt in 1936. Reelected in 1940, Talmadge fired university faculty members whom he considered communists or sympathetic to racial equality, causing the Southern Association of Colleges and Schools to withdraw accreditation from all of the state's public colleges. In 1942 Ellis Arnall, a young progressive strongly opposed to Talmadge's actions, ran for governor and won.

In the 40s, there was a small period of safe space for progressive change in Georgia. This was created by the progressive leadership of Ellis Arnall as governor. With his election [in 1942] . . . the colleges and universities, including GSCW, regained their accreditation, which had been lost due to Governor Eugene Talmadge's witch-hunt for communists in the colleges. Governor Arnall ended the poll tax, which opened election participation to the poor, and he enfranchised 18-year-old voters. ("GSCW in the 1940s: Mary Flannery Was There, Too")

Georgia State College for Women had been established in 1889 to provide women with a practical higher education that would enable them to engage in business, industry, or teaching. When Helen enrolled, GSCW was part of the University System of Georgia and had a four-year liberal arts curriculum. President Guy H. Wells and Dean Ethel Adams strongly encouraged the Jessies, as the students were called, to be active learners and welcomed the establishment of a training center for navy WAVES on campus. The beautiful setting and strong curriculum attracted promising female students, including Helen and her classmate Mary Flannery O'Connor.

I attended Georgia State College for Women from 1943–46. . . . The 1940s were a decade of enormous social changes in the South and in the world, and these changes had great impact on the college and the women who were students during that time. . . . For me it was here that I was encouraged to read and think critically about social and economic problems including race relations in the South, to believe that women could be leaders, and to act on that understanding for equality, for democracy, and social justice. So when I say to friends that I was radicalized at a small women's college in Georgia in the 1940s they find it hard to believe. But being a student at GSCW and living in Georgia in the 40s was a radicalizing experience for me and many others. . . .

The 1940s were a time of great change in Georgia and at GSCW. First, World War II opened up the world for all of us. There was emphasis on women power in industrial work and women's leadership. Women were being recruited into many traditional male jobs. Women were incorporated into the armed services and GSCW had WAVES on campus. These were young women from all over the country bringing a more diverse and cosmopolitan population to the campus. . . .

At GSCW we still had a lot of older spinster-suffragette teachers: strong independent women who were among the first generation of women to vote. They not only provided models but also ideas from the older women's movement. Combined with liberal ideas about political and social change from the new faculty of younger men and women, the ideas of the older teachers produced at GSCW what might be called today not only liberal arts but civic education, education in democracy or education for social change along with informal women's studies. We were taught by the older women faculty that at a woman's college women can be presidents of organizations, not just secretaries. Women can vote and speak up on issues. Women are not beauty queens. All are beautiful. Women are not cheerleaders. We play the sports. Women's colleges were centers of leadership training for young women. During the 40s we were strongly encouraged to enter the professions and go to graduate school. ("GSCW in the 1940s: Mary Flannery Was There, Too")

President Wells hired Emily Cottingham to be the campus director for the Young Women's Christian Association. In 1934, the national YWCA had taken the bold step of adopting a charter to further interracial cooperation between African American and white students. Supported by President Wells, Emily Cottingham encouraged Jessies to become active local and national agents of change, especially concerning racial justice.

The college was also led by a college president who was committed to democracy, self-governance of students, freedom of speech, [and] equality, and [he had] a deep interest in improving race relations. When Guy Wells came to GSCW in the 30s some of his first words at chapel were "I believe in democracy." One of his first acts was to bring a woman into the administration: Dean Ethel Adams. He was very concerned about race relations and prejudice against Negroes. Both President Wells and Dean Hoy Taylor encouraged students to attend interracial meetings to meet educated blacks who were articulating their grievances and needs. They relied on the YWCA to carry out that mission and gave that organization considerable freedom and influence on campus. The YWCAs nationally were much more radical than the YMCAs in those days. The YWCAs had strong mission statements about desegregation and were promoting interracial meetings throughout the country. YWCAs were very active in most women's colleges. At GSCW they provided speakers for religious emphasis week and speakers on current affairs for weekly current affairs discussions. This activity also brought the accusation by the Women's National Association for the Preservation of the White Race that Agnes Scott College and GSCW were centers of communist activity since discussions of desegregation and interracial meetings were considered communistic.

In 1943 Guy Wells employed Emily Cottingham as YWCA Director. Emily was a young woman who grew up in Douglas, Georgia. She had been active in YWCA activities at Wesleyan and Duke and UNC Chapel Hill where she received an MA in social work. She had been involved in interracial meetings, and she told Dr. Wells that she would like to continue that. In a recent interview, she said that Dr. Wells told her the school had already been in trouble for allowing students to attend interracial meetings and their college budgets were cut and faculty fired because of it, but that he wanted students to continue attending such meetings. . . . [He said,] "don't tell me. Do it, but don't tell." Such activities were to be secret and as students we were told when we went to meetings at Paine College in Augusta and Atlanta University, "don't tell or it will get Dr. Wells in trouble." We went in Emily's car or rode with some faculty or local folks who supported the activity. In 1945 I was one of the students to spend the weekend at Atlanta University in the dormitory with black women, eating in their cafeteria with them. I remember sitting next to a young black woman, who got up and moved. My roommate apologized and said "I am sorry but she is prejudiced against white people." That was a shock. I thought white people were the only ones who could be prejudiced. ("GSCW in the 1940s: Mary Flannery Was There, Too")

There were some progressive folks back then. There were all these socialist women who had worked in a great program that the Y used to run with immigrant women and working women who came into the factories. That's why they started building a lot of these dormitories in big cities. They were for these working women. 1915 is when they started. By the '20s and '30s, the women who were working with these immigrant issues moved into the student Y. They had students working in the factories during the summers. Matter of fact I did that one summer while I was in college. ("Interview with Helen Lewis")

"Summer 1945—Students in Industry" was a YWCA summer project. A number of students participated in this. Marion Bessant and I went to Hartford, Connecticut,

on a [G]reyhound bus. (It took three days on the bus). We lived as a group in a co-op house at the Hartford Theological Seminary. Among the group were a young black man from Harvard and a Japanese American man, a student at MIT who had been in the internment camps with his family from California. We all had to find jobs in industry, and then at night we had speakers from labor unions and social service agencies talk to us about social and economic issues. Both the black student from Harvard and the Japanese American student had great difficulty finding work. The black man worked in an iron foundry at very hard labor, and Yoshira Befu was finally employed by a Quaker family to do garden work. (We were there on VJ Day). For Mackie [Marion Bessant] and me this was our first trip North, and we discovered that we talked funny, and were thought to be ignorant because of our accents and expected to be racist. The parents of the young black man from Harvard didn't want him to participate when they heard there would be two young white women from Georgia. They were afraid that we would mistreat their son. To their astonishment, we became the best of friends.

The Y also sponsored weekly informal suppers, which included faculty and students discussing current affairs. Topics included post-war employment, compulsory military training, fair employment practices, peace plans, national elections, candidates and issues. After the War, some of us gave speeches at Kiwanis Clubs in the state on peace plans and the United Nations. We had lots of hope for peace. ("GSCW in the 1940s: Mary Flannery Was There, Too")

Having grown up in rural Georgia, Helen was keenly aware that many black farmers were leaving the state to seek better futures elsewhere. She realized that this meant the remaining tenants and sharecroppers, black and white, faced even worse conditions and higher levels of poverty.

The first thing I ever wrote was when I was vice president of the state Baptist Student Union, and I was asked to give a speech. I had written this paper in a college class about the plight of the sharecroppers. And I go to the University of Georgia for the state meeting of the Baptist students, and I get up and make a speech about the Christian duties to deal with the sharecroppers, how the farmers are oppressing their workers. Well everybody loved it, thought it was just great, and they wanted to publish it in the Christian Index, a Baptist magazine. They published my sharecroppers article with my picture, and I was so proud! I think I got hate mail from every Baptist farmer in south Georgia about what radical things I was saying. That was my first experience of writing something that I was so proud of and others declaring it to be this awful thing. ("You've Got to Be Converted: An Interview with Helen Lewis")

from "On Conserving the Nation's Human Resources" (1944)

The cotton plantation area of the South contains the largest number of America's poorest and most dependent landless families. Of all the farms in the United States, the South contains two-thirds of them. Eighty-five per cent of the farms in Georgia are operated by share tenants (estimated by Miss Matthews). . . .

The patched overalls and faded gingham dresses of the tenant and wage hand families are as characteristic of the cotton country as are the twisted, unpainted cabins. The same families that produce the world's cotton crop are in need of basic cotton products. Death rates among children are much higher in cropper than owner families, and the white croppers' children die in about the same proportion as the Negro croppers' children. The likelihood of death in a farm home follows the land-tenure line and not the race line. . . .

The farm tenant women have none of the modern household conveniences. These women bear even heavier burdens. They work along with their men in the fields. They bear more children than any other group of women in America. . . .

Generally speaking, farm tenants and wage hands do not participate in community affairs. They are the inarticulate benefactors or victims of the public policy or private practices of those who control the religious, educational, political, and economic life of the community. . . . In rural churches one sees only a few people in overalls. Yet many of the South's landless farmers have only patched overalls and denim jackets.

In most plantation counties a larger proportion of Negro than white tenants are church members. In short . . . the rural Negro church reflects that status of the farm tenant, while the rural white church reflects the status of the landowner. . . .

Many white and practically all rural Negro children walk to their schoolhouses. The Negro schools are the most inadequate and many convene in church or lodge hall. The teachers' pay is so small it is often impossible to find a capable teacher. Many counties spend more to transport five hundred white children to and from an accredited school than they spend upon the total education of five thousand Negro children.

The white people of the South have been determined to keep Negroes dependent and servile. The "cropper" plan comes natural after the War Between the States and continued as a way to keep the Negro "in his place." But we find a greater number of the tenant farmers of the South are white, and the number is increasing while the number of the Negro tenants is decreasing.

Two-thirds of the tenant farmers in the South are white and only one-third are Negroes. . . .

Worn-out, eroded, gullied, lifeless and barren hillsides are important from the standpoint of the national welfare, and the dilapidated houses on many farms are a matter of serious public concern, but the hopeless and fruitless lives of the people who occupy these dilapidated house and who struggle for an existence upon these impoverished lands assume the appearance of a national tragedy. The problem demands consideration from the standpoint of conserving the nation's human resources.

Helen's experience at GSCW was not all work and no play. In 1945, she became an assistant editor for the yearbook, working with a day student, Mary Flannery O'Connor (1925–1964). Born into a devout Roman Catholic family in Savannah, O'Connor moved to her mother's hometown of Milledgeville as a teenager. After her father died, she lived at home and attended GSCW. For the 1945 yearbook, Helen wrote the text, and Mary Flannery created cartoon illustrations. Flannery O'Connor went on to become an important figure in American literature before her early death at age thirty-nine.

I would call her an observer and critic more than a participant in most college activities. Her writings and cartoons were that of an objective observer who reported with great wit, creativity and ridicule the campus activities. She did include herself in the cartoons, along with WAVES, students, dogs, faculty, spotlights and construction sites. She could see the ridiculous side of things. Her writings were both comic and dead serious in her evaluation of student laziness, ways of dressing, and deficiencies in our education. She was both documenter and critic of college life. . . .

Her most famous and creative set of cartoons were featured in the 1945 yearbook. She displayed the campus for the end papers and introduced each section of the book with drawings to fit the theme: "A Pilgrimage through Jessieville." I often say I did the writing "because I could write better" and then quickly add "yearbook style." I say we worked together on the book, but in actuality we both worked on the yearbook. Working together with Mary Flannery was working separately, and then putting the work together. I don't remember much "team work" or real collaboration or joint planning with Mary Flannery. . . . She always worked individually, and the work was always fantastic and brilliant. She was our [James] Thurber, and we all expected her to become a famous cartoonist. ("GSCW in the 1940s: Mary Flannery Was There, Too")

The Children's Crusade in 1946

When Georgia became the first state to allow eighteen-year-olds to vote, so-cially conscious students like Helen worked hard to engage their peers in the political process. Understanding the importance of this new constituency, the League of Women Voters in Georgia established campus leagues, and Helen became active in the GSCW League.

from "*Are* They Old Enough to Vote—Georgia's Youth Take Up the Ballot" (1945)

And so comes the story of how the young voters at the Georgia State College for Women are preparing themselves to vote intelligently: At this college in the historical old Georgia city of Milledgeville, there are approximately 1,000 students. Bright-faced young girls each day pass the old "mansion" which once housed the Civil War governors of the state. . . . But today these young girls have thoughts and ideas as new and bright as tomorrow and the city is a focal point of much of the thinking of the New South and the wide-awake southern girl. A new position for women in the form of a Naval Training School for WAVES also stands here behind big columned porches. Here are girls living among past history, but living for future history that they will help build.

The registered voters number 225 on the campus, but each girl believes that to be entitled to the right of the ballot she should have the ability to understand issues upon which [she] may and must vote and have a definite interest in her government. Each one of these students has had at least three more years of education than the average citizen of the U.S. so the ability to understand seems guaranteed. Information, knowledge, and the creation of an interest in government now are following as direct results of recent move-ments on the campus.

The League of Women Voters in Georgia first realized certain lacks in the State's young voters and added to their program the plan for college leagues. Shortly thereafter, GSCW girls organized a League on their own campus. Theirs is the first organized in the state and therefore the first in the nation ever organized in a place where the 18–21 year-old members can engage in active citizenship at the same time that they study it.

Newly organized, the League first discovered that training students for intelligent voting would not be as difficult as first imagined. Many of the students already had a real interest in government. A number of them were among the college youth who so sincerely and enthusiastically supported Arnall in his campaign for Governor in 1942. . . .

Even though they are prepared and can vote intelligently, the opposition now says, "Why should they vote?" "Is there any reason that they should vote?" The "old-enough-to-fight, old-enough-to-vote" slogan has been greatly publicized and does hold a great deal of truth, but the truth lies deeper in the fact that the nation needs its young people in peace as well as in war.

Youth is idealistic and has a viewpoint usually less prejudiced that that of the older voter, who tends toward conservatism. The younger voter is usually uncommitted and brings a measure of independence in his use of the ballot. He has the courage to form his own conclusions; so youth is needed to balance the voting strength of the older conservatives. . . .

The right to vote will also give the youth an active part in determining issues, which will decide his destiny. The U.S. cannot afford more "lost generations" such as we had during the Depression. Young people are intensely interested in a stable and better world and have the courage and determination to fight for it. They are determined that the 1950s will not be the "frivolous fifties."

"Are they old enough to vote?"

From Georgia and the campus of the Georgia State College for Women comes an answer for all the Nation to hear and heed.

"Are they old enough to vote?"

Georgia says: "Yes!"

Ellis Arnall could not run again for governor in 1946 because of an amendment to the state constitution that lengthened his term to four years but prohibited him from seeking reelection. His old nemesis Eugene Talmadge ran for the Democratic nomination, but progressive Democrat James V. Carmichael challenged Talmadge in the primary. That same year, federal courts struck down the Democratic Party's all-white primary. Talmadge vowed to restore the white primary and maintain Jim Crow segregation laws. The 1946 gubernatorial primary thus emerged as a battle between populism and progressivism.

With eighteen-year-olds going to the polls for the first time, the "Children's Crusade," a statewide effort mobilizing young voters to support Carmichael, gained national attention. At that time, statewide elections in Georgia used a county-unit system of votes, whereby counties cast two, four, or six votes, depending on their classification as rural, town, or urban areas. Carmichael received more popular votes, but Talmadge won the nomination by receiving a majority of the county-unit votes. As the Democratic candidate, Talmadge was again elected governor. Yet before taking office, Eugene Talmadge died, on December 21, 1946. His son Herman aptly observed that a third of the people of Georgia would follow his father to hell, and a third of them wanted him in hell.

We were strong Ellis Arnall supporters, and because he was not able to succeed himself as governor, the progressive candidate in 1946 was Jimmy Carmichael. He ran against Eugene Talmadge and Ed Rivers. We formed a political campaign group called Student League for Good Government in Georgia. Similar student leagues were formed at other Georgia colleges to support Carmichael. In a rally and straw vote, there was 95% vote at GSCW for Carmichael. We organized students from each county to work in their home counties that summer for the candidate. George Doss of the University of Georgia and I were chosen to run the state office in the Piedmont Hotel in Atlanta as part of the Carmichael campaign, where our cause was called the Children's Campaign. We had students flying planes and dropping leaflets, three sound trucks on the road, students developing county campaigns, and vans of young people canvassing, making speeches and writing to local papers. Although Carmichael won the popular vote, he lost the election to Eugene Talmadge by the county unit vote.

What happened was the weird situation of Gene Talmadge dying before he took office, his son claiming the office, Melvin Thompson the elected Lt. Gov claiming the office, and Ellis Arnall refusing to move until a legitimate Governor was decided by the court. So Georgia had three Governors for a while until the courts decided on Thompson. Herman Talmadge and other pro-segregation, racist politicos kept up the fight to stop integration. ("GSCW in the 1940s: Mary Flannery Was There, Too")

from "Report on Summer Experience in Campaign Headquarters for Governor of Georgia, 1946"

This is not the story of a lost battle but rather one just temporarily disarmed or like the popcorn machine on Peachtree "temporarily out of seasoning," for a fight such as ours does not die. . . . The people of Georgia elected Jimmy Carmichael, but our vicious county unit system caused his defeat. We are reminded again that we are the only state in the nation to have such a system. . . . Jimmy Carmichael received 100,000 more votes than ever were polled for a victorious candidate for governor in all of Georgia's history. Mr. Tal-

"The Children's Crusade," from the *New York Times*, 1946, showing Helen (*far left*). Photograph used by permission of Redux Pictures, copyright *New York Times*.

madge isn't the choice of a majority; he is not even the choice of a plurality. His victory is that of a minority. . . .

Headquarters was almost all the fifth floor of the Piedmont. There were the main reception room, Maynard Smith, campaign manager's office, pressrooms, women's division, veterans' room, and living quarters. My room was used during the day as a conference room by Sims Garret and Frank Swift, and I was never surprised to find men's shaving things all around. Sims came by the office one day and asked if I'd moved his shaving brush from "our" room. Several visiting GSCW women looked at me with glances that said, "What did you say you did in headquarters?" Allen always helped out at such points, and at this particular one he informed them that Jimmy's shirts were in my room also and that several other men shared the room.

Headquarters was really the place for me to catch up on my flirting. . . . All of these old, and some not so old, politicians would come by without their wives, and they all felt like 16. I put on my broadest grin and sweetest talk. They loved it.

Being in Student Headquarters, we received no pay; but, through Bobby Troutman and his alumni contributions, we had all expenses paid. We really had some with three sound trucks on the road and two airplanes in the air the last week. . . . We all ate heartily, being school children with likewise appetites. I took advantage to eat my share of shrimp cocktails. I love them. Our work consisted of getting out material to all students and alumni of the various schools, organizing young people's groups in the counties to work on election day, making records for radio broadcasts and sound trucks, keeping the sound trucks running and dropping leaflets by plane, and writing letters and such. . . .

Besides the regular student work, I often got things to do dealing with the "larger campaign"—ours was just the Children's Crusade. One of the most interesting and most fun was some subversive research. We were working along with the PAC [Political Action Committee] getting out some propaganda for the workers showing pictures of Gene's guards with their bayonets standing over the workers in the barbed wire concentration camps. The *Constitution* wanted a long story on the facts of the case, so Allen and I were assigned the task. We made trips to the Citizen's Fact Finding Commission and the Carnegie Library. In the library, we went through the newspapers for Sept. 1934 to March 1935 and dug up the facts. I was astounded. I never realized that such violent strike breaking was carried on by the Governor of Georgia and his state troops. We really wrote it up how the guards evicted women from mill-owned houses, put them in jail, and put others in their concentration camps. The *Constitution* ran it with a picture of one of the atrocities. Allen and I both felt so important. We were practically associate editors of the *Atlanta Constitution*.

Another job I liked lots was peddling radio programs. We made up three 15-minute records, a woman's program, a student's program, and a veteran's program, and we wanted them used all over the state on the smaller stations and we wanted the local Carmichael clubs to sponsor (pay for) them. So I was given this amazing list of stations and towns all over the state and with my best telephone personality called everywhere and scheduled the programs and circulated the records. I got dreadfully confused at times when 16 stations wanted the veteran record at 8:30 on Monday, and we only had four copies of said record. I wanted to go back to Milledgeville.

The campaign is now over. I thoroughly enjoyed being in politics, and I am thinking seriously of running for the legislature in two or four years. Now that I've gotten over the initial numbness of defeat, I do not feel defeated. I feel definitely set-back and that's what has happened. It is a great set-back for democracy in Georgia to have again old Gene in power. But we'll be back in greater strength and greater numbers in four years to beat him. We'll continue to fight through these four years for good government in Georgia and block him in as many of his vicious schemes as possible. We must keep fighting in the battle for human rights.

An Unruly Wife

In the first half of the twentieth-century, American society continued to hold strong expectations for women to marry, and this expectation seemed especially prevalent in the U.S. South. As veterans returned to work after World War II, many working women returned to domestic life, and postwar patriotism reinforced social norms concerning marriage. Helen later recalled these kinds of social expectations after she began dating Judd Lewis, a graduate student in economics at Duke University.

I never really intended to be an academic. I intended to be a journalist and a politician. I really wanted to be the owner of a county newspaper and run for the Georgia legislature and be in Georgia politics, but I went to Georgia State College for Women and got encouraged to go to graduate school. . . .

I went to Duke. I ended up marrying a man who was going to be a college professor. I changed my goals so we could go off and teach together. We would have joint teaching careers, and it would be so beautiful, an egalitarian partnership marriage.

I was at Duke for just one year, and then went back to Georgia and worked in the governor's office, writing speeches for the Governor of Georgia for one year. My husband to be [Judd Lewis] followed me there, and we got married, and he went to Emory. ("You've Got to Be Converted: An Interview with Helen Lewis")

I really didn't want to get married, but there didn't seem to be any way to escape. It was what you were supposed to do, and everyone expected it and pushed it and planned it. And there I was—big wedding and everything. (Picking Up The Pieces: Women In and Out of Work in the Rural South)

I was quite an activist at that time, but my husband was not involved. The first year I was married, I was working at the governor's office, and that summer I took a job with

Helen at her wedding, 1947

the college YWCA and was organizing these interracial meetings and got arrested in
Atlanta in 1948. ("You've Got to Be Converted: An Interview with Helen Lewis")

from Helen Matthews Lewis to Dr. and Mrs. George Beiswanger [professor of philosophy at Georgia State Women's College], July 26, 1948

On Friday night the 16th of July [1948], a group of students from various
Southern colleges—all YW or divinity school people—met at the Georgia
Workers Education Service for a get-acquainted meeting as part of the pro-
gram of activities of 8 men students who are in a Student-in-Industry project
sponsored by the Fellowship of Southern Churchmen. . . . The boys are from
Univ of N.C., Univ of Miss., Univ of Va., Yale Divinity School and Wisconsin
Graduate School, Duke University, and North Carolina College. There is one
Negro boy in the group. . . . We had been meeting about 20 minutes—had
played two recreational games—when 5 policemen came in, broke up the
meeting, gave us all tickets for disorderly conduct and disturbance and gave

Ruth Warren a ticket for holding a public dance without a license. It was fantastic and unbelievable that they could do it—but they did. There could have been no more orderly meeting anywhere, or less disturbance. It most certainly was not a dance. But come Saturday morning and Sunday, both Atlanta papers played the matter up considerably, quoting policemen and some neighbors to the building—but not once checking with any of us to get the correct story. These headlines concerning "mixed dancing"—"Whites and Negroes jailed"—and that sort of thing brought much distress to girls, families, friends, etc., especially since they listed all names and addresses. There were three Negroes and 18 whites in all. Beside the student in the project, we invited a Negro couple from Morehouse College to come meet the people.

The hearing intended for Monday afternoon was postponed a month by the judge who was afraid of Klan trouble if we showed up. Due to the misconception brought about by the sensational news stories, there was a considerable crowd gathered at court that afternoon—much disappointed when we did not show up. . . . After it occurred, the chief of police and mayor were very disturbed over the action of the policemen—stating that we did nothing wrong, or illegal and that had they been on duty it would not have happened. We feel the matter will probably be dropped soon. However, one girl lost her job as a result of the publicity, another lost her apartment, another almost lost her job and many families have come near nervous breakdowns. I have lost all faith in both Atlanta papers. . . .

Obviously it was a trumped up affair and the police had no idea they were breaking up a group like ours . . . a group of preachers and YWCA girls— they are not happy!

from "Dr. B." to Helen Matthews Lewis, August 8, 1948

Dear Helen, I should read the newspapers more carefully! I took in the headlines "Mixed Dance" etc., thought it some usual monkey business, and just didn't read the story. Can you believe it?

You may not approve, but I am sending your letter to Ralph McGill [owner of the *Atlanta Constitution*] whom I have met and to whom I occasionally write. I think he ought to know how badly his paper managed the affair, and your letter does the thing perfectly. Tell me frankly if you think I have abused your confidence, and I won't do it again.

Incidentally, the incident confirms me in my decision to be more than just a classroom and sitting room discusser of the whole problem. I've been getting awfully tired of just tossing out ideas to the young. It doesn't look so good to one's conscience. What one can do in Milledgeville remains to be seen. My idea is that general explosions don't count, but there are concrete, specific points at which levers can effectively be applied. The job will be to find one of those points at which to go to work. And that's one responsibility I have set for myself this coming year.

I moved with my husband from Atlanta to Charlottesville, and I finished up my master's at the University of Virginia. Floyd Nelson House was there. He was an old Chicago sociologist, and a lot of training in those early days goes back to those old Park, Burgess, and McIver people in sociology. I had anthropology both at Duke and Virginia. At Duke I had been Weston LaBarre's first graduate assistant, so I helped out with all his classes, and did a lot of library research and took classes in anthropology. Clifford Evans and Betty Meggers, his wife, were at the University of Virginia. I got to know them real well and took a lot of archeology from Clifford Evans and got interested in the Mayans and wrote papers on them. ("You've Got to Be Converted: An Interview with Helen Lewis")

I have been a little different from a normal "academic" in that I had been involved in the early civil rights movement, before when I was in college, so I was already interested in social justice issues. I was more outspoken than many others. You are supposed to be "objective and value free" if you are an academic, and just look at things from the outside and not get involved, and I tended to get involved. ("Unruly Woman: An Interview with Helen Lewis")

In 1944, the Swedish political economist Gunnar Myrdal (1898–1987) published *An American Dilemma: The Negro Problem and Modern American Democracy*, commissioned by the Carnegie Corporation of New York. Myrdal's thoroughgoing critique of race relations in the United States, including the inequalities of New Deal legislation, made a big impact and contributed to the 1954 *Brown v. Board of Education* Supreme Court decision ending segregation in public schools. Writing her master's thesis in 1949, Helen compared many of Myrdal's points to the struggle for women's rights in the United States.

from "The Woman Movement and the Negro Movement: Parallel Struggles for Rights" (1949)

It is the contention of this thesis that there are many important similarities between the Negro problem and the women's problem. These similarities are not merely accidental. The ideological and economic forces behind the two movements—the emancipation of women and the emancipation of Negroes—have much in common and are closely interrelated. Negroes and women have both been under the yoke of the paternalistic system, a pre-industrial scheme, which gradually became broken in the nineteenth century. Both groups were then strongly influenced by the Industrial Revolution, and for both groups the readjustment process is not yet consummated. The problems remain, even though paternalism is gradually declining as an ideal and is losing its economic basis.

It is the purpose of this paper to point out some of these similarities and interrelations in the status and history of both groups. Rather than treating both problems as unique, it is hoped that in concentrating on the similarities of the two that it will thereby give perspective to both problems. . . .

The mind and personality are largely developed by social interaction. Social factors mold the individuals around the stereotype. It seems justifiable then to infer the differences in personality and mental expression between Negro and white and between men and women are, in the main, no greater than the existing differences in opportunity for participation in the social world. . . .

This paper is interested in the "differences that make a difference." That is, it is only so far as differences are treated as involving or related to social opportunity or inferiority that they are relevant to this discussion of sex and race statuses. . . . The judgments and evaluations of inferiority are given to the personality traits and statuses ascribed to women and Negroes.

A male acquaintance of mine recently had an automobile accident as a result of an exceptionally stupid mistake on his part. After distractedly turning left on a red light, he was struck by another car. The driver immediately rushed over, opened the door and inquired of my friend, "Are any of you ladies hurt?" He was immediately embarrassed to find the driver a man. Upon telling the story, the friend remarked that this was the most humiliating part of the accident.

Both sex and race roles are segregated in our society so as to remove both groups from the occupational positions which are identified with the highest achieved status. The members of both groups are thereby prevented from competing for status with white adult males. . . .

During World War II both Negroes and women were allowed in jobs previously closed to them. Even though this was a necessary move to achieve full production, traditional objections to the training of women and Negroes in the skilled mechanical trades still were hard to break. Though the needs of war extended the breakdown of many obstructions, even then opportunities for upgrading and supervisory jobs for women and Negroes were limited. Since the war, some have been able to remain in these traditional white man's skills; however, with the wartime emergency and F.E.P.C. [Fair Employment Practices Committee] gone, many have been forced back into their traditional jobs. . . .

The problems of wages and earnings for both are mainly these: 1) that wages have been and are low when measured by the demands of health, decency and comfort; and 2) that different scales of pay usually exist for so-called women's and men's jobs, for Negro jobs and white jobs, and different scales often exist for individual men and women and individual Negroes and whites when the occupational equipment is alike and the quality and volume of work substantially identical. The phrase "equal pay for equal work" has been a slogan for both groups in their attempts to ameliorate this situation. . . .

The problem is not always equal pay for equal work, because it is difficult to discover more than a very few instances in which men and women or whites and Negroes do the same work, in the same place, at the same time, so the question is often rather . . . segregation of jobs than of equal pay. . . .

Both groups in their struggles for status have put great emphasis upon gaining political participation and legal rights. With the American revolutionary tradition and democratic creed, it is most natural that both groups would have great faith in the vote. . . .

American women had begun lecturing against slavery and found that in so doing they had to defend their right to do so, thus leading to demands for their own political and legal "emancipation." In the anti-slavery societies and the work for abolition, women began to agitate the question of their right to speak, vote, and serve on committees, and it was from these experiences that the Women's Rights Convention of 1848 in Seneca Falls developed.

It is now common for all committees considering city-wide, state-wide, and nation-wide problems to appoint a Negro and a woman to present the "Negro-point-of-view" and the "woman-point-of-view." Everyone tends to look upon these members as representatives only of their group, and the appointees themselves tend to consider all issues from their "point of view." Negroes and women are considered very important minority groups, and both parties do some catering to them. No political convention would now be held without at least one woman speaker and one Negro somewhere on the program—at least to sing. . . .

The education movements for both Negroes and women have been integral parts of the general movements for status. . . . It was argued in Colonial America that education of women was an infringement upon the domain of man and the education of slaves was an infringement upon the domain of the planter. . . .

Just as there were similar arguments against education for Negroes and women, there was similar reasoning in the agitation for them. . . . There was much validity in the objections to education for both groups on the grounds that education was responsible for Negroes as well as for women getting out of their places. . . . In a very real sense the Negro colleges and the segregated women's colleges created a self-consciousness which resulted in the movements for "rights." . . .

The present day segregated colleges for both Negroes and women are the objects of varying sentiments. There are those who argue for the segregated schools as an escape from categorization, humiliation and discrimination in order that their students can be individuals. . . . Some argue for the segregated school on the grounds that the Negroes do no learn enough about Negro problems in other schools, or become race conscious and join the movement and fight for their rights. . . . For the woman's college, some argue that women get no training in "leadership" or experience in "running" campus politics and other organizations in coed colleges due to the male-dominated tradition. . . . It is still true that women and Negroes are not welcome in all white male schools, the discrimination existing on the professional level in particular, and the segregated colleges are necessary in that respect. . . .

Defensive beliefs function to make people's actions seem expedient, in line with current ideals, or, at least inevitable. Termed by someone "vital lies," these excuses and distortions seem necessary to justify and rationalize the various discrimination, and necessary also to defend and perpetuate the relationships.

Social stratification in Europe had been based on dominance and subordination between men and women, and slavery had been existent in many times and situations. Therefore, many of the justifications of both these institutions were ready-made and the 18th- and 19th-century defenders of the old order had but to draw from this body of thought.

The first rationalizations for both were directly religious. . . .

In the slavery question, the traditional justification for slavery was that the Negro was a heathen or infidel. . . . [In the woman question, it was] the old church doctrine that woman through her greater wickedness fell more readily than man into evil practices. . . . Another objection or justification for opposition to religious education for women and Negroes was that neither had souls and thus they could not gain salvation. . . .

The defenders of both slavery and the subjection of women had first to deny the argument that all men have a natural right to freedom. . . . Defenders declared that chaos would reign should the *status quo* be upset. . . . The ideas of biological inequality, and of innate inferiority were the product of the same rational, secular society which produced the Natural Rights, equalitarian doctrine. The "race" ideas were born out of the conflict between the obviously existent, non-equalitarian relationships and the faith in human liberty and democracy.

The natural-rights, equalitarian doctrine was used to oppose the doctrine of racial and sex inferiority, and yet called for both dogmas to justify the blatant exceptions to it. As [Gunnar] Myrdal points out [in *An American Dilemma: The Negro Problem and Modern Democracy*], a country without the fervent belief in democracy could live happily in a caste system, with a less intensive belief in the biological inferiority of the subordinate group. Race and sex prejudice are then functions of equalitarianism. The former are perversions of the latter.

From the race and sex ideologies are drawn the justifications for the daily discrimination and aggression against women and against Negroes and defenses to keep both in their places. . . .

In a very real sense the movement for the emancipation of the slaves and the early woman's movement were one and the same. The organized woman's movement grew out of the other, and the early philosophical debates on both issues have many similarities.

That the women psychologically identified themselves with the slaves was obvious. The similarities in status, though there were tremendous differences both in actual status and in tone of sentiment in the respective relations, were felt to be almost identical [as shown in the writing of Elizabeth Cady Stanton].

Though the competition between the two movements appeared and a rift occurred [over the Fourteenth and Fifteenth amendments, after the Civil War], there was a deeper relation, however, which still exists today. Leaders in both movements often see the problems as common and have, like

[W. E. B.] Dubois, made ardent appeals for women's interests as well as of those of the Negro. Women have played a considerable part in the organizations of the Negro movement. The Y. W. C. A., women's groups of the Protestant churches and similar women's organizations have been leaders in interracial work in the South. Such organizations as the Association of Southern Women for the Prevention of Lynching have developed. . . .

Women and Negroes both must be allowed to participate more fully in the economic, political, and social life of our nation. A change in the methods of the industrial world, perhaps providing more part-time work, may be necessary so that woman may pass freely from the home to the factory without such violent changes of attitude as to disrupt the harmony of the self and render the personality inconsistent.

It must be recognized that a woman's life today usually falls into discontinuous sections, and that the question of vocation or family should not be a compulsory either/or proposition. It should be accepted and society should arrange things so that its women could work at several different periods in their life. That the vocation will probably become an avocation during the years when they are bringing up a family is quite necessary, but with the previous training and their planning for later work, women, instead of being confronted in the 40s with relative unemployment and the loneliness, frustration and suffering which go with it, would be ready to use their experience and talents creatively outside the home.

Perhaps this would solve our present day problem of the frustrated, "idle" women. The Bureau of Labor Statistics lists 20 million women essentially idle. They have no children under 18, they are not members of the labor force, they do not work on farms, nor are they aged or infirm. Many of them are petted by devoted and hard-working husbands, but they remain still unsatisfied. Many are over 40 and belong to a generation which frowned on work for any but poverty-stricken women. Their husbands have worked hard to give them a life of ease. Now that they have it, it is a burden. This is because an untrained woman has difficulty finding satisfying tasks to fill her days. Social work, which once busied many women, is now largely handled by professionals. As a result many of these "idle" women fall back on increasing rounds of club meetings and card playing. They read a great deal of low-grade fiction and escape readily into dream realms of movies and soap operas. . . .

The specialization of the husband's occupational role has also made it more necessary for women to be allowed to participate more creatively in the economic world. The husband's specialization has narrowed the range in which sharing of common human interests can play a large part. The woman whose interests still remain so completely segregated is deprived of her husband's companionship during the long hours of the day when he is away from home and then the evening finds him preoccupied and disinterested in the affairs that concern her. . . .

With a society so in need of an alert citizenry, of a great number of individuals conscious of the full meaning of all their social relations, it seems a stupid waste to have two large classes of its people, women and Negroes, existing in an unreal world willfully maintained for that purpose. Nor will the white men be able to develop fully socialized selves, in so far as they are formed by their relations with the only partially self-conscious Negroes and women. . . .

The most confusing part about the dilemmas of both groups is that every woman finds herself classified with all women, and every Negro finds himself classified with all Negroes. They become categorically endowed with all the virtues and all the faults ascribed to the group, and people act toward them as if these were present. People are forever saying that all women are thus and so, and all Negroes are thus and so. Members of both groups are confined to being the mythical characters: "the American woman" and "the American Negro." Neither are ever looked upon and judged as individuals. A Negro may never become just a good singer or a good poet or a bad criminal. He is always a good Negro singer, a good Negro poet, and a Negro criminal. Women are likewise disturbed by never being described as individuals and always being assessed in terms of womanliness. . . .

As noted earlier, however, these personality traits ascribed to race or sex groups are really only aspects of the whole gamut of human temperament, and in specializing personality along the lines of sex and race we actually extirpate artificially "unfitting" personality traits in some children and create artificially proper personality traits in others. All women and Negroes are not thus and so, and a pattern of life entirely satisfying for one kind of woman or one kind of Negro will be a torment for another.

Society should perhaps provide greater freedom for individual differences. We have begun to recognize genuine individual gifts as they have occurred in either sex and either race in such fields as writing, art, music; recognizing that beneath the superficial classifications of sex and race, the same potentialities exist, recurring generation after generation, only to perish because society has no place for them. This is the groundwork for building a society that would permit the development of many contrasting personality gifts in each sex and race. Educational institutions could be shaped to develop to the full the boy who shows a capacity for maternal behavior, the girl who shows an opposite capacity, the Negro who shows leadership ability and aptitude in "white man's skill." No skill, no special aptitude, no vividness of imagination or precision of thinking would go unrecognized because the child who possessed it was of one sex or race other than the other, no child would be relentlessly shaped to one pattern of behavior, but instead there should be many patterns in a world that has learned to allow to each individual the pattern which was most congenial to his gifts. . . .

Where we now have patterns of behavior for women and patterns of behavior for men, patterns of behavior for Negroes and patterns of behavior for whites, we would then have patterns of behavior that expressed the interests of individuals with many kinds of endowment. Recognizing the whole gamut of human potentialities, weaving a less arbitrary social fabric, we would have a society in which each diverse human gift would find a fitting place.

The peculiarly unhappy positions of the woman and the Negro are realities and not illusions. All the hopeless conflict among impulses which they both feel, they have legitimate right, even moral obligation, to express; all of the rebellion against stupid, meaningless sacrifice of powers that ought to be used by society, constitutes the force, conscious or unconscious, which motivates the two movements and will continue to vitalize them until some adjustment is made. . . .

The whole philosophy of human rights has now accepted both Negroes and women as human beings with the equal and inalienable rights of all members of the human family. The Universal Declaration of Human Rights of the General Assembly of the United Nations notes that "everyone is entitled to all the rights and freedoms set forth in this Declaration, without distinction of any kind, such as race, color, sex, language, religion, political or other opinion, national or social origin, property, birth or other status."

The chief task of all social movements, then, must be at first to impress upon the rest of society the right of unsatisfied and unexpressed human impulses to constitute a real problem worthy of attention. This they will never bring about until there is a sufficient number of people who are socially sensi-

tive and adaptable that they feel within themselves as their own the impulses
and points of view of both races and both sexes.

*Virginia didn't give a Ph.D. They did make an exception and say they would work out
a Ph.D. program for me, but at that point I needed to work and make a living, because
my husband was still in school, and he was finishing a Ph.D. in Philosophy. The wife
working, and the husband going to school. ("You've Got to Be Converted: An Interview
with Helen Lewis")*

Helen's Chowchow Recipe

*Helen began developing her cooking skills as a young wife. She drew on her
mother's experience, using fresh vegetables from the garden. Helen recalls that
"chowchow was something we always made at the end of the season using the
last of the green tomatoes. When I needed it as a cook, I asked for the recipe."*

Chowchow: a green tomato relish, which is great to eat with pinto
beans, black-eyed peas, turnip greens, or green beans

1 gal green tomatoes
1 dozen onions
1/2 cup salt

Chop and mix tomatoes and onions; add salt, cover with water, and
cook 10 minutes.
Add:
1 qt vinegar
3 lbs sugar
1/2 dozen green peppers, chopped
1/2 dozen red peppers, chopped
1 dozen cucumber pickles (or use jar of cucumber pickle relish)
3 hot peppers, chopped

Cook 15 minutes, and can in hot sterilized jars.
(Unpublished correspondence with Judith Jennings, 2010)

*I took a job with the Bureau of Population and Economic Research and ran a pretty
big survey research project for the Bureau of Roads and spent a lot of time in the south
side of Virginia, interviewing folks about a new factory that was coming in, doing an*

impact study on what the effect of that new factory was going to be, organizing interviews, something that today would have counted as a dissertation. But in those days they didn't let you count paid work, paid funded research, for a dissertation. ("You've Got to Be Converted: An Interview with Helen Lewis")

Judd and I left UVA, Charlottesville, for Richmond in 1950 or '51. After the Korean War started, the government imposed price controls. He got a job as an economist working for the government. I got a job with the American Red Cross as a social worker. I was a caseworker and most of my cases were families of servicemen in Korea. I was like a field officer and kept the men informed about their families and brought messages to the families as well. I had quite a few African American families and became quite familiar with Jackson Ward and other "colored" neighborhoods.

I also worked with disaster relief when two hurricanes hit Richmond. That's when I learned about all the slum landlords and power structure of Richmond. We had to repair or rebuild houses damaged in the storms and sort out the ownership of the houses, which people thought they owned.

My supervisor at the American Red Cross in Richmond was Suzanne Williams, a very aristocratic and elegant lady. She taught me how to make Old Fashioneds, but she always used Virginia Gentleman bourbon.

Helen's Old Fashioned Recipe

Make One Glass at a Time
Put 1 tsp honey into cocktail glass, and dissolve in small amount of hot water.
Add 1 slice of lemon and 1 slice of orange and mash.
Add 2 or 3 dashes of bitters and muddle.
Add one jigger of bourbon and several cubes of ice.
Keep mashing fruits and muddling liquids.
Top with soda.
Enjoy!

Judd and I left Richmond in 1955 to go to Clinch Valley College in Wise, Virginia. The college started in 1954 as the first branch of the University of Virginia. Judd had changed his field to philosophy, and we were both going to teach at the new college. (Unpublished correspondence with Judith Jennings, 2010)

Chapter 2

Breaking New Ground, 1955–1977

Patricia Beaver

> I grew up in north Georgia. And when I moved to the coal fields that was a shock because there were a lot of similar characteristics, like the old Hard-Shell Baptists, as we called them in north Georgia, and a lot of music was the same. . . . But coal, the whole industrialization of rural people made a big difference. And so that's where I got really interested in what coal does to traditional Appalachian culture.
> — Helen Matthews Lewis, quoted in Lori Briscoe et al., "Unruly Woman: An Interview with Helen Lewis"

Helen Matthews Lewis moved to southwest Virginia in 1955. Witness to the impact of the coal industry in central Appalachia, Helen became an activist educator and an outspoken critic of the devastation occurring in the resource-rich region that she now called home. Teaching and learning from her students, Helen fundamentally reframed for a new generation of scholars and activists the most basic assumptions about Appalachian culture, communities, and inequality.

Helen's husband, Judd, had been hired to teach philosophy at Clinch Valley College, a branch of the University of Virginia in Wise, in the heart of the coalfields. At that time the University of Virginia would not employ both husband and wife in permanent positions. So for five years, Helen held temporary and part-time positions at the college, while she worked with women in Wise County to help start a local public library, learned from her students about the impact of coal on their region, and called for a coal severance tax to support public schools.

Helen sought the PhD in order to be qualified for a full-time position at

Clinch Valley College. Awarded a National Science Foundation grant in 1962, she traveled to the University of California in Berkeley to study for a summer. She then turned her attention to Appalachian coal research. In 1964 she entered the PhD program at the University of Kentucky. Grants from the Bureau of Mines helped her to conduct research on coal miners and their families and to develop expertise on the industry from the inside out as she interviewed miners in their workplaces and miners' wives in their homes. Her research, in collaboration with Edward Knipe, was groundbreaking in both its subject and its methodology. She earned the PhD in sociology from the University of Kentucky in 1970, with her dissertation "Occupational Roles and Family Roles: A Study of Coal Mining Families in the Southern Appalachians."

Helen came to southwest Virginia during a pivotal time for the coal industry and coalfield communities. She watched the 1950s bring mechanization of the mines, consolidation of control by major mining operations, massive unemployment, decline of coal production, accompanying increases in poverty, and major out-migrations from the region. At the same time, many big coal companies, largely untaxed and unregulated, made large profits. Living in Wise, Virginia, and teaching students from the coal communities, Helen saw firsthand the impoverishment of the coalfields and the wealth of the industry, and she recognized the connections between the local economy and the industrialization of this rural area by an extractive industry whose ownership and interests lay primarily outside the region.

Stereotypes of Appalachian people as poor whites, unlettered, isolated, and culturally inadequate, were invented and replicated during the late nineteenth and early twentieth centuries by successive waves of visitors and helpers. For decades scholars attributed Appalachian exceptionality to an isolated folk tradition, and by 1960 anthropologist Oscar Lewis's theory of a self-perpetuating oppressive culture of poverty had gained momentum as an explanation of Appalachian poverty. In the 1960s and 1970s, images of mountain people as degraded, white, isolated hillbillies continued to be featured in America's popular media as they had since the late nineteenth century, and these stereotypes received national attention with publication in 1965 of Jack Weller's *Yesterday's People: Life in Contemporary Appalachia.*

In response to these models of deficiency and to her lived experience with economic decline in central Appalachia, Helen presented academic talks and public lectures, proposing that Appalachia was an ecologically and historically complex region with a diversity of subcultures. Writing and speaking about the region where she lived, Helen grew into a public intellectual, concluding that "stirring up dialogue has some great value."

In 1970 Helen introduced a new interpretive model for Appalachia, that of internal colonialism, inspired in part by Charles Valentine's critique of the culture of poverty (*Culture and Poverty*, 1968) and by the work on Western colonization of the Third World by Albert Memmi (*The Colonizer and the Colonized*, 1965), Frantz Fanon (*The Wretched of the Earth*, 1965; *A Dying Colonialism*, 1967), and Pierre Jalee (*Pillage of the Third World*, 1965). Interpreting the Appalachian region as an exploited zone of natural resource extraction called for new definitions of Appalachia's communities and solutions to Appalachia's problems, including changes in the very structure of society. Helen's "Fatalism or the Coal Industry?" first published in *Mountain Life and Work* in 1970, is a key text that redirected Appalachian scholarship away from blaming the culture for the poverty of its people to examining the impacts of the coal industry on Appalachia. This work and her subsequent articles examined the theme of colonialism in Appalachia, and she and her coeditors Linda Johnson and Don Askins collected articles that expanded this theme in *Colonialism in Modern American: The Appalachian Case* (1978). Elaborating on Appalachia's subordinate role in the national and emerging global economy, the articles in this volume simultaneously critiqued the region's structural dependency and initiated the public discussion on transforming those relationships. Her work redirected emerging Appalachian scholarship and was the catalyst for scholar-activists like John Gaventa and Stephen Fisher to move the theoretical analysis into its next phases.

Helen's experiences in Appalachia's coalfields and university classrooms served to radicalize her even further. She moved to East Tennessee State University in 1967 but was fired two years later for "nurturing radical students." She returned to Clinch Valley College in 1969. To the lessons learned from Paolo Freire's *Pedagogy of the Oppressed*, published in Portuguese in 1968 and in English in 1970, Helen added her own perspective born of firsthand experiences. The political and theoretical implications of her unfolding analysis led to a new pedagogy of empowering students from their own positions of strength through their engagement with and documentation of the communities in which they lived and worked. Her activist teaching strategy embraced local knowledge, participatory research, and popular culture. She developed a social welfare program emphasizing rural social work, which laid the groundwork for one of the first Appalachian studies programs in the region and for her collaborative and participatory research of the next decades.

As a radical teacher, researcher, and activist, Helen lived and worked at the nexus of social movements in the region calling for political, economic, and environmental justice. At the same time, she moved to the forefront of a new pedagogy that envisioned student empowerment and community engagement through the developing field of Appalachian studies.

The Teacher and Librarian as Community Activist

In 1950 the United Mine Workers of America (UMWA), under the leadership of John L. Lewis, signed a labor contract that improved wages and occupational health and safety, yet resulted in mechanization of the mines, consolidation of control by major mining operations, massive unemployment, and migrations of large numbers of people from the region. The 1950s saw declining coal production, increasing poverty, and a widening gap between the poverty of the region and the wealth of the coal industry.

I moved to the Central Appalachian coalfields in the mid-'50s when the coal industry was being mechanized and half the population of the coalfield counties was leaving for northern industrial centers. Half the miners were unemployed and the area was soon to be discovered and labeled as a poverty pocket and become a center of social activism. I was teaching sociology [at Clinch Valley College] and sixty percent of my students were from mining families. From them I began to learn about coal mining, about what happens to a mountain region controlled by the coal industry. I became very interested in trying to understand what happens to a rural region when it is industrialized, and industrialized by outside ownership, by an extractive industry.

People said the coal industry was dead, but the coal was still being mined and the industry was healthy. I became concerned about how the area of the state, which produced the greatest wealth, could be the poorest part of the state, concerned about lack of roads, health care, education. I decided to concentrate my research and writing on understanding more about the Appalachian coalfields. ("My Life and Good Times in the Mountains; or, Life and Learning in Central Appalachia")

It was a time of great unemployment. So the first thing I did was go down to the United Mine Workers to talk to them about what was going on and why there weren't retraining programs and what kind of programs did they have to help all these miners that were being laid off (at that point, half the workforce was gone). The answer was they had nothing going on! I was real depressed about that. But they did let me study a lot of stuff

Helen at the Clinch Valley College Library, late 1950s

in their files. I spent months going through them. I was interested in what the grievances were all about, what was going on, just understanding the union and the coal industry.

Also I started working with the students to get the coalfield history, to get their own histories down, because these coal camps were being demolished and depleted and people were going everywhere. So some of the assignments the students did were to write histories of the communities, and we collected this huge book of community histories, which is still in the library at Clinch Valley. ("You've Got to Be Converted: An Interview with Helen Lewis")

"A Community Study of Esserville," by Beth Bingman

I came to Clinch Valley College in 1964, when I was seventeen. I had attended schools in county seat towns in southwest Virginia, eastern Kentucky, and southern West Virginia. I came to Clinch Valley because my family lived in Wise and knew many faculty members, including Helen and Judd Lewis. Even though I grew up in Appalachia and knew something about the region, my life experiences and understandings were of small towns in the upper South, not of the coal camps. Doing a community study as part of Helen's sociology class expanded my understanding.

Esserville, the community that I studied with another student, was only a mile or two from my parents' home, on the highway between Norton and Wise. The coke ovens, still burning in the early 1960s, were clearly visible from the highway, particularly at night when fire shot from the top of each brick "beehive." Less visible were the houses where the families of the men who worked the ovens lived. Our community study took us into those homes, as well as into the businesses along the highway. The excerpts from the 1966 study I did with Kay Baker, archived at Clinch Valley College and reproduced below, give some sense of what we learned:

> The camp in Esserville consists of a commissary, an abandoned house, and twenty-two occupied houses. These houses are three and four room dwellings with electricity, but without plumbing and are in poor condition. One of the company houses is rented by a man who works for another coal company, and this house is in better repair, however it is not in good condition. The camp houses are very dirty inside. Water for these houses has to be carried for some distance and any effort to keep a house in the vicinity of the coke ovens clean is nearly futile. The roads are not paved. A few families have planted gardens but not the majority. [The camp, commissary, and coke ovens, owned by the same coal company operator, formed a distinct part of the community, which also included privately owned homes and businesses and an elementary school.]
>
> The pay is on a piece-work basis—$5.88 for each oven "pulled." Some men can pull three ovens a day, but this is unusual and some only pull half an oven. ["Pulling an oven" meant removing the coke from the oven by hand. We estimated the average worker pulled an oven a day. We noted that while there was some reluctance to talk about it, the men were paid in scrip and were in debt to the company store or commissary where most families shopped.] When asked what would make things in Esserville better, people outside the camp either did not know or suggested things like more work and factories. The people within the camp suggested

a water system, improvements in the houses, garbage collection, and a playground.

This survey was not scientific, but it is accurate as far as it goes. To really know how people in Esserville, especially in the camp feel, one would have to live with them and even then the feelings would not be the same. Unless we looked forward to raising several children on $5.88 an oven, we could not feel as they feel.

In 1957 I was librarian at Clinch Valley College, and we received a call from Florence Yoder, Virginia State librarian. The state was anxious to establish library services in southwest Virginia. Would we help? The American Association of University Women (AAUW) was just being organized in Wise. I suggested to the group that this could be a good project.

Someone said the VFW dance hall on the Norton-Wise Road was seldom used and we might talk them into letting us have it for a library. We looked at the building. There were problems: the heating system, cleaning the building, then getting shelving. But after several conversations, beating around the bush, talking about libraries, educational needs, civic duties, and talking to other VFW members they agreed to let us have a go at it.

Someone said we could get prisoners from the jail to work with us. I took several prisoners who helped clean, paint, put up shelves, and move furniture. When the books and other equipment came they helped shelve books and get the library set up. One of the young men was very interested in the books on criminology. I thought, "success already, we have reformed a criminal." Later I learned that his next arrest was not for brawling and drunkenness but a white-collar crime: check forgery. He had graduated into a higher profession.

I found out later that the folks at the jail called me Long Chain Charlie. They had never had a woman come check out prisoners and work them before. If I had known it was not a proper thing to do I might have been less happy to do it. But I made some friends with prisoners. One old trustee began saving me all the coffee grounds from the jail for my compost heap, which I picked up every week also.

The library officially opened November 23, 1958. We had to continue to seek support and donations to keep the lights on, to repair the furnace, to buy coal and keep the operation going. We built a strong support system all over the county. The response to the library was great. Circulation: 10,000 books a month. The state library called the demonstration "wildly successful. . . ."

In July 1960 the demonstration library became the Wise County Public Library. We were very proud. I feel like the library came to Wise County largely through the work of the women in the county. They were the front line troops. We had support from men in civic clubs, the VFW, but the main work was done by the women, and they have continued to this day. . . . We formed a Friends of the Library to keep bringing money and funds to provide special things. I also filled in as Acting Librarian for about six months or a year in between librarians. . . . Of all the projects I have worked on in my lifetime, I am most proud of the role I played in the start up of this library. ("The History of the Beginning of the Wise County Library—As I Remember It")

So [following the successful library project] I go to them and say, I have another proposition for you. This one is a tax on coal, and the money would go to improve the schools. Some of the local coal operators wanted to be involved. They were going to do it! But then they got called by Westmoreland Coal Company folks and were told not to, so they didn't show up for the meeting. All those folks we had talked to and thought would come to the meeting did not come.

But finally there was one representative in the Virginia legislature from Buchanan County, who did propose a severance tax, and eventually it was passed, but the big coal companies brought their big people in from Philadelphia and places like that and were able to block the first efforts. They stopped it, and it was only going to be about one cent a ton, something really innocuous. It was ten years later, I guess, before the tax was ever passed. ("You've Got to Be Converted: An Interview with Helen Lewis")

from "Proposal for a Severance Tax on Coal, Wise, Virginia" (1960)

Senator Donald A. McGlothlin of Buchanan County has introduced a bill in the Virginia Senate, which would allow the counties to levy a tax of up to three cents a ton on coal mined within their counties. This is an enabling act. It does not require them to levy any tax.

A tax of 1 cent a ton would produce estimated revenue of $62,000 a year in Wise County. This would be a very small levy to the coal industry—at the most only 1/3 of 1% tax. It seems very unlikely that any coal operations would be hurt by such a small levy. At present the coal operators pay only property taxes locally and much of the great wealth which comes from the local area leaves the area and the state completely, producing no revenue for the area or the state. This produces an ironic situation in which the area of the state with the richest natural resources has the lowest level of education, poorest roads and other public services. Instead of the local resources helping provide funds to improve local schools and services, the wealth goes to other areas and states to improve schools and services there.

Although some members of the coal industry are strongly opposed to the tax, it seems inconceivable that all members of the industry will oppose it. Some members of the industry live in the area, educate their children here and are concerned for the area. Some of these men do support such a levy and wish to see such a tax used to improve education in the area.

You are urged to support this proposed legislation by writing your representatives and urging others to do the same. Let us bring the education in Wise County *at least* up to the state and national averages.

Researching Coal and Developing an Analysis

One of the battles I was fighting at Clinch Valley College was getting a real position rather than being [part-time]Wife-of-Somebody. . . . So in '62 I applied for a National Science Foundation Fellowship at Berkeley and did the anthropology institute all summer with [Allen] Mandelbaum, [Eugene] Hammel, and [Robert] Murphy. That was so exciting. That was my first trip west. I rode the train all the way from Williamson, West Virginia, into Berkeley and got off and spent the summer there. The deal was, if I went back to my school and taught anthropology and came back the next summer, it would be a Ph.D. program from the University of California at Berkeley.

So I get back to Clinch Valley at the end of the summer and the librarian had left. There was nobody to run the library, and I was asked to do that, and I just practically cried. I wanted to do anthropology. Instead I did the library again. People in the University of Virginia administration promised all sorts of things, that if I would be librarian again I would get a full-time position, which they later forgot about. But I did the library for two more years, and I would have been doing it probably until today, but I said, "I am not going to do this any longer." I applied to the NSF again and got a National Science Foundation faculty award, which would pay my full salary until I could get my Ph.D. I could go to school anywhere in the world with it.

I went to the University of Kentucky because I'd decided I wanted to deal with Appalachian issues, and that was where the only people were who had written anything or done anything in Appalachia. Tom Ford was there and Marion Pearsall and James Brown. . . . But Jim Brown went away the year I arrived, and Tom Ford was chairman of the department, so he didn't have time to teach. . . . There was not one Appalachian course of any kind. I went there to study and write about Appalachia; instead I end up

Helen visiting a pony mine in Virginia, mid-1960s

taking "Marriage and the Family" for the third time, and I'd been teaching it for ten years! I had to take everything over.

I wrote the Bureau of Mines and asked them if they'd ever done any studies on coal-mining families or attitudes of miners, things like that. The head of the research division wrote back and said, "No, but would you be interested in doing some?" I was particularly interested in changes in the coalfields because of mechanization, from the old hand loading methods up through continuous miners, and the changes this technology was making in the ways miners viewed their work. I got Ed Knipe from the University of Kentucky to join with me in doing the study for the Bureau of Mines. Ed and two male students would go down underground and interview the miners, study the work organization. Two women students and I would go and interview the wives, and it was wonderful data. But our project director at the Bureau of Mines became critical of the Nixon administration and he got fired, and we got fired. We had finished up one part. So much for doing research for the Bureau of Mines. ("You've Got to Be Converted: An Interview with Helen Lewis")

In their methodology, Lewis and Knipe emphasized the importance of under-standing regional dialect and the occupational language of coal mining, and of building relationships of trust. Recognizing the cultural importance of storytelling, their methodology also includes the use of projective, or hypothetical, stories of familiar life experiences to which respondents might be able to respond. Gifts to miners' families of photographs of miners on the job served as a tool for bridging the isolation of the miners' world of work and their world of family.

from "Toward a Methodology of Studying Coal Mining," with Edward E. Knipe (1968)

THE INTERVIEW AS SOCIAL INTERACTION

The interview is a form of social rhetoric and the main business of sociology is to gain knowledge of social rhetoric. How were interviewees rewarded for giving their time, effort, and knowledge? We found two types of rewards, which we were able to give. One was the photograph. Before the miners and their wives were interviewed, the male observers spent time in the mine where the miner was employed. Usually one day of this observation period included taking of photographs of each man on the job. The film was taken to the photographic lab, developed, and printed. The next day the photographs were given to each man. In some cases, enlargements were made. The men could take home not only their own picture, but also the picture of their workmates. Not only were the miners themselves indebted to the interviewer for the photo, but the wives and family were given an introduction to the interviewer. One of the roles was that of "picture taker." This enabled the interviewer to establish a rapport with the family of the miner before he met them.

The photograph had other value in recording the work situation and the task performance of each employee. It also served to reveal and emphasize some characteristics of the relationship between the man's occupation and the family roles. Through the family's response to seeing where the husband-father works and what specific task he performs, we were made aware of the difference between coal mining and most other occupations. The miner is more separate and isolated from his family and the wife and children have meager knowledge of the job requirements or the specific setting in which the husband-father works.

The second role of the interviewer is that of a member of a quasi-family group. The interviewers worked in male-female teams. The male would interview the husband and the female would interview the wife.

The interview sequence goes as follows. First, general introductions are made, the male interviewer taking the lead, introducing the female interviewer first to the husband and then the wife. This was at times awkward because the female interviewer is introduced to the husband by first name, but the male interviewer does not know the first name of the miner's wife. The introductions are made on a first-name basis for the interviewer and a Mrs. for the interviewee. Generally the male interviewer and the husband are on a first-name basis. Each interview is different depending upon the leads of those being interviewed. In some cases coffee was offered, and all four parties sat in the living room or the kitchen talking. Once it was felt that sufficient rapport had been obtained, one of the interviewers would suggest that they separate. This could be easily facilitated if coffee were served in the living room. The female interviewer would go with the wife when she went into the kitchen to put the dishes away. This is a legitimate role for the female and is one that can be naturally assumed. When the interview started in the kitchen, the male interviewer could suggest that he and the husband retire to the living room. With the portable tape recorder many of the interviews with the miner were conducted on the front porch or in the yard. In either case, the two-person interview team could successfully separate husbands and wives.

The body of the interview consisted of a set of pre-established questions, which form general topics to be discussed. Although the interviews differed in length, a number of basic responses were recorded, which enabled the researchers to tabulate information in a systematic fashion.

The termination of an interview is often as important as the beginning. Instructions were given to interviewers to terminate the interview in such a way as to facilitate later follow-up interviews. The most effective way of doing this is to terminate the interview with the same type of casual conversation that characterized the beginning. This was often done by getting the husband and wife back together with the two interviewers. Often a period of ten or fifteen minutes at the end of an interview signals the end of the interviewee-interviewer relationship and the introduction of a relationship between two couples on a less formal basis. During this period, remarks referring to the possibility of a follow-up interview are introduced along with statements of gratitude concerning the interviewee's cooperativeness. In this manner, the interviewee answers as a friend or acquaintance rather than a subject. This general pattern was followed, and none of the interviewers were given the impression that they could not return.

The political rediscovery of Appalachia, beginning with the presidential election in 1960, made Appalachian poverty, and by extension Appalachian culture, subjects of national debate. Visiting West Virginia in his campaign for president, John F. Kennedy questioned the promises of the affluent society and the failure of the American dream. These questions brought new attention to the region by journalists, scholars, and activists and generated a flurry of media attention. After Kennedy's death, Lyndon Johnson declared a "War on Poverty" in the United States, although he soon faced an escalating international war in Vietnam.

I went back to school at the University of Kentucky and began research on coal mining communities. I read all the old books such as John C. Campbell's The Southern Highlander and His Homeland. *Two new books also came out about that time: Harry Caudill's* Night Comes to the Cumberlands *and Jack Weller's* Yesterday's People. *In 1967 I was invited to give a talk about the Southern Appalachians at the Institute of Southern Culture, Longwood College, in Farmville, Virginia. Margaret Mead was the key speaker. I was very excited. This was my first official paper I had written about the region. I saw it also as an opportunity to respond to Jack Weller's book. I felt that he had only described one segment of Appalachian reality, that he didn't portray the diversity of the region. . . . I was not very critical of the subculture model then. I also accepted most of the conventional history of the region.*

In describing the settlement of the Cumberland-Allegheny area I wrote, "Up until the Revolution, it was an area to pass through or skirt around and those who finally settled here were the dropouts from wagon trains or the disillusioned returnees from the West. Most of the area was difficult to access and offered few advantages to the farmer in comparison with the fertile fields of the Blue Grass. . . ."

Some local folk took great exception to my use of the phrase "drop-outs from wagon trains." Others took exception to my describing class differences. And there occurred a lively exchange of letters in the local newspapers. Some suggested I go back to Georgia— I should look at the stars instead of the mud. I learned a good lesson—to be more careful of using rather smart-aleck phrases such as "wagon train drop-outs," although I meant it in a positive way, and rely more on local people's own words and wisdom and think about who was going to read it. I found, however, that stirring up a dialogue had some great value. ("My Life and Good Times in the Mountains: or, Life and Learning in Central Appalachia")

Informed by living in the region and in response to Jack Weller's publication,

Helen presented a new analysis of the region's cultural diversity and the class relationships that had developed with industrialization in southwest Virginia and eastern Kentucky. Discarding the received wisdom that defined Appalachian culture as a homogeneous folk culture, she distinguished among three subcultures: traditional mountain culture, which had been the subject of Weller's analysis; coal mining communities; and middle-class or town culture. The following excerpt discusses coal-mining culture.

from "The Subcultures of the Southern Appalachians: Their Origins and Boundary Maintenance" (1968)

One can delineate a statistical area, and it is this Appalachia which is the focus of poverty programs, the Appalachian road building program, and the economic development programs. This type of enumeration does not tell us much about the way of life in the Appalachians.

SUBCULTURES AND VALUE ORIENTATIONS

Values are seen as mechanisms that both sustain and retrain. They explain and make tolerable the conditions of life in which one is situated and, as such, they frequently become barriers and deter changes needed to achieve different conditions. There is no better place to observe this than to see how certain Southern values have thwarted reasonable and efficient desegregation.

In time, coalmining changed some of the values, but it also helped preserve and protect some of the mountain ways. Coalmining continued the physical isolation and added a social isolation due to the segregation of the town folk from both the miners and mountaineers. This served not only to prevent disruption of some of the mountain culture, but also to produce a homogeneous coal camp culture. Coalmining did not require education, and this cut down on integration into the larger society.

Separated from kin, the men entered into a dark, dangerous occupation underground. Working with a small group in a dangerous situation and living in a closed homogeneous community, there developed a strong peer-group orientation, which replaced the strong family orientation. The family might still be important, but one's buddy comes first. As one miner said in a recent interview, "You can't let your buddy down, you never know when your life may depend on him."

Mining, danger, and risk dominated the coal camp, and there was a high degree of identification with and loyalty to the work group even outside the work situation. The male "secret society" met nightly on the commissary steps to talk over the day's work. Hunting, drinking or fighting together on the weekend made the work bearable. An over-compensating masculine aggressiveness dominates the industry. Coalmining is a man's work, and outsiders are women and children.

The work did develop a more active aggressive exploitative attitude toward nature. One does control nature, digs out coal, cuts off sides of mountains, changes and pollutes streams and air, and causes floods. However, one not only exploits but is exploited. Aggression and conflict replace the passive acceptance, which is the adjustment of the mountaineer. The miner became part of the industrial, technological revolution but was still isolated and separated into a closed society.

Changes are now occurring which portend greater movement into the larger society and a more syncretic integration. Many factors are breaking down the isolation caused by both the mountains and coalmining, including the improved transportation and communication facilities. The breakup of the homogeneous coal camps and the development of patterns of commuting place many miners in the heterogeneous towns where they are participating more in social organizations and are losing their group consciousness and awareness of separateness. The change to more skilled, specialized mining jobs breaks up the cooperative, informal small-group arrangements in underground mining and lessens the intensive interaction and informal solidarity. The emphasis on skills and training in mining now encourages education and training which is the major bridge to the greater society.

When the boundaries are no longer important and the identifying value systems are no longer functional, the comparisons and group identifications, which represent a specialized adaptation to a particular situation, will no longer be needed. The differences will no longer make a difference and they will slowly fade away. The mountaineer will work hard and will work all the time, whether he needs to or not. He will compete for position and goods, which symbolize success. Instead of reticent and retiring, he will become blasé, gregarious, and sophisticated. He will become a joiner and worry more about society than about his family. The coal miner will become a skilled, highly specialized laborer, commuting to his place of work. The closeness of friendships will give way to more formal contacts through clubs and associations. He will fight, not the company, but crab grass, and join the PTA.

Those who tabulate progress will be pleased.

Radical Teacher

Helen joined the faculty at East Tennessee State University, in Johnson City, at a time when social movements of the 1960s were sweeping American colleges and universities. Idealistic young people came to Appalachia as VISTA (Volunteers in Service to America) workers and Appalachian Volunteers (organized initially by the Council of the Southern Mountains). The Vietnam War drew disproportionately high numbers of recruits and draftees from the region, some of whom returned to speak out against the authority of corporate America on the region's campuses. The conservatism of the region's institutions was challenged by a new generation of activists, schooled by civil rights, feminism, and the antiwar movement.

[By 1967] Clinch Valley still wouldn't give me a full-time job, and they had promised they would, after I did the library work for them and finished a Ph.D.

I got so mad at them [Clinch Valley] I quit and went to East Tennessee State and took my grants with me. Ed Knipe went, too, since we shared the Bureau of Mines grant. ETSU gave him a full-time job, me a full-time job—both of them half-time teaching, half-time research. President Culp had just come in. . . . It was one of the most exciting teaching experiences I ever had, and the sociology department was growing. They had no anthropologists, so I was doing most of the anthropology. We started one of the first graduate programs at East Tennessee, and we attracted all these interesting students.

Charles Dyer, who had come back from Vietnam, started a petition to have a referendum on whether or not ROTC should be compulsory. That got the administration alerted that something was happening in Sociology. We were also gaining students when every other department was losing them. People were flocking there because it was exciting. I did a lecture on rock music with overhead projectors and a light show, a content analysis of the meaning of the words in the songs, and people flocked to it. I had seen something like it at Berkeley, so I was putting on the California scene.

[In 1969] just one week after [Chair] Paul Wilson was being congratulated for the growth of the [Sociology] department, Ed Knipe and I both get notices in the mail that our contracts would not be renewed. And they hadn't talked to Paul about it. . . . The dean who had been congratulating him the week before was telling him that we were nurturing radical students.

And then the story starts that I had told my students to burn their draft cards. I don't think I ever mentioned burning draft cards or that anybody even did it. It was story after story: that I had a sign on my door that said "Jesus was a hippie too." But I didn't.

Helen in Paris, 1964

The minute that Ed and I were terminated, students went into a fit and organized this big march on campus and a funeral for the sociology department. . . . They got a casket and funeral music and wreaths and put up signs all around the building about the funeral. . . . Then they cut off all the money to our department. . . . This woman wrote an article in the Johnson City newspaper about what was going on, and she quoted all these students, and one of them said that I had framed pictures of Marx and Lenin in my office. I had Durkheim and Max Weber.

I just went back home. I was still married to Judd, and I just went back to my house, and I didn't have a job. ("You've Got to Be Converted: An Interview with Helen Lewis")

After Helen returned to Clinch Valley College, she developed her first Appalachian studies courses, as well as a rural social work program. Helen took half pay and used the rest of the salary for speakers for her Appalachian seminars and a Wednesday public forum for community people. She brought noteworthy voices to campus, including musician Jean Richie; attorney Harry Caudill, author of the critique of the mining industry *Night Comes to the Cumberlands*; and physicians who would talk about black lung.

[In 1969] I started the social work program [at Clinch Valley College] and taught sociology and anthropology. At Clinch Valley I had all these wonderful students and I had this money. Since the social work program was being funded by outside sources, there was money for speakers and money for trips

I developed an urban study course and took students to New York to visit the Puerto Rican neighborhoods during January, and to Boston and Cincinnati. I invited people from Welfare Rights, and students took placements with these organizations. The Union Reform movement was going on at that time, and that's when I got in trouble with the Union. ("You've Got to Be Converted: An Interview with Helen Lewis")

"Helen Lewis as Teacher," by Jack Wright

I didn't know it when I was a student, but [Helen] was ahead of her time. She practiced experiential education. . . . In her Appalachian class, we all had to do a project. I didn't want to write a paper, so she said, "Well, what would you like to do?" I said, "Maybe I could do a concert or a festival, or something like that." She told me she had $350 she'd give me to do that. In 1969, that was a ton of money.

So I made contact with a guy named Dock Boggs who lived not far from me. I'd been visiting him and got to know him. He was a real friendly chap, about 70 years old. And we had a local street singer named Bill Denham, who was blind. He made his living playing guitar and harmonica. . . . He wasn't a brilliant musician, but his music came from the heart. Dock introduced me to Kate Peters Sturgill, who was also a musician. . . . She had been on the radio in the '40s. She and Dock were good friends. . . .

But Helen gave me that money, and I offered Dock 60 bucks, Bill 60 bucks, Kate 60 bucks, and 60 bucks to Earl Gilmore, who was a black piano player and dancer. He was gay, and that was back before you could really be out, but he wore earrings and a nose ring in 1969. . . . He ran the black choir in his neighborhood coal camp over at Clinchco in Dickenson County.

I also got a letter from Mike Seeger, Pete Seeger's brother, who told me he would like to come, and that he'd come for whatever I was paying Dock. . . . That was a big thing at the end of the course on December 4, 1969. I called it the Appalachian Folk Festival.

[We had] a huge turnout. Well, relative to the size of the college. We filled the lounge, which held about 200 people. It was the first time that a lot of town and county people had come to the college for an event other than athletic or graduation ceremonies. That impressed some people at the college. I charged a dollar a person to get in, and I took in about 200 bucks. A couple of students played, too, including myself. I had never done a solo gig in front of that many people before. And I had never emceed before. I had access to a little reel-to-reel tape recorder, so I've got a recording of the concert. ("'Looking into My Culture': An Interview with Jack Wright")

Problems with coal dust, black lung, and underground safety produced calls for reform and challenges to the leadership of UMWA president Tony Boyle. With grassroots support from miners, black lung activists, and War on Poverty workers, Joseph "Jock" Yablonski challenged Boyle's leadership in the fall 1969 election.

I invited Yablonski in to talk. He didn't come, but I had gone up to Grundy to hear him speak and tried to get him to come down. I didn't realize then that the Union was that bad. The head of the Union in Wise, a Boyle supporter, started in on me, knew that I had invited Yablonski. The chancellor says, "Well, the Union's against you, and the coal operators are against you too. I'm having a hard time." (It seemed like everything you did in those days got you into trouble.) I started my students studying taxes and land ownership and going to the courthouse and going through records and going to the bank and finding out who the Board of Directors of this and that were. It was wonderful. My program was kind of the first of the new style of Appalachian studies, activist oriented. I became this person. ("You've Got to Be Converted: An Interview with Helen Lewis")

I had started taking students to urban centers to teach Urban Sociology, and how are you going to learn about urban sociology if you don't go to an urban setting? So I arranged for us to go to New York City and spend the January term living at the YMCA in Midtown and visiting with some of the Puerto Rican communities. And a group of young Puerto Rican activists and militants, The Young Lords, had taken over this church. So we visited these people in this church. They wanted to start a breakfast program for kids and do some things like that. They were kind of copying what the Black Panthers were doing. And the police, they let us in, but they were threatening to go in there and break them up. And these Puerto Rican kids talked to us and told us, "You know, anybody who tries to go against the system or change things gets killed." And they named Martin Luther

King, and John F. Kennedy and Robert Kennedy, and they said, "And we will probably get killed when the police come in." All of us were just sitting there shocked, that we were in this position. So we leave, and we go up to Times Square and we walk in this music store, and Taj Mahal is singing "Death, Oh Death," and it's a song by Dock Boggs, who is an old banjo player from Norton who had come to our class and talked about his life and work and had sung these songs. And we looked out and around the top of the building—you know, where the news is shown—and it said "Jock Yablonski and family murdered." We were all standing there, and we were the same group that had invited Yablonski to come speak. And talk about shock! And one of the students said, "Remember what that fellow said in the church?" Well, we sat up all night long, this whole class, crying and talking and trying to figure out what it was all about, in the middle of New York City. Talk about learning experiences! Jack Wright was in that class, and Beth Bingman was in that class, and a lot of other folks who were and are still activists in the mountains and very much involved in social change. ("Unruly Woman: An Interview with Helen Lewis")

The following excerpt was written in 1970 as a rationale for the social work program that Helen developed at Clinch Valley College in 1969. With an Appalachian focus, the program included a course entitled "Appalachian Seminar" that drew on Paulo Freire's *Pedagogy of the Oppressed*. Her rationale, along with the class outline and bibliography, were passed around the region among academics who were planning Appalachian studies curricula.

from "Appalachian Studies—The Next Step" (1970)

The area, itself, should become a learning laboratory and students should see the area as a learning environment. . . . The concept of teachers must also be enlarged. Skills should be taught by models, or people who know, who are competent, and they may be welfare mothers, coal miners, or bankers. Teachers of skills need not be in the profession. Administration and teachers should concentrate primarily on providing access to resources. Education must eliminate the "banking" concept of education in which the student is a depository, a receptacle that receives, memorizes, repeats, and files and stores.

Instead of a "banking" type education, education must be a "problem-solving" one, not a transfer of information, but a dialogue in which students and teachers are jointly responsible and critical co-investigators together. It bases itself on creativity and stimulates true reflection and action upon reality. This is true liberal arts education, which can "liberate" Appalachians.

Appalachian Activism and Appalachian Studies

Helen's application of the internal colonialism model to the Appalachian coal-fields of the 1960s altered the direction in which regional activists and educators set their course and provided new ways to begin thinking about regional culture and class. The following excerpt represents an essential piece in the movement of cultural workers and scholars away from Appalachian subculture and deficiency models toward broader analyses that took into consideration global industrial forces. Helen Lewis and Edward E. Knipe presented an elaboration of the internal colonialism model in "The Colonialism Model: The Appalachian Case" at the American Anthropologist Association meeting in 1970; it was later published in *Mountain Life and Work* and *Colonialism in Modern American: The Appalachian Case.*

from "Fatalism or the Coal Industry?" (1970)

Walter Lippmann, in the introduction [to *Public Opinion,* 1954], spoke of the way men perceive social reality as "the world outside and the picture in our heads." What are the pictures in the heads of those who are interested and involved in the uplift of Appalachia? What are their views of the situation? Unfortunately many of these students, workers, change agents, helpers, organizers and general meddlers are completely unaware of the preconceptions, definitions, and models which guide their proclamations and programs for the area. This has led to conflicts and confrontations concerning programs for Appalachia. Appalachia has been the ground for many battles throughout its history: family and clan feuds, coal mine wars, battles between strip miners and land owners, and now individuals and groups at war over how to solve the problems of Appalachia. Some of the recent confrontations between members of the Council of the Southern Mountains can be seen as confrontations of two different views of Appalachian problems and two different strategies for helping solve the problems. One can also go further, take a step behind the "views" and look to where these protagonists are "located" in the social structure to explain their views.

I would like to outline two opposing views of Appalachia and suggest some of the implications of each for the solution to Appalachian problems. The first view is termed the Appalachian Subculture Model and the second the Colonialism-Exploitation Model. In simple terms it is either fatalism or the coal industry.

The Appalachian subculture model is what Charles Valentine in *Culture and Poverty* [1968] calls a "difference" or "deficiency" model." By this view one sees the Southern Appalachians as a subculture with unique and different customs, values, style of life which developed historically and which is passed on through each succeeding generation. It is almost always compared with the greater society or mainstream America and the differences between the two are pointed out. The Appalachian is fatalistic while mainstream Americans believe they can control their environment and their lives. The Appalachian is impulsive, personalistic and individualistic while mainstream Americans are rational, organized, can handle impersonal role relationships and have a social consciousness.

Some emphasize the subcultural traits as obsolete . . . , while others emphasize the traits as a pathological, disorganized, defeating value system. . . . Mostly these approaches describe and generalize on Appalachian character and general values. Some speak of the adaptive nature of the subculture and explain how such values are tied to conditions of poverty, lack of resources, isolation, powerlessness and the group's location in the total socio-political-economic system.

A major problem with this type of view, and the resultant descriptions of Appalachia, is that they emphasize a stereotyped view of Appalachian values with little concern for the socialization process and the content of what is transmitted from one generation to another. It is assumed that middle-class or dominant American values are not transmitted in Appalachia. If we are concerned with the causes of Appalachian problems, we must view them differently than if we are concerned with the effects of these problems. In the former case, we are concerned with the factors which led to those behaviors described as belonging to those in the Appalachian subculture. In the latter case, we want to know how these behaviors are transmitted from one generation to another. Pure description answers neither one of these questions. They do not tell us why these conditions prevail and do not tell us why these conditions cause certain values, norms or behaviors of the people.

Yet many helpers, social workers, community organizers, teachers, preachers accept and operate on this view of Appalachia. In so doing, they focus in on the values of the Appalachian and say that these must be changed. Unfortunately, the subcultural model has been the predominant one influencing most of the poverty programs. One seeks to improve the schools, motivate children to achievement, change the values, break down the isolation, bring the area into the "mainstream." One does not question the institutions

and avoids recognizing the need for radical change in the society. The whole-
sale and intemperate acceptance and promulgation of this model and these
strategies have been extremely pernicious and wasteful of money. They have,
if anything, helped create an Appalachian subculture by convincing the Appalachian that he is inferior, backward, lazy, and has "bad" values. He should
catch up, "get with it." This image has been projected upon Appalachians by
all major institutions from the mass media to anti-poverty programs. It is
untenable and unjust to characterize Appalachian culture patterns as deficient
or pathological versions of mainstream American culture.

Some of the outspoken critics of the subculture model claim that the subculture proponents blame the underdevelopment of the region on the Appalachian
character rather than the exploitative conditions institutionalized in the region.
In their search for the causes of the problem, they see Appalachia as a subsociety structurally alienated and lacking resources due to processes of colonialism
and exploitation. Those who control the resources preserve their advantages
by discrimination. The people are not essentially passive but these "subcultural"
traits of fatalism, passivity, etc., are adjustive techniques of the powerless; ways
in which people protect their way of life from new economic modes and the
concomitant alien culture. These values are reactions to powerlessness.

The claim of colonialism has become more popular with young "change
agents" in the mountains, VISTA workers, students, young professionals, lawyers and churchmen working in the area. The emergence of books on Algerian
and Third World colonialism have also encouraged comparisons. Except for
[Harry] Caudill most of the writings stressing this interpretation of Appalachia have been in the mimeographed, underground publications, "movement"
newsletters and the student press. This speaks to the location in the social
structure of those who promote this view. Most are outside the established
institutions and many are involved in counter- or alternate institutional movements. Many poor also champion this view.

The colonialism interpretation has been particularly applied to that por-
tion of the mountains in which coal mining developed, that section labeled
by the Appalachian Regional Commission as "Central Appalachia." . . . There
are no systematic, thorough studies of the land and mineral ownership for the
region. This "oversight" itself might be considered "evidence" of the protection provided colonizers. Even the Appalachian Regional Commission after
a number of years of data collection and analysis of various aspects of Appalachian poverty and economic potential has only lately turned its attention

to the Central Appalachian area. . . . One must go to the radical student or movement publications to find any studies, or to the Bureau of Mines statistics on such things as coal production, to find documentation.

Certain income distribution is characteristic of colonialism. Coal mining produces different kinds of distribution of resources than those produced by manufacturing industries. It requires a less complex and a shorter range of skills, which leads to an income distribution with a small elite and a large number of people at the bottom.

Education distribution and migration patterns also reflect the economy of exploitation. Despite some improvements in schools and a greater number of high school graduates from local schools in recent years, the median education has improved only slightly. The industry attracts the uneducated, and the high school and college trained leave the area. Even with mechanization the skill requirements have not increased to the point of attracting the better educated.

The outside coal interests exert political control in subtle and often unseen ways for the local inhabitant. The protection of investments and property through state legislation and the judicial system began early. Seldom does the outside owner have to deal on the local level with local politicians. He can work through the state capitals, and the state courts and the counties are relatively impotent in ability to tax or control the industry.

The courts have been used to legitimize what were fraudulent, inadequate or at least "inconclusive" leases to property bought at the turn of the century by speculators from the illiterate and unwary mountaineers.

The condition of racism associated with the colonialism model is well illustrated in Appalachia. [Albert] Memmi, [in] *The Colonizer and the Colonized* [1965], points out that it is not only the colonizers but the colonized who go into businesses that engage in this practice. In the region, one finds that the smaller independent coal operators are even more conservative in their political and economic ideology than the outsiders. Most of these small operators are dependent upon the larger companies for leases or money for equipment or their coal sales facilities. A number of local millionaires have emerged in the area through strip mining, selling equipment and truck mining. It is interesting to observe how many of these make their money and then retire to Florida. Perhaps Florida serves as the "homeland" for the native who joins the colonists.

That the coal interests came into the region uninvited; that cultural patterns changed as a result of this intrusion; that the area is controlled by representatives of the industry cannot be disputed; and that racism exists to perpetuate this pattern has been illustrated. Since these conditions exist it would appear that recommendations for change should consider these factors. Changing the values of Appalachians will not change the system of colonialism. Nor will knowledge of the situation.

Those who view Appalachia in this way present very different solutions to the problems of Appalachia. They emphasize the need to change the structure of society. They advocate the redistribution of goods and resources, which would give power to the poor. They see the revolt of Blacks in America and rebellion of Mexican-Americans as resulting from similar colonialism, and they look for and work for a strong movement of the people. They do not look to social work, education and psychiatry or programs designed to change attitudes to motivate and assimilate the Appalachian into mainstream culture.

There is an interest in developing Appalachian pride, reemphasis on the culture as good, emphasis on Appalachian studies to rediscover the lost history of struggle, and to start a revitalization movement and develop an Appalachian identity. Those who follow this point of view look to parallel organizations for services or radical alteration of existing dominant institutions with respect to the values, attitudes and interests which they serve. Although some will dismantle and some radically change, all emphasize the need to make the service institutions responsive to the people: the institutions should change; there must be radical shifts in power relationships and the class system. Professionals must learn respect for subcultural systems and recognize the legitimacy and creativity of the subculture rather than regarding them as problems to be changed.

This view, although it seems to address itself more to the causes of Appalachian problems than the first model, does present us with problems when we come to strategies for change. Where is the "homeland" of the exploiters? How can one "throw the bastards out" and take over the resources when one is also part of the same national system? How does one begin a meaningful revitalization movement? Do the colonized always revolt? There is evidence that the most severely oppressed people and subsocieties have seldom rebelled or risen up effectively. Those helpers or change agents who are the proponents of radical change in the mountains are also very expendable, and have little power of their own to back up such a movement. There is also a tendency for them to exaggerate a single cause: it's the coal company, and postulate a nirvana when this one source of trouble is eliminated or conquered. Stop strip mining! Pass a severance tax on coal! Take the resources! This also becomes a rationalization for failure. Since the corporations are so large and powerful and unapproachable, and the institutions so corrupt and unresponsive, little can be done. So they just sit and wait for the revolution and maybe sing a few folk songs while they are waiting. They worry so much about changing society they may forget to help a friend. Some are even calculating enough to be willing to "throw a few bodies" at the system.

There is also a tendency on the part of the revolutionaries to over-protest the deficiency model, and to stereotype all the mountain culture as good. They go native and begin to extol a life style, much of which may be an adjustment to oppression. Some would be very reluctant to allow Appalachian people to live a suburban, middle-class style of life even if they wanted to.

As we have looked at the two models we find differences in responses to the conditions in Appalachia stemming from the acceptance of one or the other. Those who follow the deficiency or difference approach—the subculture model—work to help to change people. Their object is to change their values and assimilate the Appalachian poor to middle-class culture. Through various programs of social work, education and psychiatry, they hope to change attitudes, to motivate and to assimilate. Those who follow the colonialism model emphasize the need to change the structure of society. They advocate the redistribution of goods and resources which would give power to the poor.

Is there a meeting ground for the two approaches? One can look at Appalachia as a heterogeneous subsociety with adaptive subcultures. The area does share norms of the total society but there are variations in different locales and situations. Creative adaptive cultural patterns have developed from historical and situational sources. Some of these are adaptations to oppression and powerlessness. Programs for change must recognize the varieties of Appalachian lifestyles and avoid uniform programs to eliminate poverty based on distorted stereotyped pictures of Appalachian life. Change must look toward changing the causes of poverty and not the results of poverty. The compromise or combination model would approach change through:

1. Increase resources and/or control over resources.
2. Radical change of institutions to meet needs and deliver services.
3. Alteration of the total social structure to provide for power and participation by Appalachian poor.
4. Change some subcultural patterns resulting from oppression through education, social work and cultural programs to motivate and stimulate creative activity among all the people.

But is it possible? Are there enough strengths left in the region to produce creative forms of action for change?

Tom Gish, editor of the *Mountain Eagle* in Whitesburg, Kentucky, talks about colonialism, outside exploitation of the wealth and the various government programs for amelioration. Although outside corporations still exploit the resources, he feels that the period of blatant colonial control and local domination is past. The coal companies can continue to mine the minerals through control over a few politicians, state courts and lawyers, and they can control labor through collusion with the United Mine Workers. In the meantime they can ignore and leave behind the many social problems resulting from technological change, illness, injury, and long powerlessness and deprivation. These will be handled (along with polluted streams and devastated land) by federal government programs. The early war on poverty programs tried to create political action, which was threatening to the local power structure and to the corporate interests. These programs have been co-opted or dropped. The focus is now on economic development, assistance and control. Regional offices of Health, Education and Welfare, Department of Labor, U.S. Corps of Engineers, Office of Economic Opportunity, Department of Agriculture and Department of Interior with headquarters in Atlanta, Baltimore, Philadelphia and Washington funnel in programs of "assistance" through regional economic planning and development organizations. Gish finds these regional organizations developing more and more like the Office of Indian Affairs, to control the natives. Perhaps this is a latter stage of colonialism in which those who are left-over, the land and the people, are now wards of the government, living on a Paleface Reservation.

The following excerpt is from a presentation at the American Anthropologist Association in 1972, which was then published in *Colonialism in Modern America: The Appalachian Case.*

from "Kinship, Religion, and Colonialism in Central Appalachia; or, Bury My Rifle at Big Stone Gap," with Sue Easterling Kobak and Linda Johnson (1972)

The process of colonization as it occurred in the Central Appalachian generally followed these stages:

1. Gaining entry: invasion and securing the area of resources.

2. Establishment of control: removal of opposition and resistance to prevent expulsion of invaders.
3. Education and conversion of the natives: change the values and social system of the colonized.
4. Maintenance of control: political and social domination.

The invasion was well planned and well executed, almost before the natives knew what had happened. A well-trained force of lawyers, surveyors, geologists and land buyers came into the mountains and millions of acres of mineral and virgin timber-lands passed into the hands of development companies at from 30 cents to one dollar an acre. . . . In the process of entry, both the missionaries and the industrialists were amazed by what they found. They sought to understand, to categorize the mountain people and culture. Letters were sent home, reports to church boards, newspaper articles of the development. Picturesque stories appeared in magazines. Some were horrified at the illiteracy, the lack of schools, medical facilities, limited diet; appalled by the lack of roads, isolation, lack of conveniences and the hard life of the women; intrigued by the songs, beautiful weaving, quaint language, marriage and funeral customs and unorganized church meetings; admiring of their courage, honesty, directness and lack of sophistication. But always they were compared with "back home": the middle-class, professional, urban, educated homes and situations from which they came.

The hanging of a local bad man, Talton Hall, became a ceremonial display of power, showing the legal conquest of the mountains with a confrontation and defeat of the family-clan system. . . . This early show of force and organization of political control made it possible in later years for the owner-operators to rely on the local authorities to protect their interests and maintain the needed law and order. After that, natives did most of the policing and not until the unionization of the mines did the outsiders have to take up guns to protect their interests. . . . The technological superiority of the newcomers made conquest inevitable. The shrewd manipulation of the machinery of law made the newcomer the supporter of law and order while the native became an outlaw. Since the newcomer wrote the history, the colonizer is adventuresome while the native is tough.

The missionaries' and educators' role was an important one: to legitimize the exploitation, eliminate some of the worst abuses, and to educate and change values so that the people would accept the new ways. . . . A former missionary reported that women were sent in to "pave the way" for the ministers. She rode horseback all over Eastern Kentucky without fear of any harm whereas the preachers would be run out. She started schools and clinics but she knew that she was really there to pave the way for the preacher to save souls. . . .

The missionaries were sincere, dedicated and sacrificed their lives to educating mountain people, nursing the sick, caring for orphaned children, and assisting families in many ways. They also had a profound effect upon family life. . . . The missionary and settlement schools were successful in educating a whole generation of teachers and middle-class leaders. . . . It was these schools which developed a dual society where children had one relationship and identity at home and one at school. The schools, books, and teachers represented another world, others' history, others' literature. Some of the teachers attempted to preserve certain aspects of mountain culture such as crafts and music.

Although churches and missionaries gave some support to certain harmless aspects of native culture and served to soften the impact and ameliorate some of the abuses of the system, the denigration of mountain culture, the development of feelings of inferiority as mountain people were "helped," also helped the industrialization process. The churches and schools taught the values of organization, planning, hard work and thrift. They legitimized the industrial process by blaming the ills of the system on the mountaineer himself. He must learn to be more "cagey" (not so gullible and taken in by the land sharks), he must learn to be more thrifty and hard-working and respectful and cooperate with the mine operators.

Some few missionaries thought the church should be more vigorous in warning the mountain people of the danger of large corporations and also in preserving parts of the native culture. . . . Even those ministers who admired the primitive, simple, real worship, found the lack of organization of churches a drawback; services were not regular enough and preachers were ineffective and inefficient. Here again, the outsider judged the family and churches as needing to be better organized; or disrupted if the native was to be fully integrated and assimilated into modern society.

Helen became a frequent speaker to academics, service providers, and church groups and liked to create colorful titles for her talks. This title links the old primitive Baptist hymn "Bright Morning Star" with bright city lights as a metaphor evoking how Appalachian culture was transplanted to urban areas by migrants, who had to learn to live in and use two cultures.

from "Bright Lights and Bright Morning Star: Bicultural Appalachians" (1974)

I am convinced there was and is an Appalachian culture distinct and different from that of the mainstream culture. It is very hard to define what values, what kinds of relationships, what nuances are particularly Appalachian but Appalachians know it exists and when Appalachians come to the city, city folks know it exists. Despite 85 years of "cultural contact" and concerted efforts to destroy that way of life, mountain culture still exists. It can be found not only in back hollows, but also in the city where mountain people live and work. . . .

It has been largely through family and religion that mountain people have maintained their particular way of relating to each other and ways of viewing life. As long as family and kinship groups remained the center of the mountain life, they provided a strong refuge to preserve and maintain mountain culture. Rather than industrialization and migration and urbanization destroying the family ties, kinship ties and networks remained strong enough to ease migration problems and take mountain culture to the cities. Kin networks also provide a support system still viable enough to provide a home base in the mountains for returning migrants. Mountain families seemed to require more commitment of members to help each other through trying times. But, in order to preserve itself, the family became conservative, resisting schools and other "brought-on" institutions. Mothers encouraged their children to drop out or taught them to be bicultural: hillbilly at home and put up with or act proper outside. Mountain culture went underground. It was a form of resistance and sabotage for survival.

When the Appalachians went to the city, they took with them a mountain family system, religion and values, which created "problems" for the cities. But it seems to me the problem is always stated backwards. The city wouldn't adjust to the mountain person. Here was a tremendous labor force, eager to work, people who came to the city not to sit on the porch and rock but to do the dirty work of the economy. It would have been all right if they had just worked, but they brought in another culture and acted like hillbillies. The problem was and is that the cities would not, and perhaps will not, adjust to the hillbilly.

The true bicultural is one who operates in two worlds with some ease, who keeps his soul and maintains his values but who learns to operate when necessary within the system. He learns to manipulate the system; to deal with the institutions; to speak the language and to use these selectively. Many of these bicultural Appalachians live in the city, but with Appalachia in their hearts. They try to maintain as much of their life style as possible. The family supports and understands and forgives those who work for the system. But the strain is great for both. The Mountaineer can't get too rich and he can't show off; he can't really join the enemy or he will be forever estranged. He must walk a tight rope between two worlds.

Mike Smathers calls this person a "cultural transvestite." He may teach or may be a welfare worker or work in the city, but he "lives at home." He compartmentalizes and may never be fully "integrated," but he is most useful in that he learns to use the system for himself and his people. . . .

In order to study Appalachia and really tackle the basic problems of Appalachia, one must question many sacred assumptions such as progress, technology, industrialization and the social class system. If Appalachians can learn to be bicultural, can researchers, planners, professionals also learn to be bicultural? Can we operate so that the research and planning is no longer antagonistic to Appalachian culture? Can professionals who work with Appalachians or "deal with" or interpret Appalachians give support to the Appalachian or provide the kinds of analyses needed by Appalachians to promote needed change or resist change? Can researchers avoid being part of the destructive process and giving comfort, aid and data and legitimization to the enemy? This may involve resisting changes rather than describing them. If we are Appalachian professionals, we must learn about Appalachian life and culture by participating in it and learning to pass back and forth between the cultures, suffering some of the same problems of alienation.

By the early 1970s, the appearance of surface or "strip" mining signaled another major change in the coal industry; massive machines and explosives were used to strip away the surface of the land to access the coal below. Again, Helen became a nexus for the social movements in the region calling for social, economic, and environmental justice.

from "Testimony Presented at Hearings of Joint Subcommittees, Mines and Mining and Environment of the Interior and Insular Affairs Committee of the U.S. House of Representatives" (1973)

I have lived, worked, and studied in the coalfields of Virginia since 1955. I have been particularly interested in the effect of coal mining on the mountain people and their way of life. The longer I have lived in the area, the more I have become concerned about the way in which the coal industry has exploited the area.

Coal mining is an extractive industry. Even at best, mining is exploitative. It does not develop an area and leaves little behind, unless it devises ways or is forced to make returns to the area through taxes and services. When the land and minerals are owned by large corporations located outside the area, both coal and profits go outside the area. Little return is made to the area in the form of taxes or jobs. It has always seemed to me to be an ironic situation that such a great wealth-producing area should have poverty, poor roads, inadequate health facilities and schools.

One of the greatest wealth-producing areas of the nation required a massive "War on Poverty" by the federal government. The war on poverty, however, did not attack the real cause of the area's problems. Rather, federal programs of education and health and welfare services took up the job of ameliorating some of the problems caused by an exploitative and socially irresponsible industry. In essence, the federal government paid for services which should have been paid for by the wealth in the area. Instead, the wealth of the area went outside the area to provide services in other parts of the country.

Strip mining may be the final chapter in the destruction of Appalachia. When the stripped and denuded hills are hauled or washed away, there will be nothing left to exploit. . . . It seems as if strip mining is a final insult added to a long history of injury. Not only is surface mining exploitative in that it removes the coal resources, but it is also a process which further destroys the land, roads, water, homes, and returns less in taxes or jobs to the area than underground mining. In addition to removing the coal, the trees, streams and mountains are also destroyed. Soil, trees, and mountaintops are defined as "overburden" to get out of the way. Mountain ridge by mountain ridge and hollow by hollow, the dwelling places of mountain people are being destroyed or damaged.

Families are left without drinking water, with dangerous mud and rockslides, with impassable roads, with dead streams and lakes, with damaged houses and with guilt and remorse on the part of those who have no alternative except to work on a strip mine. Mountain people are given the cruel alternative of destroying their own homeland in order to continue to live there. Their dwelling places are also considered "overburden"; regional planners suggest that people should be removed from the hollows to the service centers. Such plans seem designed to serve the strip mine industry in that they may strip without fear of heavy blasts wrecking houses, flying rocks breaking car and house roofs, mud sliding into yards or blocking roads, or angry people.

The people who live up the hollows are angry and very depressed. Many who complain may resort to more destructive behavior. Most people in the area feel powerless in the face of such arrogant power and social irresponsibility. They are afraid to speak up for fear of reprisal against relatives who work for strip mines. Strip mining does put bread on the table for a few—at the expense of many more. . . .

Honorable members of this committee, I strongly urge that you consider legislation and that you adopt measures such as are contained in Representative Kenneth Hechler's Bill HR1000, which applies exclusively to coal—coal apart from other minerals.

This bill calls for the phasing out of mountain strip mining in eight months and all strip mining in eighteen months. The bill also provides for assistance and training for those who would be displaced from their jobs and might be seeking new employment.

from "Remarks Made to Energy Crisis and Strip Mining Hearing, Interfaith Council on Corporate Responsibility" (1974)

In the early days in the mountains, families were isolated, transportation was poor, and there were few ministers about. When people died they were buried at the time and later, usually in the spring or summer, after winter broke, preachers would tour the area and preach the funerals. . . . I figured that's why you are here—to preach the funeral for Appalachia and Southwest Virginia. As you memorialize us, I give you a few notes to include in your sermon. It has been a slow death and a long struggle for survival. . . .

Appalachia has had a long history of exploitations, and strip mining is just a last cruel chapter. . . . It has been an area rich in resources. Descriptions of the area, when early explorers came here, tell of the bounty of land and forest.

The first exploitation was probably the game, which hunters and trappers destroyed for coats, and elegant food for the tables of gourmets outside the area. . . . Then, the wealth in timber was discovered. The Vanderbilts built a castle in North Carolina in the midst of a virgin forest, which helped finance it. The lumbering industry unmercifully cut away the most valuable deciduous forest in the world, one of the finest forests of the world's temperate zone.

The discovery of coal by geologists, industrialists, and New York and British financiers at the turn of the century is a sad and well-documented history of colonization. Coal mining has removed billions of tons of coal with little return to the area. It was a rich area, great in resources always exploited for the outside. Strip mining may be the fatal deathblow. It is like insult added to long years of injury. Those who once lived off the land and forest—hunted, fished, farmed—became timberers, coal miners, and then strippers to survive. But survive they have!

What have we lost?

An area which could have been developed rather than ravaged. Instead of the poorest, it could have been the richest with the best services of any part of the country. It is also an area with a rich culture and a life style and philosophy this country badly needs. It is a land of independent, proud, and courageous people, a people with a deep appreciation for the land and their fellow man. The death of Appalachia will decrease the whole nation.

Some of my more theologically oriented friends say that for every death there is a resurrection. Perhaps, as you preach the funeral for the region, we can look for new hope, new life, new vitality to rise from the mud and salvation of our region.

Only an area as rich as Appalachia could have survived this long. Unless the system is changed, the exploitation will continue until the resources are exhausted. We will be sacrificed for profits and the energy needs of the nation.

Greed has produced exploitation of people, destruction of land and resources, pollution of the environment. Corporations in New York and Philadelphia hold our destiny in their hands. I think they have already decided that our hardwood forests, our streams, our hills, our homelands, must go. Voices of the people are ridiculed. James Reilly, a Vice-President of Consolidated Coal Company, said, "Conservationists who want strip miners to restore the land are stupid idiots, socialists, and commies who don't know what they are talking about. I think it is our bounden duty to knock them down and subject

Helen speaking at Clinch Valley College graduation the year she left, 1977

them to the ridicule they deserve." We have voices, but they have power. It is only as we see where the real power is—an attempt to change that system —can we see a resurrection in the mountains.

There were great years at Clinch Valley then for about six years [1969–77], until we got a new dean who started trying to put clamps on everything. . . . The coal operators got upset with me because I decided when I got fired at ETSU that if I got fired again, I would be doing something. If they want to fire you, they'll find a way to fire you, so you might as well do the things you want to do and accomplish the things you want to accomplish. If you just pussy foot around and try to be safe, you won't get anything done and they'll still fire you. Might as well accomplish all you can. Instead of asking permission, ask forgiveness; do it and then ask forgiveness. . . . . The strip miners at that time had this real PR guy who was determined to get three of us fired. . . . I actually resigned. I was not fired. ("You've Got to Be Converted: An Interview with Helen Lewis")

from "Response to the Region: The Role of a Small State-Supported College in Central Appalachia" (1977)

Having recently resigned after twenty years of teaching at Clinch Valley College, I have to look back on the history of the college and understand the changes which have occurred during that time. . . . As a branch of the University of Virginia, Clinch Valley took the role of polishing up and sending away some of the "brightest and best" to complete their education at the university. Many of these were to return as physicians, lawyers, business leaders, but a "good" student was encouraged to leave the area in order to "better oneself"—to be successful elsewhere. . . . The job of the college was to uplift, raise the cultural level and help the mountain youth enter the mainstream culture. The following chart attempts to outline a view of the position and role of the educational institutions as related to manpower preparation and placement:

The Position and Role of Colleges in the Social Structure

Type of Institution	Manpower Preparation
Prestigious national university	Managers of large national and international corporations; leaders in the professions, arts, medicine, law, education, administration of national government bureaucracies; policy advisors to presidents
State liberal arts and professional university	State government leadership; college faculties, physicians, corporate lawyers, ministers, education administration, managers of regional businesses
State engineering technical university	Agricultural, engineering, business leaders, civil planners, mining engineers, managers of forestry, teachers, social workers, inspectors, government employees, local planners, accountants
Small regional state colleges	Local managers of banks, commercial businesses, small manufacturing, teachers, social workers, inspectors, government employees, local planners, accountants
Community colleges	Skilled technicians, skilled factory workers, computer scientists, paraprofessional medical and social service workers
High schools	Clerks, clerical workers, small industry, manufacturing, services, miners, stockmen, file clerks, sales persons
Local technical schools	Blue-collar workers in mines, factories, construction, maintenance, mechanical skills, roads
Drop-outs of the system	Manual laborers, surplus labor pool, unemployed

The reform zeal of the '60s and early '70s affected Clinch Valley and was facilitated by the liberal arts approach of the college. Programs were begun in social work and special education. The faculty began to help write grant proposals for community groups, discover those areas outside the towns, and recognize the class structure in the mountains. The environmental damage from increased strip mining alarmed the biologists, bird watchers, ecologists, and sociologists on the faculty. Many became outspoken.

The college began to produce a group of young graduates in the area who became more highly critical of environmental damage, exploitation, and control by the coal industry and collusion by local government. The social movements of the '60s and early '70s also produced a revitalization movement in Appalachian culture, and the new ethnicity re-emphasized pride in local history and culture. . . . Clinch Valley developed one of the first and most influential Appalachian studies programs in the region with emphasis on social and economic history and reinterpretation of the industrial history of the region. Hillbilly was beautiful. Students were encouraged to remain and work to prevent the destruction and exploitation of the mountains and a way of life.

This activity did not impinge too much on the local economic community because funds for most of the poverty programs, special education projects and reform movements came from the federal funds. However, as many of these programs became controlled by local interests, conflicts erupted with the newly trained "change agents," and there was considerable pressure on the college to change its emphasis.

The mid-'70s brought another major change to the region, and the college is in the process of changing and reacting to that. . . . The energy crisis and boom in coal production in the area has resulted in new economic growth, prosperity, and considerable local wealth, especially from surface mining. New businesses began to come into the area: shopping centers, Pizza Huts, mining equipment dealers.

The Appalachian Regional Commission and regional development brought other small industries to the region, and the road building and growth center strategy began a need for computer experts, more sophisticated accounting, banking, business management skills and less social service, poverty workers and critics of society. New wealth and power in the towns began to transplant the older professionals and land-owning power. Their interest in education was different. . . . Graduates were needed in business management, personnel management, banking—a new type of expertise for the growing businesses of the area. There was also a need for less critical and active social-change-oriented graduates or criticism of the mining industry because "coal puts biscuits on our table." There were rumors of big contributions from local wealth, which might be given to the college, if certain changes were made.

The newer young faculty coming from the business and p[...]
were more congenial with the new industrialization and be[...]
"plug into" the new wealth and power of the region, which o[...]
professors. The new industrialists, with emphasis on progr[...]
no advantage in emphasizing "old mountain ways destroyed by industrialization.
Appalachian studies were seen as provincial and should be limited to preserving
the more harmless elements, such as music and crafts. . . .

The new faculty of modernizing intellectual elites is training graduates to
meet the new needs of the new prosperity. The graduates are trained as tech-
nocrats, managers, planners. There is a new boom in the area and a need for
new mountain-style "Kens and Barbies" to organize banks, develop resources,
manage capital. The college can produce young moderns, and they don't have
to migrate to get ahead or be hillbilly if they remain. They can change the old
home place into a helicopter pad and live in a growth center.

The decline in the more humanistic, liberal arts education also denotes
a change to a more uncritical, value-free, technical education which doesn't
question the ends but becomes proficient in the means: how to manage, how
to control, how to intervene. The humanistic, liberal arts approach puts more
emphasis on the ends, dealing with such questions as what is the good life,
justice, human needs. It emphasizes the need to understand the total social
and cultural system of which one is a part.

CHAPTER 3

Local to Global, 1975–1985

John Gaventa

> It is important to develop pride in the region's rich heritage, but it is also important to see Appalachia as part of a worldwide process of development and change. We must deal with economic and political questions and build an understanding of what is happening in the region and how it is related to the global economic system.
> —Helen M. Lewis and Myles Horton, "Transnational Corporations and the Migration of Industries in Latin America and Appalachia"

I first met Helen Lewis in 1974, about the time her work reflected in this chapter begins. I was living in Clairfield, Tennessee, trying to understand how a British-owned multinational had developed its corporate power in rural east Tennessee and east Kentucky, as well as working with a bold group of citizens to challenge that power. This work informed my later book *Power and Powerlessness: Quiescence and Rebellion in an Appalachian Valley.* While students in Oxford, England, Richard Greatrex and I had done some very rough videotapes in Wales of the 1974 Miners' Strike. Helen invited me over to one of her classes at Clinch Valley College to show the tapes. As happens with many people Helen meets, I became a friend and colleague on a number of projects thereafter. I also think of Helen as a mentor in the sense of someone who inspires in others the ability to see their work differently and who helps them see new possibilities to which they can aspire.

In an article in the 2005 *American Sociological Review*, Michael Burawoy, a well-known scholar and past president of the American Sociological Association, argues that "the world needs public sociology—a sociology that transcends the academy—more than ever. Our potential publics are multiple, ranging from media audiences to policy makers, from silenced minorities to social movements. They are local, global, and national." I once told Michael that Helen represents the model of a public sociologist. She has an enormous ability to transcend the academy, to link and incorporate different worlds without losing her own core values and identity. In this section, we see this strength in at least three different ways: in her move from the local to the global and back again; in her move from teaching in classrooms to engaging broader publics; and in both of these, in her commitment to using her academic and teaching skills to speak truth to power, enabling others to do so along the way.

At the time I met Helen, she was finishing her book *Colonialism in Modern America: The Appalachian Case,* coedited with Linda Johnson and Donald Askins. In this book, she and her coeditors understand the region by drawing on colonial theories used by liberation thinkers to explain development and underdevelopment in other parts of the world. With such an analysis, and for such an inveterate networker and activist, it would be only a matter of time before Helen's work began to reach beyond Appalachia to forge links elsewhere.

In the first set of projects described in this chapter, Helen used video and visual anthropology to understand life in Welsh mining valleys, an area described by Michael Hechter as an internal colony in the British context. In later excerpts toward the end of this chapter, Helen writes with Myles Horton about the comparative role of transnational corporations in Appalachia and Latin America, outlining the importance of global understanding. Throughout her career, Helen has been able to build such global links, but always to do so without losing her deep local and regional roots. Her work is a conversation between regional culture and global political economy and as such spans disciplinary as well as geographical boundaries.

For Helen, the sociological world has always been bigger than its academic boundaries. At Clinch Valley College, she and her students engaged in the communities, not just the classroom. In her Welsh project, she used her networking skills to build links among miners, academics, and broader publics in the two regions that last to this day. When she returned from Wales and found she had lost her office at Clinch Valley, she moved from the classroom to become a full-time public sociologist—perhaps sooner than she had intended, but in ways that came to her naturally. Moving to a base at Highlander Center, she led a program to strengthen the ways in which community members and medical professionals could work more effectively together, as part of a network of community-based health clinics across the region. When her leadership was needed, she stepped in to become the acting director of Highlander in 1978–79. With funding from the National Science Foundation, she created public forums across the region to bring scientists, industry leaders, activists, and community groups together to discuss occupational and environmental disease. With funding from the National Endowment for the Humanities, she worked with filmmakers in Appalshop to produce a series of documentaries on the history of the region. In all of these roles, Helen again crossed traditional boundaries: taking her insights as sociologist and researcher out of the classroom to much broader publics.

It was in this latter role that Helen began to move from being a public sociologist, who used her knowledge to *inform* broader publics, to being a *participatory* intellectual, who used her teaching and networking skills to *enable* others to learn and to act for themselves. And when this approach empowered relatively powerless communities to challenge powerful interests, Helen's work demonstrated the potency and risks of speaking truth to power. At Clinch Valley College, she challenged powerful strip-mining interests in her writing and testimony on the social and psychological effects of blasting, and she left her job as a consequence. In Kingsport, Tennessee, she and others challenged the dominant knowledge of the chemical industry, and public reprisals followed. Local and global systems have the ability to absorb the critiques of lone public intellectuals, but Helen's work dared cross another boundary: she used her skills to enable the collective action of others. For her, sociology is not only about understanding the world, but also about changing it through redressing unjust power relations with more humane and democratic ways of knowing. And as much as any single writing reflected in the following pages, it is this courage and commitment to step out of the prescribed box, to challenge the boundaries of power, that continue to inform and inspire others to step out of their boxes as well.

Coal Mining Communities in Appalachia and Wales

While I was still at Clinch Valley [College], the groundwork was laid for my work in Wales. . . . John Gaventa, who was a student at Vanderbilt, was working in the mountains with Marie Cirillo and came to talk about his plans for his dissertation as a Rhodes Scholar in England. He then began coming back to the States with videotapes, which he'd show for my classes, and we devised a scheme to have an exchange of people between the Appalachian and Welsh coal fields.

So I got a postdoctoral fellowship from the National Science Foundation on energy-related research and went to Wales. . . . John Gaventa was over there. His friend Richard Greatrex, a Welsh filmmaker, had been in the States for a year working with Vanderbilt Center for Health Services and was going back home. He agreed to do videotapes in the mining communities if I would provide him with room and board. So I piggybacked this whole Welsh videotape production on my fellowship. Most weekends John would come to Wales, and he and Richard and I would videotape Welsh community scenes. We also used the grant for an exchange; we brought Hazel Dickens, Mike Seeger and that group of musicians—Rich Kirby, John McCutcheon, some of the Brookside mine women, Charis Horton, and people from the River Farm. It was an invasion of the Americans in this mining community where they hadn't seen Americans since World War II. ("You've Got to Be Converted: An Interview with Helen Lewis")

from "Industrialization, Class, and Regional Consciousness in Two Peripheral Regions: Wales and Appalachia" (1983)

The industrialized coal mining areas of South Wales and Central Appalachia share several common features: similar highland environments, a history of rural subsistence agro-pastoral economies, colonial experiences as a result of capitalist expansion, and industrialization based on extraction of minerals. Both regions have maintained viable subcultures and developed regional consciousness despite (or because of) their industrialization and integration into an international economy. In both areas class-consciousness and labor militancy also developed among the coalminers.

Michael Hechter [in *Internal Colonialism: The Celtic Fringe in British National Development, 1536–1966*] presents the hypothesis that industrialization of peripheral areas results in a process of exploitation and underdevelopment that encourages the continuation (or invention) of distinct cultures and a regional consciousness. He applied this hypothesis to the Celtic fringe of Great Britain (Scotland, Ireland, and Wales). This paper, through comparison of Wales and Appalachia, explores Hechter's perspective and examines the relationship between class-consciousness and regional consciousness.

The argument is made [by Hechter] that traditional cultures were revived and regional consciousness arose in these peripheral areas as a result of domination and exploitation by the larger society. Although the highland environments provided protection for both groups and enabled them to maintain or develop cultural patterns different from the larger society, regional consciousness was neither a result of isolation nor a reaction to the standardization and uniformity demanded by industrialization. Rather, the exploitation of each region by the larger society resulted in the denigration of the culture and the exploitation of the people, experiences that led to the development of regional consciousness.

Although highly industrialized, both regions still display a strong mixture of rural and industrial patterns. Many similar rural, highland cultural traits are maintained: egalitarian relationships; bartering and neighboring; large family-kin groups; non-conformist, independent religious behavior; community music; hospitality; expressiveness; and pride in local culture. Many of the people of Wales and Appalachia remain basically rural mountain people with strong ties to the land. Hunting, hiking the hills and woods, keeping dogs and ponies, gardening, and maintaining small landholdings are especially characteristic of Southwest Wales and the Appalachian coalfields.

As internal colonies, peripheral to and serving the larger economic order, Appalachian and Welsh cultures have been denigrated, and as a result revival and preservation movements emerged in both areas. A strong regional consciousness developed in both areas in the 1960s. Recent efforts in Appalachia have focused on preserving the music, crafts, regional history, and traditions through Appalachian studies in the colleges and community festivals. The Welsh have insisted on Welsh-language instruction in their schools and nationalism has reemerged as a political force.

Both regions were underdeveloped for the advantage of their more dominant and powerful parts of the country; for Wales this was largely for England; and for Appalachia, the financial centers of the North and East. Both became economically disadvantaged areas. Wales, like Appalachia, ranks lowest among British regions on all indicators of employment, housing, education, health, environment, and personal income. Wales and Appalachia both send a higher proportion of their population to front lines in wartime than England or other regions of the United States. Young unemployed Welshmen and Appalachians have always been good recruits.

Both areas have been classic lands of emigration. In periods of mine closures and economic depressions, large numbers of economic refugees leave to seek employment outside the region. Parts of Appalachia were peopled by Welsh emigrants and now, as Appalachians, they have emigrated to Northern and Midwestern urban centers. For many, the mountains remain home, and continued ties keep the communication and people flowing back and forth. Many urban centers have Appalachian ghettos with accompanying prejudice and discrimination against the migrants, who are labeled hillbillies and bri-arhoppers. In English cities, enclaves of Welsh form social clubs for support against similar discrimination. Welsh jokes about Will and Dai in the city and "briar" jokes about urban Appalachians portray the newcomers as country bumpkins.

While rural areas were slower to organize than urban areas, the mining experiences in both regions resulted in the development of strong militant labor unions and class-consciousness. In Wales, Marxist educational programs produced miners with socialist political rhetoric. . . . Although both Social-ists and Communists organized in the American coalfields during the West Virginia and Harlan County, Kentucky, strikes, there were no long-term educational programs, no miners' libraries and labor colleges to provide the Marxist socialist education prevalent in the South Wales coalfields. Although Appalachian miners changed politics from Republican to Democrat in the 1930s, there was no Labour party for workers to join as there was in Wales.

Appalachia is a larger and less compact region than Wales with a greater communication problem. Fewer opportunities exist for communication be-tween communities. The region lacks the kind of institutions that bring people together in Wales: pubs, working men's clubs, miners' institutes, regional sport conferences such as rugby, or music competitions. High school football carries out some of that function in America and fiddlers' conventions and bluegrass festivals are similar to the Welsh Eisteddfod.

The integration of the economies of both Appalachia and Wales into the multinational advanced capitalist society has been occurring in the 1970s and 1980s. Today, multinationals with automated processes, computer technology, and capital and industrial activities throughout the world find moving labor is unnecessary. Nations now must compete for industries and jobs and trade off surplus labor and resources. Appalachia and Wales remain rich in both labor and resources and continue to face similar problems. Large energy corpora-tions now manipulate production, investments, public opinion, and informa-tion. They can control communities, regions, and countries. . . .

In Appalachia, many union operations have closed or been sold to non-union operations. There seem to be concerted efforts on the part of the coal industry to limit the power and influence of the union and to diffuse class-consciousness and struggle. There has been a major emphasis on harmony and cooperation between miners and operators and attempts to curtail antago-nisms and struggle. . . .

This paper raises important questions: Is the key variable in the development of regional inequalities in peripheral areas industrialization, coal mining as an extractive industry, or capitalist expansion? How traditional is traditional culture and what accounts for its invention or revival? I suggest that early isolation and lack of integration into the mainstream society made possible some survival of older patterns in Wales and Appalachia, but that the revival and development of village culture in Wales were more modern developments in response to exploitation and oppression. Nonindustrial northern Welsh claim that industrialized southerners aren't real Welsh and don't speak the language properly. In South Wales mining villages, they say that "coal brings culture" and their opera societies, jazz bands, and choirs are defined as Welsh culture. In Appalachia, there are similar conflicts between the traditional folklorists and the revivalist musicians and storytellers. A countrywoman watching the Hillbilly Parade in Pikeville, Kentucky, says that the marchers are not real hillbillies; they don't live and eat like hillbillies. An older Welshman complains that the young college kids come home telling him how to be Welsh.

This paper also raises questions about the nature of class and regional consciousness. Is class-consciousness more progressive than regional consciousness? Can regional or ethnic consciousness, which grows out of experiences of exploitation, analyze the reason for the exploitation and inequalities and reach the same point as that reached in class analysis? Can class-consciousness emerge but fail to take the analysis to the root cause of the inequalities? Can class-consciousness and regional consciousness together develop an analysis and conceptualization that locate the source of power in society and provide a means of joining together workers and community? Can both be co-opted so that people only seek equal distribution of the same pie? Should regional consciousness be joined more supportively with class-consciousness, could it give additional support and aid in the analysis of the root causes of inequality and exploitation?

After my trip to Wales, I returned there every year between 1976 and 1984, but I missed three years (1984–1986). And I missed the whole British coalfields strike. . . . A lot of my international interest grew out of coal. I've dreamed of visiting coalfields all over the world. I've gotten really interested in the role of women in the coalfields, and some of that grew out of the dissertation. . . . One of my theses, which proved to be true, was that mining families do tend to be mother-centered. Women take a lot more responsibility and authority than in other families in the mountains because of the dangers inherent in mining. Plus the husband is removed from the family so much, isolated underground, and he's strongly bonded to his peer group down there, which competes with the family relationships. ("You've Got to Be Converted: An Interview with Helen Lewis")

"My Old Black Mountain Home" or "Deep in the Heart of Dyfed" or "What I Learned in Wild Wild Wales"— A Poem of Sorts, read at the Rose and Crown, Wales, April 24, 1976

I came from old Virginia
Where the corn and tobacco grow
Where the coal is soft and smoky
And the people all talk slow.

I came to live in South West Wales,
To look and live and learn
How people in these valleys
Work and play and earn.

I bought a van—'twas Austin blue
And left old Swansea town
To make my way to the open moors
And a home called Rose and Crown.

Driving on the wrong side,
I lose my way four times.
I drove through towns I couldn't pronounce
Lower and upper Cwns and Ystradgynes.

I drove and pushed the van 6,000 miles,
From Brynaman to Swansea town,
Up and down the valleys
But mostly to the Rose and Crown.

To Llanelli and to Pontypridd,
From Heathrow to Dyfed twice;
To Abergavenny and Pontypool
And over Bettws Mountain in the ice.

To Llandeilo, the castle and Gwinfe,
A trip to Birmingham and Keel,
Up and down the Rhonddas
To the Red Lion and Myddfai for a meal.

I saw the old ironmaster's home,
'Twas a castle in Myrthr Tydfill.
I saw where the riots started
In Tonypandy on the side of a hill.

I rented a little cottage
In Upper Brynamman on Bryn,
With Richard and John in the household
And visits from one or two friends.

We made a lot of videotapes
At schools and pubs and clubs and mines,
Of people singing, dancing and shouting a bit,
But mostly speaking their minds.

What have I done in my travels?
What have I learned in my stay?
I'll tell you a few of the highlights
In my work, which is better called play.

I learned about lager with a bit of lime
And in the 30s it was very hard times.
A pint is larger than you think.
A pony can also be a drink.

A fiddle is not a violin.
Enjoying oneself is not a sin.
A hobble is not a funny walk.
And a chat may not be a talk.

I've had the greatest welcome
And made some lasting friends.

Helen reading this poem at the
Rose and Crown Pub in Wales,
1976

So I'll be back for Christmas
By jet, boat or a broom in the winds.

But when I reach the U.S.A.
And "How was it?" asks my mate,
I'll give a smile and a little wink
And say, "It was bloody great."

Merry Christmas, 1976

"Helen Lewis and Wales," by William R. Schumann

Helen Lewis's place-based critique of capitalism and experiential-
activist teaching style were some of my earliest inspirations to pursue
an academic career, and as it turned out, her cross-cultural research in
Appalachia and Wales opened a pathway I have followed ever since. As

a young college student visiting Highlander in the early 1990s, I first met Helen through my mentor, Patricia Beaver. We did not really speak much at the time, yet Helen always managed to remember me during chance encounters over the next several years. In 1999, Pat invited me to join her and Helen for a summer course in Wales in 2001, just as I was set to leave Appalachia for graduate school in Florida. I was told that the course would be a reunion of sorts, commemorating Helen's Welsh coalfield research of the 1970s and early 1980s, but also an opportunity for me to develop a comparative research agenda centered on politics and culture in mountain regions. It was not too long before I was on board.

That summer was not just a nostalgic tour of familiar places and old friends, but also a taking-stock of social and economic change in a mining region that had witnessed an accelerated economic decline since her last visitation, a kind of mirror image of what Appalachia might become. After a couple of weeks abroad, Helen and Pat paid me the ultimate compliment of asking me to take over the trip in the future. Of course I said, "yes!" Every other year since then (i.e., 2003–9 and counting), I have enjoyed the privilege of leading new Appalachian studies students into Wales (in partnership with Pat) to take Helen's work into new directions.

While based on her original course template, the Wales trip has now morphed into a participatory course that places students in the service of community-based social justice agencies in Wales's former mining valleys. Following Helen's pedagogy, I involve students in a research agenda that does not separate ideas from practice. Through internships, students engage on a practical level in the question of how political and economic power is both constituted through and challenged by networks of civil society. We continuously assess what our efforts mean in terms of achieving sustainability in postindustrial sacrifice zones like Wales, but try to do so as a way of bringing back home fresh perspectives on positive social change. Though Helen is now "retired," I believe her contributions to Wales and Appalachia continue in this way: not only do former students keep in touch about how Wales shapes their work in Appalachia, but their efforts have directly contributed to a wide range of community regeneration projects in Wales.

One highlight of the trip for me is pointing out to students the Rose and Crown, a pub that served as Helen's home base in the 1970s. She is still remembered and asked about it by the older generations who met her then, and those connections have opened numerous doors for me to pursue just futures for Appalachia and Wales today.

Helen walking with dogs near Rhosamman in the Black Mountains of Wales, 1970s

Helen Lewis is always a networker. While carrying out her National Science Foundation project in coal mining communities in South Wales, she also began to support exchanges between Wales and Appalachia, including bringing to Wales miners from Harlan County and women miners linked to the Coal Employment Project. Several sources say that her meeting with women miners helped to inspire the critical role that women in Wales played in the bitter national miners' strike a few years later. The exchanges also went the other way. In May 1979 Helen and I, at Highlander Center, worked with Hywel Francis, then the head of the Miners Library at the University of Swansea and director of a Coalfields Oral History project, to bring a delegation of Welsh miners to tour the Appalachian region. As the excerpt below shows, the contrast of politics and culture in the two regions was great. While the Welsh miners were highly political, and while their movement had deep international links, they were shocked by what they saw. But the links have continued. In 2001 Hywel Francis was selected to serve as Member of Parliament from the Aberavon Constituency of Wales, and he continues to visit the Appalachian region.

from "Welsh Miners in the American Coal Fields—Culture Shock and Response" (1979)

There were many startling and surprising experiences for the miners, and I have tried to pull out some, which caused the most shock or response.

They were alarmed at the idea of a separate women's convention, which was being planned by the Coal Employment Project, and saw this as divisive. They were surprised when UMWA District officers in Charleston, West Virginia, said they thought it good since the women needed support and had special problems the Women Miners' meeting might deal with. By the end of the trip and many women miners later, some of the group was admitting mining was good for women who needed to support their families if there was no other employment. They still felt it was not needed in Wales where there were many other good jobs for women—a conclusion I felt from my observations was overly optimistic.

Coming from a strong union and a 100% unionized industry, and one of the most radical unions in Britain, non-union operations were hard to understand as was internal criticism of the union. They were so shocked with remarks they heard about the UMWA, that early in the trip the group decided they should not visit and talk with any non-union, anti-union, or dissident groups. They feared they would be meddling in UMWA politics, legitimizing one faction or approving of non-union situations. It was hard to explain that this decision meant they would have to stay in Washington or go home. It was hard for them to understand how strong union persons could call the union president obscene names or how a local could be strong when it was in great conflict with the International. They were greatly disturbed by the apolitical nature of American miners. They met a number of militants and could identify with their comments and observations but found it impossible to take the discussion into the political realm.

They were frightened in Harlan County to see scabs transported in armored trucks. Their fear grew partially from seeing *Harlan County USA* and from miners all along the journey warning them of "Bloody Harlan." They would not go to the picket line even with the local District officials—but attended and spoke at a rally for the Jericho miners [in Harlan County].

They missed the solidarity of mining communities and the organization of the lodges. They longed for that sense of union brotherhood and comradeship. In each district, we visited the District offices, sometimes finding people to meet but even when we had appointments, the officers might not show up.

They brought presents to present to each local or district and sang songs and brought greetings. They were accustomed to more formal proceedings and presentations, and they took the Americans off guard with their prepared greetings and nice presents. Before leaving the country, they visited UMWA Headquarters and presented gifts and sang songs under the bust of John L. Lewis. No officers were there to receive them, but it was a highly emotional experience for them as it symbolized a sense of unity and brotherhood they sought but had to find only in their own singing.

They were stunned by the attitudes and the reality of coal owners—private ownership—company control. Early they began to talk of some of their problems of nationalization and bureaucracy of the coal board only to find American miners thinking that they favored private ownership. Quickly they began to speak out for nationalization, related their history of change and the advantage of a nationalized industry to promote safety. On return to Wales they reported on the total control of communities by companies, brainwashing by corporations and vicious tactics to destroy the union.

They spoke up loud and clear about safety throughout their visit. Nationalization was given credit for investing more money into new equipment and safety devices. Ivor England was shocked when a U.S. Steel guide said they could not afford to install longwall. He said the National Coal Board would spend 10 to 15 times more experimenting in new equipment than U.S. Steel.

[On return] Len Jones said they had been amazed at the enormous scale of strip mining. "They simply ravage the countryside out there and there are big battles between the state and the coal companies to make them restore the land. But you have to see these operations to believe them."

In an interview on return, one said the American Dream had turned into a Nightmare where there are "big brother" towns run and controlled by multinational companies. [Others pointed out the internal contradictions they saw here]:

Scabs are transported to work in armored cars.

Appalling poverty existing among so much wealth and luxury.

There is a sense of tension coupled with warmth and generosity of the people.

Helen (*center*) with a group of visitors, including Richard Greatrex (*seated*), 1970s

There's a tremendous disillusionment in America.

Political vacuum in the U.S. where the two major parties are so devoted to the perpetuation of Capitalism with a big C.

There is a brightness and inquisitiveness about the Americans. They want to know about different social systems.

There was aggression and tension in the air as ordinary human beings were forced into positions which made them act inhumanly.

"Helen Lewis: A Very Modern Mother Jones," by Hywel Francis

When I first met Helen Lewis in the mid-1970s, I was struck by two things: her radical community-focused values and her ability to translate those values into action and tangible achievements, without much fuss, in a unique democratic, nonhierarchical feminist style. She has in her own way, through her work at Highlander and many other places, including South Wales, become as influential an adult educator as Myles Horton.

Helen's friend John Gaventa and I had discussed during John's visit to the South Wales coalfield in the midst of the successful British Miners' Strike the need for trade union and community links between our two coalfields. It was Helen who made this happen due to her productive sojourn in the western Dulais, Swansea, and Amman valleys in 1975–76.

Her work as a visiting research fellow during that year with me at the South Wales Miners' Library in Swansea University established the firm educational and cultural foundations upon which, over the decades, many hundreds if not thousands of community and trade union activists here benefited. Through her teaching and learning strategies she was able to facilitate leadership training and better international understanding—indeed, solidarity would be a better word—between our communities in Appalachia and the South Wales valleys.

The first fruits of this important work were trade union exchanges in the late 1970s, culminating most significantly for me with the three-week study visit of six rank-and-file South Wales miners from Brynlliw and Mardy collieries.

It was during that momentous visit that I met another of Helen's friends, Pat Beaver of Appalachian State University (ASU), who has done much, if not most, of the subsequent educational and cultural exchange work to sustain relationships, including a visit of the Onllwyn Male Voice Choir and biennial ASU student study visits.

At the heart of Helen's strategy was her belief that radical community-based education at Highlander and the South Wales Miners' Library was the key to progressive social change, locally and globally. In that respect I always think of her as a modern Mother Jones, and for that reason we in the South Wales valleys will always cherish her fellowship, her comradeship, and her pioneering spirit.

Community Health Clinics

I returned from Wales to find my program and courses at Clinch Valley had been eliminated. The former Chancellor tells the story today that a coal operator offered the college $7 million to close out the program and get me and my students back in the classroom and not meddling with their business.

My last year at Clinch Valley, I went on half-time and started working some with Highlander, with their community health clinics project. . . . We got into the health

project because Arnold Miller and the reform ticket had just won the United Mine Work-
ers election, promising to improve primary health care. . . . Highlander's involvement was
to provide education and training, and help mining communities gain confidence and
develop and perspective on the kinds of health care they could have. ("You've Got to Be
Converted: An Interview with Helen Lewis")

from "Medicos and Mountaineers: The Meeting of Two Cultures" (1971)

In the coalfields there were some historically unique experiences, which still affect the native-medico relationship. Most doctors came into the area with coal mining and were always outsiders. The coal camp doctors were identified with the outside exploiters and urban cultures, and many were considered by the natives to be exploiters themselves. Only recently have some natives become doctors or nurses and returned to the area.

The role of the doctor as exploiter or his identification with the coal operators and outside exploiters has affected ideas of both native and other outsider middle-class and professionals in the area toward medical facilities. Many distrust the "local" facilities and go outside for all care since they judge the local facilities and local doctors as being for miners and mountain folk and thus inferior. This is also part of a more general "put-down" of the area, which happens in any situation of colonialism or outside exploitation. The native culture is judged the same. Studies in Algeria found natives were very distrustful of modern medicine and refused to use the facilities until they were under native or local control. It was not a distrust of modern medicine, but a distrust and fear of outside exploitation with which the doctor or medical facility was identified.

Let us look at some general comparisons of the values and situations of the medicos and the mountaineers. . . . The doctor and other medical profes-sionals are socialized to relate to people impersonally, objectively, rationally. Medical personnel move in organizations as roles, not as persons, and interact with people as a doctor, a nurse, a patient, a client, a surgeon. Activities and behavior are directed, coordinated, arranged in a rational hierarchy of author-ity and responsibility. For a mountain man this is really weird. For him, people are persons, not roles, and they react to others personally, emotionally, as kinsmen, friends, or foes. People are liked or hated, loved, respected, but never treated impersonally as a thing. To be treated as a thing, a number, is a demoralizing, dehumanizing experience, which professionals learn to accept and live with. The doctor and technician and nurse are socialized to be professional: to be impersonal, to be objective. The mountain man would say "nonhuman."

How does the mountain person relate to the professional? If he cannot break down his shell and make him act like a human being, then he reacts with awe and suspicion, or he tries to defend himself and gets accused of stupidity and uncooperativeness. I wonder how many times the term "uncooperative" appears on medical reports. The mountain man in his general rejection of roles, authorities, and expert opinions doesn't want to know the doctor's degrees, but he wants to know who he is, what he is like as a person, is he honest, does he really care, will he try to help me, or will he hurt me? For the doctor to be called by his first name or a nickname such as "Doc" shows a degree of acceptance as a real person, someone with personal value. . . .

Among professionals, planning is essential, organization is foremost, and there is an assumption that life and nature and people can be ordered, controlled, and changed. Mountain people tend to accept life as it is, live more day-to-day, and make the best out of it they can. You put up with what the good Lord provides. What will be will be. You will do something if the good Lord is willing and the creeks don't rise.

Mountain culture is also an expressive culture. Although people in organizations and local institutions see mountain people who come for help, treatment, welfare checks, etc., as very repressed, shy, withdrawn, and uncommunicative, it is because the mountain person does not know how to relate to impersonal roles. Meet him as a friend in his own backyard, and you find him most creative in his expression and his conversation. His philosophy of life is varied and deep. He has been studying and thinking on many things and has such beautiful things to say.

What are the implications of these differences for the professional working in the mountains? How can he be really helpful to people? If I had some advice to professionals coming to the mountains or to mountaineers turned professional, I would say, "Listen to *people,* learn from *people,* work with and help and treat *people.* Try to learn from the mountaineer how to be a human being and how to use your skills, knowledge, and energies within the mountain culture." I would say, "Unlearn your 'professional' training, be unprofessional, be human."

Because of his training to be objective, impersonal, act within the system, the professional in the mountain culture tends to become immoral and cynical. The personal values of the professional tend to be the standards set by the medical or legal or educational occupation or organization. Their policy becomes his policy. You do your job and become indifferent to good or evil. You are a professional, a hired gun, doing the will of the profession, the company, or the organization. One must either have no inner values or hide them; they must not intrude on one's behavior. One must be committed to the profession, be tough, hardheaded. One can disclaim personal responsibility for what the organization or society does. "I can't judge that. I'm only a doctor, a nurse or technician." Some of the younger people coming into the profession say this is a sickness of our society: the unquestioning acceptance of the policy of the organization and the premises of society.

For the professional there is a lack of wholeness, a form of schizophrenia. In the mountains this is in contrast with local culture. Just as church reflects the culture of social gatherings, cocktail parties and banquets also reflect the culture of the organization, the occupational role. Whenever professionals get together, whether they are medical people or sociologists, there is much display, much showing off of what one knows. There is lots of agreement that we precious few really understand. Each individual is on guard. He must never leave his real self unprotected or undefended. One must never appear ignorant (like getting a bad grade in school). One must already know it or already have been there. So it becomes very hard to really swap ideas, to really ever learn anything, or to approach an idea openly. A professional will rarely ever admit to being overwhelmed by something new. One is ashamed of being caught not knowing.

At play, action takes place within incredibly narrow limits. Golf is a well-organized controlled game. Even nature is organized, and the "obstacles" are controlled and planned. There is much passive watching of organized sports and well-regulated parties. One knows how drunk one can get without being shunned. The banquet has lots of conversation, but mostly supportive banter. There is almost no sensual attention to food and no sharing. Everyone has his little portions carefully supplied, and you are terribly embarrassed if you eat the wrong salad. All remain aloof, untouched. Everything is under control, planned to the last detail. What if something unexpected happened? It is impossible. Action is stereotyped and constricted, constrained and policed. Would you dare to slurp your food, stretch out on the floor, and take a nap? You would make a "spectacle" of yourself and could never participate again.

Where are the real selves? None were invited! Only doctors, nurses, administrators, sociologists, and we must all play our roles. The sociologist's role is to classify and to analyze behavior and social systems, which I have done. I have played my role, and I take no personal responsibility for what I said. My real self was not invited.

Note: I am indebted to the following for many of the ideas and examples: Marion Pearsall, University of Kentucky; Jack Weller, *Yesterday's People*; James Branscome; Charles Valentine, *Culture and Poverty*; Charles Reich, *Greening of America*. To none of these would I assign the blame for the outcome.

I started visiting clinics and meeting the administrators and board members. High-lander's philosophy is that people learn from each other, so the first thing we did was identify the clinics' lead people and then start pulling them together to talk and find out what their problems were and how we could help. . .

One of our goals was to give these administrators confidence that they could deal with medical experts, and to teach the medical experts that they could deal with com-munity boards, that there's a different way of practicing medicine. Many of the doctors wanted to do that but didn't know how, so we developed some workshops where doctors and board members and administrators would meet with each other. People could say things to other doctors that they couldn't say to their own doctors, so we had a series of very good workshops.

The boards thought doctors had to see a lot of patients so they could make money and be self-sufficient as clinics. But it wasn't important to be self-sufficient as long as the Union was able to put that money back in, but then in the 1978 Union contract, they lost the Health and Welfare fund. As a result, most of these clinics became federal government subsidized with big pressure to be cost-effective, and they had to start cut-ting out all these extra programs.

We recruited some very good doctors from several medical schools, like Harvard, and some of them still live here and are doing really good work. In addition, we formed an Association of Coal Field Clinics, which tried to fight the loss of health care, educated people about what their health system was all about. An organization of Appalachian health providers came out of that, which kept going for several years. ("You've Got to Be Converted: An Interview with Helen Lewis")

from "Rural Healthcare in Appalachia" (1977)

The Highlander health project was started to give support and assistance to some of the rural community-controlled health clinics in the Appalachian region. These clinics are the most progressive approaches for providing health care for rural people which have developed in the area. Operating with community boards and salaried staff they provide basic primary health care through a community-organized and -controlled non-profit corporation. Most of these clinics emphasize broad community health goals rather than narrow medical treatment. Rural health problems include environmental and living problems such as water quality, sewage, diet, housing and occupational hazards. Community health clinics provide a local structure through which these problems can be considered.

Most of these clinics face considerable difficulties. Unlike urban areas, they have problems recruiting health professionals because training programs based in urban hospital settings have not encouraged rural practice. Also, the professionals are trained in medical and organizational skills but have little experience or training in working in a community setting with community boards. Because they have salaried staffs and community boards they face prejudice and hostility from the medicine-for-profit system; and they lack a network of kindred organizations, which can give support or share resources.

Part of our program has been to try to develop a network of community clinics to enable them to communicate and learn from each other, and develop ways to work together and share resources.

There has been something of a social movement in the region as numerous communities have developed community clinics. Developing a community clinic is a community building process. Since health is a non-controversial issue in most rural communities, it is an issue around which community citizens can unite and mobilize their efforts. Community groups have formed health councils, built health facilities, raised funds, applied for grants and recruited health professionals. But, too often when the professional staff enters the scene, the community board is overwhelmed by the mystique of professionalism and drops out, leaving the operation of the clinic to the experts. The board becomes little more than a body to legitimize or endorse the decisions and actions of the professional staff.

Part of the Highlander health project was specified as "developing board education" to assist community boards to learn more about controlling and managing their health care system. . . . What I have been doing for the past year is visiting clinics, carrying news (gossip?) from place to place, observing, working with staffs or boards on projects at particular clinics, trying to learn and understand the relationships between staff, board, community and the larger health system. In the process I have developed a few tentative conclusions about boards and their roles.

I am convinced that boards can and should be more actively involved in the planning and operation of the community health program. . . . The task is not an easy one, and I would estimate that adequate board education and work to keep the board fully involved would take 1 / 3 of an administrator's time or should involve a special educator for the task. My observation is that few administrators or other health professionals have the time or feel it is important enough to allocate the time and effort to develop a program of education and experience which will provide the board with the knowledge, information and skills needed to really control their clinics.

But, I have also seen some active boards with knowledgeable members. Where board members have had the opportunity to learn and have developed confidence in their own judgment they become quite competent in dealing with the intricacies of clinic administration. Essential to the development of an active, educated board is a desire and a commitment on the part of both the board and staff to the ideals of community control, shared decision making and democratic procedures.

Along with building buildings, hiring staff, and setting up office procedures, each community health program needs to develop an education program to fit their particular situation. The program should be designed for both board and staff for neither is fully equipped to develop a good health program for the community alone.

Some guidelines for such an educational program might include the following:

The professionals need to share certain types of information with the board to enable them to evaluate different forms and styles of medical care and clinic management. This could involve board members working as aides in the clinic or periodic demonstrations or seminars by the medical staff. Field trips to other clinics, visitors, reading materials, speakers from other programs and workshops with board members and staff from other clinics can contribute to this learning task.

The board and staff need to think past the limited medical model, the doctor's office syndrome, to understand the possibilities for a comprehensive health care center with emphasis on preventative medicine, education for self-care and healthful living situations. The particular needs and health problems of the local community should be studied together and a unique plan designed for that place and situation. Board and staff can work together on health surveys and research projects in the community.

The board and staff need to experiment with more democratic organizational patterns allowing more flexibility of roles and shared problem solving. Others in the community should be recruited into responsible roles so that the clinic can utilize the expertise wherever it exists among community persons, board or staff. This makes health care a community wide project and endeavor.

The staff needs to rely on the board for information and skills in dealing with local problems, local institutions and people. The specialized, scientific training of the staff results in an impersonal, objective professionalism in health care. The board can help re-educate the staff in how to deal in personal, humane, helping ways while still respecting the autonomy and integrity of the patient-person.

The board staff needs to understand the relationship between health problems and environmental conditions and the relationship between the health system and the larger socio-economic system of which it is part. The politics and economics of health care should be a part of the education program for these issues continually impinge upon and threaten the existence of community clinics.

This is not meant to be a complete recipe for successful "board education." It seems to me that as the board and staff and community work together to learn how to develop a health care system to meet their particular problems, the clinic becomes a center for a lively community education program.

Environmental Health

My work with health led me to a project funded by the National Science Foundation to have a series of forums all over the region on environmental problems. One in Kingsport, Tennessee, concentrated on chemicals; one in Harlan County concentrated on coal; and one in Charleston, West Virginia, concentrated on chemicals and coal. ("You've Got to Be Converted: An Interview with Helen Lewis")

from "'It Shakes You Up'—The Social and Psychological Effects of Surface Mine Blasting" (1978)

Probably the best statement that can be made about the social and psychological effects of blasting is that *it shakes you up*. This happens on many levels: personally and physically, it disturbs an individual or an individual family living near the blasting site; socially and psychologically, it disturbs a community or group or families living near a blasting site; politically, it may disturb all those who experience the disruption or must deal with those affected by the blasts.

First a set of definitions, which set the perspective from which I come: As a sociologist, I am interested in the social and psychological effects of surface mine blasting on individuals, families and communities. To try to delineate what makes a "social" impact as different from economic, political or environmental impact is difficult. *Social* pertains to the relationships between people as they "interact" and behave with and toward each other and develop patterns, behavior, histories and traditions. *Psychological* refers to the meanings the events have to the people, how they feel, how they define the situation and how they face, react or cope with the events in their private and public lives. How do they evaluate these happenings, how are they reacting to the changes which occur and what expectations do they have for the future?

Blasting—others have defined that technically as to what physically occurs to produce explosion, noise, dust, flying rocks, vibrations; socially, it results in several types of disturbances to the people. Socially, it is a *trespass,* which can be defined as "to make an improper or uninvited inroad on a person's time, attention, patience, etc.; to intrude on or upon the rights of domain; to encroach on; infringe." Blasting is a trespass, which does physical, social and psychological damage to the persons in a very dramatic, uncontrollable way. In the long run, other problems of strip mining, erosion and siltation of the streams which result in flooding, stream damage, and destruction to the water supply may be more disastrous to people of the area but blasting—shakes you up. Although a flood may be defined as an act of God—placing explosives cannot be so defined.

Blasting is an *intrusion*—to interpose (oneself or something) without invitation, fitness, or leave; to come in rudely or inappropriately, to enter as an imposer or unwanted element.

Another definition: *Gossip*—to talk mostly about other people's affairs, to go about tattling; to tell tales. As a sociologist, this is what I do. . . . I have been a gossip of surface mining for some time and will draw on interviews and observations during the past 10 years to show psychological and social impacts.

In 1975 a large strip mining operation got underway in the western end of the City of Norton [Virginia]. In 1976, 14 residents of the 13th St. section, the area joining the strip mining, filed suit in Wise County for damages from blasting to their homes. The families charged that "emotional trauma, suffering, great emotional anguish and inconvenience and suffering" was caused in addition to the damage to their homes.

As they increased operations, rocks rolled down on the schoolyard, and other sections of town began to feel the repercussions. A prominent upper-class woman became disturbed when her nice china began to shake in the china cabinet. The blasting was shaking the foundations of the social system. People organized, brought suits, "stormed" city council.

It has been a learning experience for the people of the area and some have been shaken out of their complacency. It changed their attitudes. They have learned that some believe that coal under the ground is more valuable than people who live above, and there are few laws or institutions to protect people from the destruction of their homes, life style, social relationships. They have learned that neighbors and family members who become rich and power-ful also become exploiters and unresponsive. They have learned that laws for protection become lost, and town councils or other governing bodies may work for special interests. They learned that dependence on one industry and reliance on it for employment and job security can produce conflict between family members and limits or silences their opposition to destructive policies.

They have learned that the coal industry does not want or plan to meet the social costs of mining but expects residents to meet those costs and thus subsi-dize their operations. They have learned the value of joining in protest and the power of organized resistance. They have learned the need to effect political change, the need for constant monitoring of both business and government agencies to prevent collusion and continued destruction.

Blasting also trespasses on traditional mountain values and relationships to the land—it invades people's sense of rightness and peace in living on the land.

Some mountain people traditionally have lived in relative harmony with the land. As subsistence farmers, hunters, trappers, and gatherers of herbs and wild foods they have developed a symbiotic relationship with the land. Religiously, they found solace and security in the protection of the hills. Blast-ing is an offense to those values. It hurts and destroys this solace and security. Surface mining leaves a legacy of feelings of anger, bitterness, betrayal, and conflict with neighbors, destroyed social relationships and community, feel-ings of powerlessness and helplessness.

Blasting is the ultimate trespass and intrusion. You can't lock your door, you can't take the phone off the hook, you can't refuse to open the mail, you can't say come back next week. You can't isolate yourself. There is no hiding place. The shock waves reach you and for many in the region, blasting becomes symbolic of the nature of an exploitative industry.

We started planning and organizing around Kingsport [Tennessee]. A former Clinch Valley student who was running a program for disabled kids in Scott and Wise counties got to talking about the great numbers of children with birth defects and Downs Syndrome. He wondered if there was some relationship with the kind of work their parents were doing, which was largely in the chemical industry in Kingsport. So a group of us got together in Scott County and involved Juliet Merrifield, who was a good researcher with Highlander, to help us out. Jamie Cohen, a young woman who was interning with us from Vanderbilt, started interviewing people who worked in Kingsport. Then Southern Exposure *wanted an article, which Juliet and the group wrote—"It Smells Like Money." Tennessee Eastman absolutely blew its top.*

As it ended up, we had a very successful forum in the Kingsport Ramada Inn, with the words "pollution in Kingsport" on the marquee. That was about the first time those words had ever been used there. A lot of businesses had agreed to be on panels, even Holston Defense, which is government-run, but Tennessee Eastman was able to keep every business in town from cooperating, and then tried to stop our National Science Foundation money because we weren't giving "a balanced view." They started red-baiting us. The groups we had been working with in Kingsport fell apart because of fear of job loss. ("You've Got to Be Converted: An Interview with Helen Lewis")

from "It Smells Like Money," with the Kingsport Study Group (1978)

No visitor to Kingsport can miss the fact that the town smells. But industrial pollution is more than an aesthetic problem, more than a problem for plants and animals, birds and fish. In Kingsport, some people are concerned that the air they breathe and the water they drink may seriously affect their health.

Tennessee Eastman Company—the largest employer in Tennessee, and part of Eastman Kodak—dominates Kingsport. The town began as a port on the Holston River, an important transportation link for settlers heading west through the Cumberland Gap. In the early twentieth century, a small band of entrepreneurs decided that the Holston River site would be ideal for a manufacturing city. It had raw materials, good communication with the rest of the country, an adequate supply of water, and good country people to provide a compliant work force. In 1920, Eastman arrived and transformed a wood alcohol plant into what is now a huge chemical complex. With it, the character of the town was transformed. . . .

Perhaps the worst health problems exist for the 14,000 employees of Tennessee Eastman and the 2,000 of the Holston Army Ammunition Plant, run by Eastman for the federal government. In its Kingsport plant, Eastman manufactures fibers (acetate, modacrylic and polyester), plastics (cellulosic), dyes and industrial chemicals. Tennessee Eastman is a division of Kodak, the second-largest chemical company in the U.S. and among the largest in the world. Behind the familiar image of every kid's first Brownie camera lies another reality for workers.

A growing recognition of the dangers of such workplaces led Congress to pass the Occupational Safety and Health Act of 1970 and set up an agency, OSHA, to enforce its provisions. . . . Since OSHA began, it has been increasingly apparent that the dangers of the workplace extend beyond the plant to the community into whose air and water it discharges its wastes. In 1976, Congress passed the Toxic Substances Control Act, which theoretically enables the Environmental Protection Agency (EPA) to control harmful substances manufactured and used by large companies.

In spite of increased awareness of environmental health hazards, there is little public concern expressed in Kingsport. Residents are understandably reluctant to criticize the industries which put bread on their tables. As the local newspaper comments, Kingsport "smells like money."

But there are hidden costs behind that smell. Workers and local residents have to pay their own doctor bills. The neighboring rural counties, down-wind and downstream, are also affected by the city's pollution. In the surrounding area the rate of babies born with abnormalities is more than twice the state average.

Tennessee Eastman also tries to avoid paying compensation to workers who think their ill health is attributable to workplace hazards. . . . Although the company has a large staff of physicians and extensive laboratory facilities, they share very little with their employees. . . . But in addition to breathing problems and lung damage, a lot of other things have happened, like blood disorders. Some people who've worked in the same division developed neurological disease. There was a group of people working together on a chemical product who developed a form of paralysis. But you never read about this in the paper. The only way you get it is through the grapevine.

Day in, day out, Tennessee Eastman releases 350 million gallons of waste water into the Holston River, sixty-five percent of the total daily discharges of all industries into the river. At times of low flow, in the summer months, all of the Holston River has to be diverted into the Eastman plant. Several agencies—EPA, the state, TVA—monitor and report on water conditions in the Holston River and Cherokee Lake on an occasional or regular basis. Yet to the concerned layperson, study of such reports indicates one factor of over-riding importance; we know very little about the extent of the damage being done. . . . The organic chemicals and metals which are discharged into the river by the chemical companies upstream are seldom monitored. Yet it is just these substances which are currently causing scientists more concern for their possible effects on human health.

What can people do when faced with these kinds of threats to their liveli-hoods? There have been hearings and meetings about the state of the river and lake, but they do not offer much help to ordinary people who, when faced with the "experts," are often silent.

Constant daily pollution of the waters of the Holston River by industrial users, past and present, is one form of environmental health hazard. Another, sometimes more dramatically visible to people in the river basin, lies in the "spills," accidental or otherwise, from those same industries. . . . On February 4, 1977, Eastman employees washed approximately 7,000 gallons of ethyl pivalate into the storm drains leading to the Holston River. . . . The chemical stayed in a mass, and a week later, citizens in Morristown [downriver] began besieging their utility commission with reports of a foul taste and smell in the water coming out of their taps. Reports compared the smell with walnuts, cherries, sewage and rotten eggs. . . . Tennessee Eastman's officials claimed the chemical was nontoxic, but under questioning it became apparent that they really knew very little about the effects of ethyl pivalate on people.

In December 1977, Morristown lost its "approved" water status. Michael Stanley of the state Water Quality Control Division said that Morristown's water supply is "the worst in the state," and "the water being pumped into their filter plan compares with water going out of a secondary treatment plant. It's unreal the kind of water they are pumping into their plant."

Tennessee Eastman declined to participate in our investigation. The com-pany said they were too busy preparing the list of chemicals they manufacture and use, which EPA requires under the new Toxic Substances Control Act. The puzzled layperson might well suppose that a company would already know what it manufactures. And whether or not this list will be publicly available in the next few years is uncertain. . . .

Tennessee Eastman's employees, lacking a union, have no place to turn when they are worried about the hazards of their workplace. Citizens' groups haven't the resources to analyze a company's products and emissions either. Employees do not know what chemical they are working with, and know it is dangerous only by the fact that they are tested, but they are not given the results of those tests. Doctors are not told what chemical makes a patient sick, so that he or she can be treated; the community is not told what is in the air it breathes and the water it drinks. . . .

We are teachers and students in the Kingsport and Holston River area, who have an interest in health and environment and a concern for the people of the area. We continue our interest and our concern beyond this article, and invite the participation of others.

The work in Kingsport came at a time of growing awareness in Appalachia and nationally about the impact of environmental and occupational health in poor communities. At the beginning of the decade, the National Environmental Policy (NEPA) had just come into effect, the Occupational Health and Safety Administration had been established, and debate was raging about toxic chemical sites in places such as Love Canal. Through Highlander, Helen applied for and received a grant from the National Science Foundation to hold forums linking scientists and citizens to build public knowledge about these issues. Over an eighteen-month period in the late 1970s, these were held in Charleston, West Virginia; Harlan County, Kentucky; and Kingsport, Tennessee. The forum in Kingsport was particularly controversial, as it attempted to put into public debate the impact of chemical pollution—in the heart of a town dominated by Eastman Kodak and the chemical industry. Despite their support from the National Science Foundation, and the presence of top national experts in the field, the forums were attacked as biased. Drawing on the 1950s McCarthy-era attacks on Highlander as a communist training center, radio ads challenged Highlander's motive for the forums, and local participants, including those from Bumpass Cove, Tennessee, were red-baited and threatened. In her report to the National Science Foundation, Helen outlines the links between knowledge and power that the project itself experienced. The project report is a significant one, as in a sense, it provides a narrative that underlies much of her life work as an academic committed to using academic and scientific knowledge to help challenge power and injustice.

from "Preparing Appalachian Communities for Changing Environmental and Occupational Health Needs" (1980)

The plan was to work with local community planning committees, hold three major forums in the Appalachian region, and follow each with community meetings to develop on-going education and health programs. Then [we would] bring together the three groups to a final regional workshop, which would form a network of concerned citizens of Appalachia, which would be a regional educational and public policy group to deal with the environmental and occupational health problems of the region.

The best education occurred before and after the forums. Because of the size, publicity and community conflicts around the issues of occupational and environmental health, some of the forums became ceremonies, part of the confrontational politics of the region.

The follow-up after the three forum/conferences concentrated on the East Tennessee area where a number of concerned citizen groups were active around problems of toxic waste dumps. There were needs and requests for scientific expertise to help community groups solve community problems. This was some of the best and most effective education. Using workshops, small meetings, providing scientists to teach skills, or providing resource materials and research assistance to the groups produced exciting learning experiences for all. Community people began to realize they must become their own experts; learn how to monitor, study, research their problems. Our role was to help make resources available: scientific expertise, books, materials, skills.

We found in the field of occupational and environmental health there was a scarcity of scientists with relevant scientific knowledge who were available and able to work with community groups. . . . Many local scientists were employed by local industries and their employees prevented them from being resources to their neighbors in their communities.

Some of the lack of available helpful scientists goes back to their scientific training: the specialization and concentration on esoteric research topics which leads to fragmentation of their knowledge and their inability to communicate their knowledge to ordinary community persons. The isolation of universities and research laboratories from community life and activities

makes them inaccessible to community people. There is a great need for public laboratories and facilities to help communities check and monitor air and
water quality, investigate health problems, conduct epidemiological studies,
detect health hazards.

The attempt to be objective and unbiased also prevents scientists from
dealing with controversial issues. They guarantee their objectivity by not dealing with a controversial issue. . . . Another problem was the narrow view
of public health held by the public health agencies. Because few had defined
environmental or occupational health as part of their domain, they did not
have the expertise or willingness to assist communities. In Tennessee, the state
health department seemed more interested in providing space for dumping
toxic wastes than in helping the communities adversely affected by the waste.

One problem was the controversial nature of the subject and the fact that
the industries, the chemical industry in particular, saw the forums and organization of local planning groups as a threat. . . . Part of the problem also came
from a difference in perspective between the project planners and staff and
the NSF staff. . . .

The NSF point of view seems to assume that all groups in a community
are equal and from a community with the same interests, such as households,
workers, industrial firms, professionals. Bringing them together and giving
equal time to each to discuss the "problem" they agree on, they will then work
together to solve this problem. This does not admit to the power relations
within a community, the gaps of information, the control of information, the
dominance and control of certain segments of the community not only over
information, but over the life choices of other persons and groups within the
community. . . .

In contrast, the project staff views the communities as made up of unequal
groups, some more powerful due to control over economic and political institutions which provide jobs and control the behavior and movement of these
groups. There are inequalities in access to information and control over scientific and technical information becomes a way of controlling people. There
is basic imbalance and conflict in the community and any intervention which
seeks to provide balance must work for power equalization, changing the patterns of control whether it is over property or information. Such efforts result
in more conflict and in those dominant segments seeking to maintain or regain
full control. To provide balance in such a setting, one must put major emphasis on equalizing access to information so that groups have more options

or choices. Their economic powerlessness may still make it impossible for them to make major changes. The trade-off may be to continue to accept poor health, or to work with dangerous substances or to allow more air and water pollution in order to continue the economic base of the community. But at least they have the information on which to make that "trade-off" decision. They also have the information on which they may work for more control over other parts of their lives.

Scientific or technical knowledge is a tool which is not equally distributed and continues to be controlled and used by those who control and dominate the community. Not recognizing that, and just bringing all segments, powerful and powerless, together and calling it balance, only encourages the continued dominance of the dominant.

The nature of power and control in our society is such that the governmental agencies (health, environmental, etc.) operate to keep the system going, by providing services to industries, helping preserve the system of institutions and supporting and maintaining their power.

Such problems will not change unless basic institutions themselves change; changes in those fundamental relationships and institutions cannot change without conflict and changing the balance of power.

The project staff was more concerned with bringing balance through power equalization, through making scientific information available to those with the least access. . . . Yet it is my dream that in a truly democratic humanist society, there will be more balance; freedom from exploitation and dominance where life and health must be traded off for job security and livelihood.

A lot has happened in the region in the field of occupational-environmental health during the 18-month period. How much can be directly attributed to the project is impossible to determine. There is a much greater awareness of health hazards by a lot of people, many of whom were touched by the project. There are a number of community and state-wide citizens groups which have developed and are active in the region. There have been state legislative investigations.

The theme of using knowledge to challenge power is one that also has deep international roots. In the late 1970s, in addition to the links that Helen brought to the Welsh coalfields, Helen and Highlander also began to deepen their links to broader international movements. The work on the impact of the global coal and chemical industries in Appalachia had parallels to growing critiques of the impact of the transnational industries in other parts of the world, including Latin America. We began to make links through the International Council on Adult Education to other groups that were using participatory action research as a way of democratizing knowledge and using it to challenge power. In 1980, Helen Lewis, Aimee Horton, and I represented Highlander at what is now seen as one of the first meetings of an emerging participatory action research movement, held in Ljubljana, Yugoslavia. While the next chapter describes this participatory approach more thoroughly, the piece below shares Helen's emerging analysis of why it was important to build links between Appalachia and other parts of the world.

When I went to work at Highlander, we talked about "popular education," we talked about "adult education." We didn't use the term "participatory research," and it was only later when some people came who were from Canada and had been working in Nicaragua and Latin American countries that they said, "Oh what you do is participatory research." We began to realize that there was a whole social movement, mostly started in the third world, and it grew out of Paulo Freire's work and Orlando Fals Borda's work and work in Colombia and Nicaragua and Peru. I think there was always something similar in both anthropology and sociology, in the activist sides of those disciplines, the "applied" side of those disciplines, and there were people who early on took a lot of interest in working with communities and making their skills available. Participatory research has been really associated with peasant movements and third-world countries more than with the industrialized, developed world. But they're coming together. ("Unruly Woman: An Interview with Helen Lewis")

In 1980, at the Appalachian Studies Conference, Myles Horton and I presented a paper to try to alert the conference and the region's scholars to the issue of transnational corporations. Myles had visited Brazil, and we had both visited Peru and other Latin American countries so we made some comparison. ("My Life and Good Times in the Mountains; or, Life and Learning in Central Appalachia")

from "Transnational Corporations and the Migration of Industries in Latin America and Appalachia," with Myles Horton (1980)

This is not intended as an academic exercise. We are not writing to secure tenure, promotion or scholarly acclaim. We are interested in presenting some of our experiences and concerns about the growing role of transnational corporations in the world. We wish to make special comparisons between their activities in Latin America, especially Brazil and Peru, and Appalachia and the rural South. We believe that such cross-cultural comparisons are essential to those in Appalachian studies in order to understand Appalachia's place in the global economic system. We hope our remarks will stimulate discussion here today and back home on the campus in classes which are studying Appalachia's social, economic and political situation.

Last year Myles visited Brazil, Argentina and Peru, attending a conference called for by the Catholic Bishops in Brazil. In his visit, he met and talked with people concerned with the problems of domination and exploitation by multinational corporations. Together, we attended an International Congress of Folk Medicine in Peru in October 1979, and met people from throughout South America. We were also able to travel some in Peru on the trip. We became convinced that United States educators and workers must become more interested and concerned about what is happening in Latin America and begin to make connections both literally and figuratively.

The pace and extent of multinational activity is increasing. Corporations are changing the nature of their activity or entering a new stage and, thereby, reshaping the competitive context, which portends enormous consequences for communities and workers in America/Appalachia.

The growth of multinational corporations or transnationals represents a new stage in capitalist development and poses new problems for third world and exploited regions, internal peripheries or colonies, such as Appalachia. Transnationals can also turn whole countries into "Appalachias" or "Latin Americanize" the United States.

The international corporation has interests separate and distinct from the interests of every government including its own government of origin. The dependence of the leading United States–based corporations on foreign profits has been growing greatly since 1964. United States corporations have been shifting more and more of their assets abroad. . . . Although the United States is still the dominant transnational, Germany, Japan, France, Holland and Great Britain are actively involved. Some of these are investing in the United States. . . .

What is happening is not just the old pattern of runaway industries looking for new raw materials or cheap labor, although that is part of the total process. The industrial system is changing from national or regional operations to a globally integrated production system. The large corporations are developing a global grid of producing subsidiaries, which utilize labor, raw materials, markets, and political systems throughout the world.

This triumph of multinationals is made possible by jet aircraft, international telecommunications and computers. . . . The corporations are large, capital intensive, technologically oriented and managerially intense. They are looking for greater growth and profitability through world markets. They seek growth centers, countries which are developing and willing to cooperate politically and economically and follow the capitalist path. Global corporations have destroyed the concept of market. They conduct most transactions with themselves. Profit maximization is the major guiding principle. Decisions are based on hard, cold, business facts. They develop global standardization of business procedures and measures, and uniformity in work habits, products, and services. Corporations transform production techniques to make for manufacturing flexibility: shifting tooling, interchangeable parts, multiple sources of goods.

The internationalization of the division of labor allows the rational placement of plants according to type of labor available. They have shaken off traditional sources of countervailing power: outgrown trade unions, consumer groups, and local and national government. Nations now compete for corporations and use their legal and financial resources, raw materials and labor to attract foreign capital for development. The free flow of goods, investments and technology may eventually equalize standards of living and wage scales. In each country where a corporation concentrates wealth, the gap between rich and poor widens.

Transnationals use foreign countries to avoid ideological barriers to sales. Migration of industries or "going transnational" is encouraged when big changes in production are needed. These give an industry the impetus to move to a more congenial environment to recoup capital investment sooner.

In Appalachia, we have just begun to understand the nature of corporate control, outside ownership, and the effects of exploitation. Now we must try to understand what it means to be integrated into the international capitalist system. This seems far more complex; yet we must try to understand how this reality changes the nature of the problems and the ways of dealing with them. We will continue to have large numbers of absentee owners of land and minerals and industries. . . . Large timber owners are returning to the area to do again what they did before, as mountains have been reforested and can provide a new crop. Oil, gas, and uranium will be developed along with coal, since the energy conglomerates own it all.

We are now the site of runaway or expanding industries from other countries, such as the VW plant in Charleston. As our wages decline, unions weaken, and state and local governments and unions "sell" their workers. This trend can be expected to continue. As a region, Appalachia will compete with other regions, and the thirteen Appalachian states will compete with each other for runaway industries and new industries. . . .

We can expect government services to become fewer and weaker as the state takes on a role of caretaker and opts for a free market economy. The government will use welfare, social services, and education to serve the needs of business, and will be encouraged to invest in expensive developments such as synfuels or other energy development.

We can expect growing attempts to control the labor force through "union busting" or more sophisticated legal maneuvers and psychological strategies. The large oil companies seek to employ more technically oriented, skilled middle-class miners to avoid militant trade unionists. The destruction of coal camps and homogenous communities is designed to produce less militant workers. The "line" is that one is not a coal miner but a skilled technician, and class-consciousness is destroyed or avoided.

The use of Appalachia as a market and the development of a local bourgeoisie to operate banks, fast-food franchises, markets, and regional offices have led to a growing role for local colleges in the training of managers for industry. The developing middle class must be trained, and colleges and universities have received funds and encouragement to meet the needs. As a result, the business education programs are the largest programs in almost every school, replacing teacher training. Business and economics are being merged in some places as skills and "right thinking" economics are taught together. Again, Appalachian colleges are serving the needs of the economic system in educating the local bourgeoisie who serve the needs of the multinationals which employ them. Today, they are not "teachers" but "managers."

Their adaptation to this role makes progressive social change more difficult. The rising middle-class managers are trained to serve the needs of their employers, with allegiances to the multinationals. It becomes much harder to identify the "outside exploiter." The semblance of prosperity keeps the middle class loyal, and it is more difficult to educate about global issues and problems. The Appalachian/American middle class receives dividends as they profit from the cheaper labor of third world countries and purchase low cost luxuries.

Appalachian studies in Appalachian colleges have a responsibility to research and educate around these changes and the implications of the integration of the region into the international economy. Cross-cultural studies are important and necessary. Workers in Appalachian industries need to understand their connections and kinship with workers in other parts of the world.

The possibility of an international labor organization seems remote. Some argue that the internationalization of industry and labor forces makes possible linkages between workers all employed by the same company. While capital can defend itself against isolated national laborers through multiple sourcing, an organized global workforce could stop production worldwide. An international workers' organization could support workers' struggles against repressive regimes and fight against second-class status for immigrant workers, no-strike legislation, and government-mandated "sacrifice" on the part of the working class.

The organization of an international work force would be difficult. Cultural and language differences are hard to overcome, but understanding the interrelationships and interdependencies is a first step. The development of coalitions of workers within Appalachia, especially in the energy field, would add great strength to the battles of coal miners, oil workers, and nuclear workers who are often employed by the same corporations. Such would be a first step for the region.

Communication between communities and workers trying to deal with environmental and occupational health hazards would begin to develop international networks to fight such hazards. There is an urgent need for systematic monitoring and reporting of the national and worldwide movements of hazardous industries and hazardous wastes.

In Appalachian studies, we must not limit our programs to the exotic, romantic Appalachian cultural history. It is important to develop pride in the region's rich heritage, but it is also important to see Appalachia as part of a worldwide process of development and change. We must deal with economic and political questions and build an understanding of what is happening in the region and how it is related to the global economic system.

We must also try to influence our regional educational institutions to de-

Helen and Myles Horton, early 1980s

velop broader courses in political economy. They must not concentrate only in training managers and technicians to keep the system running, but must provide a broader education so the managers and technicians can understand what they are doing, why, and to and for whom.

Appalshop Multidisciplinary Arts and Education Center, Whitesburg, Kentucky

While making the connections to global political economy, Helen's work also always comes back to interpreting and reunderstanding the role of culture. As an academic, she had communicated her insights largely through the written word, yet her experience with video in Wales and her close connections to Appalshop, an arts and education collective in Whitesburg, Kentucky, also lured her to experiment with the use of film as a research and communications tool. Both of these themes came together when she was asked to serve as the academic humanities scholar for a film series on the history of Appalachia.

Appalshop started a proposal to do a series of films on the history of the region. When it was funded, I got so excited about it I decided I wanted to do that. In getting the National Endowment for the Humanities funding, Appalshop won out over several universities, a kind of landmark. Then we were able to recruit a wonderful group of scholars as our advisory committee and seriously use them. Out of that grew Strangers and Kin, the first of the history of Appalachia series.

The kind of training I had as a teacher—it's always been words, books, papers, rather than pictures. But things we see, we never forget. We really learn from films, especially when we're emotionally involved in them. I've been puzzling about how people learn, how you teach, how you move people to change. If we're going to change the world, we've got to deal with the media, because that's the main thing people look at these days. We're bombarded with television. They do affect us. You've got to be converted, and there's got to be some way to do that.

At Appalshop I helped develop more cooperation between "the 'shop" and academics. I think I was able to help academics gain a little more understanding of Appalshop and vice versa. I became almost like a professional humanist. At times I felt like I had tattooed across my forehead HUMANIST. Introducing and connecting people is one of the things that I've been best at. I think I'm a facilitator and a catalyst and a thinker-upper of ideas. I like to pull people together and say, look, you should go and see so-and-so and do such-and-such. ("You've Got to Be Converted: An Interview with Helen Lewis")

from *Strangers and Kin: A History of the Hillbilly Image*—Notes on the Making of the Film on the History of Images about Appalachia (1984)

For this film, we concentrated on those periods of change and culture contact where contrasts and conflicts resulted in the emergence of stereotypes. We looked for the shifting of images from one group to another or a reversal of images for a group, such as change from noble savage to ignoble savage; brave, intelligent pioneer to illiterate country bumpkin. The persistence of certain images is noted: paradise, primitive, independent, slothful, etc.

In order to script the film, we decided to arrange the history of the images thematically instead of chronologically. This would more clearly show some of the ways in which a particular image persisted or became reversed, shifted to another group, or changed meaning. We realized that history should not be portrayed as periods or events tied up in neat packages but shown instead as a dynamic process involving the complexities of conflicting forces.

So we organized the images into the following categories:

1. Enemies of Progress: Uncivilized, pagan, backward, lazy, lawless, arrested frontier, barriers to progress: wilderness must be tamed, Indians must make way for settlement and agriculture, settlers must make way for industrialization, communities must make way for modernization. In both the late nineteenth and early twentieth centuries, journalists portrayed the Appalachian Mountains as the lost frontier.

2. Noble but Doomed: Noble Savage, nature's doomed aristocrats, archaic, obsolete life style, innocent, pure, courageous, but must die or move, inevitable growth of industrial technological system, morally superior, but expendable.

3. Objects of Paternalism: Pathetic, illiterate, dumb, ignorant, poor, backward, ungodly, victims of exploitation, dependent, genetic deficiency, need to be lifted up, saved, protected, educated, changed.

4. Preservers of Tradition: America the Paradise, Garden of Eden, Survivors, pure Anglo-Saxons, Real Americans, Pioneers, humanistic values, the best of nature, models for tomorrow's post-industrial society, remnant's of past glories to be preserved, lessons for today.

The script sought to weave these images and events into a story of how these types of images arose and persisted throughout history. Looking at the four types of images, the tension can be seen between nature and technology and the ways of dealing with the victims or the saviors.

"Leading Scholar of Appalachia Leaves the Academic World to Work with Wild-Eyed Kids," by Herb E. Smith

When Helen joined the Appalshop staff, we could hardly believe it. We were a bunch of young people trying to figure out how to survive while making films. Helen was an internationally known scholar and a leader in the emerging group creating Appalachian studies. I was twenty-nine, and most of the others in the project, Marty Newell, Scott Faulkner, Elizabeth Barret, Frances Morton, and Mimi Pickering, were about the same age. What is unusual about the six filmmakers is that we were so close in age. Don Baker was a bit older, but Helen (fifty-seven at the time, I think) was of our parents' generation.

I still don't know why she took that leap of faith from the safety of steady pay to the risky realities of making documentary films. It was a brave and unpredictable leap of faith, and I still don't know why she did it, but I know it changed Appalshop and all of the Appalshoppers, especially me and [my wife,] Elizabeth Barret.

Helen helped us as we entered our thirties, became parents, and wrestled with all of the challenges of being adults. [Our son] Evan was born in December 1981. Helen helped us as Elizabeth and I moved into a new phase of our lives.

Helen's lack of self-righteousness taught us how to accept our weaknesses. Her analysis challenged us to think harder and deeper. We would say things like "mountain people are smarter, better looking, and have more fun than people from other parts of the country." Of course, we would laugh and say things like that to be what we thought was funny. That is the nature of people in their twenties. Helen helped us get past that kind of silliness. We knew we were playing games, but it took Helen to call our hand.

from "The Filmmakers Speak: Interview with Helen Lewis and Herb E. Smith" ("Appalshop and the History of Appalachia," 1984)

Lewis: One of the things that has been interesting for me because of my own training and background is trying to learn to see things visually and understand visual images and what you can do with them. There'll be so much in a historical situation that you'll want to put in, so much information—we know all of this—and then you have to leave it out, and you settle for just one or two images for that 50 years. We learned a lot.

When we finally got down to the script [for *Strangers and Kin*], Don Baker wrote it. I worked with him a lot on it. I'd bring him stuff. The process was really pretty interesting. Maxine Kenny, Don Baker, and I worked for several months doing all the research and pulling together all the kinds of images, and made three or four big notebooks of Xeroxed materials from all sorts of sources. . . . And then we put in visuals, photographs. Then we put in descriptions of films, and then we started trying to put those in some sort of pattern. . . .

I was reading this thing about American Indians: "American Indians have been seen as noble but doomed; enemies of progress; objects of paternalism; and models for tomorrow . . ." and I said, "That's it. That's it. These are the categories!" The categories fit this little box—you know, being a sociologist, I love little boxes. . . .

So we then tried to write the script around those four things. Well, it got so confusing, and things were never that clear. We would find an image and we'd find a film, and we'd say, "Well is that 'noble but doomed' or is that 'enemy of progress'?" It got terribly confusing, and it made a very complicated script. The first script went through all four of those boxes. . . . Then Herb E. took it for production.

So we got Lucy Massie Phenix and Gurney Norman together, and Lucy says, "It's not a good film script. It's a good play, but it's not a film script." They convinced us that the actors had to be real people, and that viewers had to be able to identify with them. We didn't have them telling any personal stories. We had other people telling personal stories, mostly older people, and I really miss some of that.

We had a lot of interviews with people, but then the actors were just coming in and doing these little things. Lucy and Gurney insisted that we really needed to make the actors real people, and let them tell their personal stories too, which is most effective stuff. . . . That original script is a delightful script, but it had to be changed to make this film. The individual stories of the actors ended up being a major part of it. That cut out a lot of the other interviews, a lot of which I still pine for. I'm sure that's always true of any film you make. You see these marvelous things that you wanted to keep in that went to the cutting-room floor.

I think John Gaventa said when he saw it, "You know what this is? It's like a primitive ritual where the native puts on the mask of the oppressor and acts out the oppressor. It's a kind of ceremony of people acting out their oppressors so that they can get control." Whether we knew that we were doing that, I don't know, but it can be interpreted that way.

CHAPTER 4

Participatory Research, 1983–1999
Juliet Merrifield

> I would like to see all aspects of my life and work come together even
> more in the future. I would like to pull together my experiences and
> knowledge in experiential education, Appalachian studies, women's issues,
> environmental health, film and video production, residential workshops,
> learn more about popular culture and popular education and work more
> effectively for structural social change.
> —Helen Matthews Lewis, application for Kellogg Fellowship, 1984

Participatory research and Helen Lewis were made for each other. They came
together at the Highlander Research and Education Center in the late 1970s,
when Helen joined the research team and made connections with the participatory research movement that was springing up around the global south. The
international movement shared Highlander's philosophy that the knowledge
of ordinary people is valuable and valid, that people can document their own
situation and use their knowledge for action. Helen, with John Gaventa and
Aimee Horton, represented Highlander at a seminal meeting in Yugoslavia in
1980, at which enduring international relationships were formed.

Helen's work runs as a thread through the early development of participatory research at Highlander in the late 1970s and early 1980s, especially around
environmental health. From the Kingsport Study Group through the series of
public forums organized under a National Science Foundation grant, to the
work with the Bumpass Cove Citizens Association and Yellow Creek Concerned
Citizens, Helen's talents for relating to local people, for gathering them up and
connecting them with others, and for teaching through informal conversation

and debate were fundamental. Both her academic training and her own experience gave Helen a deep understanding of communities and how they work.

By the time the work of this chapter starts, participatory research was firmly established at Highlander. The international links had been made; the concepts had been explored and developed through practice in projects on environmental and occupational health and on land ownership. In this later period, Helen's work addressed a particular challenge of participatory approaches to research and development: how do people learn the skills to document and analyze their situations in order to bring about change? And by focusing on working with women, and their place in the local and regional economy, culture, and community, Helen added a feminist perspective to Highlander—not alone and not the first, but nevertheless an important contributor to the work.

Helen's talents as an out-of-the-ordinary teacher enabled her to grapple with the processes through which people learn to change. The work on the economy started with a workshop, as so many things at Highlander start. The 1984 workshop on women's work, which led to the booklet *Picking Up the Pieces,* was a classic Helen Lewis event, formed around an interesting idea with no sense of where it might go, an eclectic mix of participants, and a lot of space for stories. None of us involved in planning the workshop had any idea whether it would work or what we would do with it afterward. But it did work, and the stories were so powerful that we put them together in a booklet to share with other women. And it did lead to something: in fact, that one small event led to almost a decade of work on economic and community development.

In her conclusion to the booklet, Helen talks about women's traditional role in family or community crisis to "pick up the pieces" and get everyone reorganized and functioning. In the deindustrialization of the Appalachian economy and the economic restructuring around the declining coal industry, she noted that women were emerging as leaders of the most creative and progressive groups. But to take on these nontraditional roles, women had to learn how to assess community needs, understand economic changes, and plan for a more just and democratic approach to development.

The Highlander Economic Education Project (HEEP) was a response to this learning need. Tried out initially in Jellico, Tennessee, and later in Ivanhoe, Virginia, the curriculum developed by Helen and others combined the now traditional Highlander approach of beginning with people's own experiences with more explicit participatory research activities. These included community surveys, mapping, and interviews with decision makers (including bankers and elected officials). In keeping with Helen's style and Highlander philosophy, cultural components were woven into the learning process: theater based on oral histories, poems and songs, history books, and exhibitions. As Helen commented, "At the community level, the economic knowledge cannot be separated from other ways of knowing."

Because the HEEP project was based on action for change, it is not surprising that the boundaries between curriculum and community development were fluid. In Ivanhoe, in particular, Helen's immersion in the community and involvement in the process of change went deep. Over a five-year period, she worked with the Ivanhoe Civic League and in particular with the woman who was leading the redevelopment of the community, Maxine Waller. What was most unusual about Helen's work in Ivanhoe was involving a theologian, Mary Ann Hinsdale, in helping the community explore its faith and discover its own "local theology." The initial HEEP class led to an in-depth collaborative research and development project that cocreated a community history book as well as a book on the process itself.

Helen's insights into working with people, the challenges and conflicts as well as the inspiration and hope, are moving and revealing. She doesn't hide from the difficulties of the role of educator for social change—not just a listener and researcher, but a challenger and critical friend. Developing critical awareness in others requires educators to work on their own critical awareness and to be open to criticism from others.

Finally, Helen has always brought together the wider context with the local perspective. During this period, Helen was not only spending in-depth time in Appalachian communities but also traveling and learning from work in other countries, as chapter 3 reveals. Her links with South Wales were maintained, and the growing strength of women as community leaders there following the 1984 miners' strike provided a powerful exchange. She continued the long-standing Highlander links with folk high schools in the Netherlands. And she made visits to development organizations in several African countries. As she says, she deepened her perspective on the United States within the global context and found exciting ideas in rural development projects, many of them led by women. These ideas and insights were integrated into the work "back home."

Walking New Paths

Ten years ago, I left formal academia in which I was both a teacher and a "faculty wife." I left both roles to work more closely with community groups, developing education programs and working with a regional media center. I also moved to a cooperative farm and live among people I work with in filmmaking, community education and various social movements, so the personal and professional are even closer together. I call up and use my professional credentials to assist community groups when needed; and I use my skills and training when needed, but I avoid the expert, professional role as much as possible. I am basically an educator and social activist, whether I am teaching a class, working with a community group, fighting a toxic waste dump, planning a film series, networking health professionals or leading a workshop.

I am not opposed to formal academic institutions. I worked within the institution as long as possible, feeling that it was important to push the institution to be responsive to community needs. But I reject much of the "academic" approach as too detached, abstract and fragmenting. I do not believe that value-free objective analysis is possible or humane. . . .

If there is one word that describes what my major educational contribution has been, it is that I act as a catalyst. I am good at pulling together people and resources, facilitating an educational encounter. (Application for Kellogg Fellowship, 1984)

In 1972, I began a series of conversations with Monica Appleby and Anne Leibig—former Glenmary Sisters who had been involved in social and education programs in the area since the 50s—about organizing an Appalachian education center that could coordinate the numerous projects and social movements that were going on in the region. We could house student groups and volunteers, teach workshops and do some farming. And frankly, my husband was tired of me filling up the house with students and volunteers, so the timing was right on several fronts.

Anne and I looked at properties for a while until we finally found something near Dungannon, [Virginia], in rural Scott County. It was close enough to Clinch Valley that I could continue teaching, and a good location for Anne and Monica to continue their own work. . . . So we piled into a Jeep and entered the property on this incredible road that wove around the top of a mountain and into the land below, 152 acres in all. The farm was stunning—a mile of riverfront with rock-faced mountains on one side and a tunnel where the railroad passed on the other. . . .

We started working on the farm right away. . . . There were so many people who helped us on the farm it's hard to remember. . . .We had long-haired hippies living on the farm, and people living in painted-up vans and makeshift camps. . . . The education center was an important feature of our work, but we also wanted to try and make a living selling organic produce. . . .We discovered pretty quickly that we weren't very good farmers.We had some really productive gardens that provided a good bit of our own food, but it never took off from there. It's difficult trying to make a living as a farmer. . . .

We had a good time at the farm with a constant flow of artists, activists, community organizers, most of whom were Appalachian natives, even though they might not have looked the part. I was still teaching at Clinch Valley at this time, so I continued living at my house inWise County. But as the farm became more organized and my marriage started to break up, I decided to move to Dungannon full-time. . . .

As we settled in at the farm, we lost a little bit of the "hippie-commune" image; and we started to become more active in the Dungannon community.We helped organize a leadership program and an education program through Mountain Empire Community College.We developed the Dungannon Health Clinic and the Clinch River Educational Center. . . . Organizing people . . . didn't make us the most popular people in town. . . . But in the end, our neighbors stepped up and protected us. . . .They may have thought we were strange, but they saw the bigger picture. Some even started coming to the farm to enjoy the activities we had going on. So this is how the River Farm started. ("Interview with Helen Lewis")

"Nomination of Helen Matthews Lewis for the Wonder Woman Foundation Awards, 1983," by Richard A. Couto

Helen Matthews Lewis has a Ph.D., a pickup truck and a penchant for the untried.

Her creativity is in the analysis and synthesis of social conditions which most of us do not yet realize are related. Her achievements are considerable. She kindled Appalachian studies, fostered a renaissance of cultural expression in the Appalachian region and catalyzed numerous community projects in the region. She did this in such a manner that the similarities of the Appalachian region to other parts of the country and the world are now far more obvious. . . . One can generally learn what others will be discussing and discovering in three to five years by talking to Helen now.

It is important to understand that Helen constantly redefines roles. She also combines many roles: sociologist, filmmaker, educator, researcher and homemaker. Her avenue to her achievements and creativity is her immersion in the lives, strength and struggles of ordinary people. She is well equipped for this task with a mind that is a brilliant combination of scholarship and common sense. She raises private troubles to the level of public issues as C. Wright Mills advised us to do. In her work and in her roles, she has provided us with an important example of being first and foremost a human, caring person. Her example is all the more remarkable because her creativity as well as her risk-taking increases with time.

But being ahead of your time sometimes exacts a price, especially for women and other minorities. . . . At the age of fifty-three, in 1977, Helen faced new and undefined challenges. . . . She was now divorced and along with several friends and former students she entered into a land trust agreement and purchased a hidden, idyllic, working farm in Southwestern Virginia, near Dungannon. The most concise measure of Helen's creativity is the stream of researchers, coal miners, government and foundation executives and friends who find their way to Dungannon, Virginia, and to Helen's A-frame house on the River Farm. Their determination can be measured by their traversing a difficult, one-lane, dirt road that leaves the blacktop, clings to the side of a mountain and weaves among rocks and trees until it comes to her house. They come for conversation and insight. They find those and inspiration and hospitality as well. When they leave the road seems far less risky.

Helen's Gardening Tips

Living at the River Farm, we certainly learned early that we were not real farmers, but we were gardeners and raised lots of good food.

1. Compost: save all your potato peels, fruit rinds, coffee grounds, tea leaves, eggshells, etc., from the kitchen and grass clippings, weeds, dead flowers from your yard, add some manure and dirt, and you have great fertilizer—homemade.
2. Plant lots of greens: mix turnip, mustard, and kale seeds with some sand, and sow a big patch both in the spring and late summer and have great mixed greens. Also spinach planted in fall and left over the winter will come forth in the spring for early spinach. Also plant chard and

arugula and other greens. Small chard plants can be brought inside and used for salads all winter long.

3. Plant lots of tomatoes, and can and dry and freeze whole tomatoes or sauce for great winter soup. A soup mix of tomatoes, okra, corn, and small lima beans is wonderful.

4. Plant lots of basil, and make pesto from fresh basil, garlic and pine nuts or walnuts, and olive oil blended. Freeze in ice cube trays, and then keep in freezer in zip-lock bags and use to season soups and pasta and other dishes.

5. Learn about your wild greens: lamb's quarters and poke salad make great dishes.

6. You can mulch between your rows with newspapers to cut down on weeding.

(Unpublished correspondence with Judith Jennings, 2011)

from "From Kingdom Come to Chestatee: The Importance of Learning History" (1984)

If we see Appalachian society as historically changing, imperfectly bounded, with multiple and branching social alignments, the concept of a fixed, unitary, and bounded culture must give way to a sense of the fluidity and permeability of cultural sets. In the rough and tumble of social interaction, groups are known to exploit the ambiguities of inherited forms, to impart new evaluations or values to them, to borrow forms more expressive of their interests, or to create wholly new forms to answer to changed circumstances.

The interaction is not causative in its own terms, but is responsive to larger economic and political forces; the explanation of cultural forms must take account of that larger context, that wider field or force. A culture is thus better seen as a series of processes that construct, reconstruct, and dismantle cultural materials, in response to identifiable determinants.

We have moved from a people without a history where time stood still to a people learning and celebrating our history. . . . E. P. Thompson says the past is not just dead, inert, confining; it carries signs and evidences also of creative resources, which can sustain the present and prefigure possibilities for the future. When we look at history we see our lives connected with the lives, struggles and understandings of previous generations.

There is a moral responsibility inherent in the historical process both backward to parents, grandparents, generations past and forward, to those who come after us. We see how events elsewhere affected the area. Our lives are part of the flow of time, action and change. There is beneath the present a ghostly, ancient remnant made of events and thoughts of other times. . . .

An historical perspective helps us see not what is *like* the present in the past, but what is *new* in a situation. It helps us to see how society changes, when things are different and when things are the same.

It is commonplace to say we all inhabit "one world." There are ecological connections: mountain chestnuts destroyed by a foreign blight; Cherokees decimated by smallpox from European invaders. There are demographic connections: Haitians migrate to North Georgia; West Virginia coal miners migrate to Chicago. There are economic connections: Virginia coal goes to Japan; strikes in Wales or Poland increase Appalachian coal production; Tennessee workers produce Datsun trucks or nuclear weapons. There are political connections: unemployed Kentuckians join the Marines to guard the airport in Beirut.

These connections hold true not only for the present but also for the past. They indicate contact, connections, linkages and interrelationships. Instead of defining the region as an integrated and bounded system, set off against other equally bounded systems, rather we look to the interconnections between the region and the world. There is a complex orchestration of antagonistic forces, of contradictory relationships.

By endowing the region with the qualities of internally homogeneous and externally distinctive and bounded, we create a false model of reality: Appalachia as a white Anglo-Saxon enclave, isolated, traditionally bound. Having fixed entities makes it difficult to understand the encounters and confrontations of diverse social groups, and discourages analysis of inter-social or inter-group interchanges, including internal social strife, colonialism, imperialism and societal dependency, the issues demonstrably agitating the real world. People are caught up in continent-wide and global change. For 500 years, there has been confrontation, killing, resurrection and accommodation. There is no Appalachian history apart from American history, European history, World History.

We need to understand the effects of human contact and influence as open systems inextricably involved in web-like, net-like connections. We need a history of configurations and relationships. We cannot understand the world unless we trace the growth of the world market and the course of capitalist development. We must relate both theory and history to processes that affect and change the lives of local populations. We need to look at, delineate the significant elements at work in these processes and their systemic combinations in historical time.

Theoretically informed history and historically informed theory must be joined together to account for significant processes and as their carriers. We must see the range and variety of population, their modes of existence before European expansion and the advent of capitalism, the manner in which these modes were penetrated, subordinated, destroyed, or absorbed, first by the growing market and subsequently by industrial capitalism. We need to look at wide linkages, at how people were drawn into the larger system to suffer its impact and to become its agents.

We must understand the transition to capitalism in the course of the industrial revolution, the impact on an area of the world supplying resources to the industrial center. Look to the formation of working classes and their migrations within and between continents.

There are no contemporary ancestors, no people without history. All have been involved in the construction of a common world. All societies and cultures have undergone major changes. We must look at the economic and political conditions that generated these linkages, the mode of production, how people confront the world to modify it in their favor. Men make their own history under the constraint of relationships and forces that direct their will and their desires.

from the introduction to *Images of the Appalachian Coalfields,* by Builder Levy (1989)

The Appalachian region has served as the source for some of the highest-quality coal in the world, but the development of that industry never benefited the region's inhabitants as much as it did outsiders—the speculators and the corporations who gained control of the land and its minerals. From its earliest days, the industry has been characterized by insecurity and exploitation. Intense competition for markets and frequent swings in boom and bust cycles created an economically vulnerable labor force and a deeply scarred landscape. The history of Appalachian mining is a tale of continual dislocation, a depressed regional economy, and volatile labor relations. . . .

When the coal boom of the 1970s brought an increase in population and the demand for housing, the coal companies made little of their land available for housing. Mobile homes began to spring up throughout the area. Relatively well-paid miners lived in town or built comfortable houses outside the coal camps and commuted to work. Thus, the prosperity of the 1970s decreased the likelihood that miners working for a company would live in the same community and, thus, decreased the solidarity among miners and their families. . . .

By 1975 thousands of acres of farm and forestland were irreparably damaged, overturned, or buried [because of strip mining]. The soil and forest, which covered the coal, called "overburden," were pushed into valleys and streams, resulting in floods, mud slides, and damage to roads, houses, and communities. Many miles of streams were polluted with silt and mine acid. Sometimes these mining practices took place despite the opposition of those who owned the land where mining was undertaken but not the mineral rights—they owned only the surface. "Broad form" deeds gave mineral owners the right to get the coal by any method they chose. These legal instruments had been supported by the Kentucky courts until a constitutional amendment was approved in November 1988 to prohibit their use. In other cases, privately owned land was destroyed by neighboring mining operations, or operators intimidated owners into selling to them. Many were forced to move from the coves and hollows of Appalachia, and communities were devastated. Families were forced to move or live near spoil banks that ruined farmland, water, and roads, as homes and land were devalued. The operators, impervious to community and individual protest, claimed that they were benefiting the region by providing more flatland to encourage economic growth. . . .

In areas where coal companies closed down their operations, remaining residents inherited a variety of hazards related to the abandoned mine workings. Underground mine fires, dangerous slag piles (such as those which caused the Buffalo Creek disaster in 1972), and burning coal refuse, or slag, endangered the whole community. Deserted mine structures, equipment, tunnels, and caves provided hazardous playgrounds for children. In areas where strip mining had replaced underground operations, they encroached on some small communities—water sources were destroyed and coal-hauling trucks spewed dust and damaged roads. The mines ruined the land, making it unfit for other uses. And when the coal was depleted, the companies abandoned these areas too, leaving the pillaged land to its residents.

Heightened political activity in the 1960s and 1970s led to the formation of such organizations as "Save the Land and the People," "Save Our Cumberland Mountains," and "Virginia Citizens for Better Reclamation." These, along with older environmental groups and newly formed coalitions and national groups, began a serious political struggle that culminated in the 1977 federal strip-mine regulations.

A decade later, many of those who fought for the legislation claim that the law has never been properly enforced. Citizen groups must monitor the activities of the operators *and* the enforcers. Some coal operators believe the regulations are too stringent and hinder the industry, but even their grudging compliance with the legislation did make a major change in the way coal is mined and land is treated. . . . Despite the limited compliance and irregular enforcement of the 1977 regulations, this legislation has had important practical and symbolic effects. The citizens' organizations succeeded in getting both state and federal strip-mining legislation to protect their land and to help many families win compensation for damages. They demonstrated that collective action works and thus encouraged others to take a stand against a coal industry that most people believe was too strong to be affected by community protest.

This recent wave of unemployment in the coalfields has also produced greater inequities in coal communities, where residents include a small number of relatively well-paid miners, retired miners, miners' widows, and a growing number of unemployed and destitute miners and their families. . . . The human costs of these conditions are devastating. Many people cannot pay for health care, and the schools are full of hungry children again. The people caught in this spiraling poverty often do not see the changes as structural; instead, they feel inadequate and ashamed of their inability to support their families. The rates of suicide, alcoholism, drug use, domestic violence, school dropouts, and racist acts are all on the rise, while the literacy rate declines. These human costs are made clear in the testimony given at public hearings held by the Commission on Religion in Appalachia in 1985. The Commission published its findings in *Economic Transformation:The Appalachian Challenge* in 1986. . . .

Drawing on the creativity and resilience that enabled them to survive long strikes, layoffs, and depressions, many of the mining families are turning to an informal economy—bartering, selling goods, making crafts, and growing food. Women who have never worked outside the home are returning to school, seeking employment in the few small sewing factories, looking for low-wage jobs in nursing homes, or attending sick and disabled people at home.

In the midst of such hardship, miners and their communities are being asked to help make Appalachian coal more competitive by working for lower wages, cutting severance taxes, and giving up environmental regulations—in effect, subsidizing the industry. Having fought so long and hard for decent wages, safe working conditions, environmental controls and reclamation, equitable taxes, and some return to the community, miners and their families resist surrendering those protections. . . .

Mineworker and community experience has not borne out the companies' contention that what is good for the industry is good for miners and their communities. Industry prosperity did not raise incomes, jobs, tax revenues, or bank deposits. In fact, the growth cost the region. Road-repair costs for coal hauling alone were higher than tax revenues from coal producers, as indicated in the Mountain Association for Community Economic Development (MACED) report. With coal development, the economic "multiplier" works backward; there are few spin-offs. In fact, coal development discourages other development and burdens the community with costs. The MACED report of 1980, *Coal and Economic Development,* projected the costs of the coal industry to Kentucky over the next fifteen years at $1.5 billion. . . . The current plight of mining communities is strong evidence that the enrichment of the coal producers has resulted in the impoverishment of the region and its people.

from "Coal and After Coal" (1996)

This is the Easter Season, and we think a lot about death and resurrection. The message of Easter is that for every death there is a resurrection. Perhaps that is the message we are looking for in the coalfields as we are told to prepare for the death of the coal industry and think about what comes next.

Is there life after coal? . . . The problem doesn't seem to be lack of coal, but it is harder to mine, deeper seams and more costly to mine. . . . Others say the real problem is the companies have invested so heavily in machinery, which they feel they must keep running to pay for their investment that they have overproduced and have mined themselves out of business. Others say that what are left are the thinner, deeper seams too expensive to mine. All agree the peak production is over and the costs of mining will increase and the number of miners will probably continue to decline.

What has happened is part of a national and international restructuring of the economy. We have experienced in the U.S. a loss of manufacturing jobs and movement of industries to countries with cheaper resources, cheaper labor and fewer regulations. We have seen the decline of steel, automobiles, textiles, electronics and increase in services and lower wage jobs, along with an increase in high tech information services. Mining has globalized too, become multinational. You don't move the mine, but switch the orders to cheaper coal operations where coal is easier or cheaper to mine, [and] there are fewer regulations. . . .

In the 1980s steel companies and land companies sold out to large energy multinationals. Both U.S. Steel and Bethlehem sold out or left mining. . . . A. T. Massey is an example of the new multinationals and their style of operations. They are part of the multinational Fluor Corporation. Integrated sales, separate relations with different mines, decentralized production with centralized worldwide sales, along with centralized capital, decision making and planning, make it possible to shift production to more profitable mines. . . .

When the mines close, they leave holes in the ground, unemployed and disabled miners and impoverished families. . . . We have greater inequalities in the coalfields. Many women are seeking education and employment. They are working in fast food, new retail outlets, sewing factories, nursing homes, low-wage service jobs. People have to be very creative in survival techniques. There is a large informal economy with bartering, selling goods, making crafts, growing food, and some illegal crops. . . .

And now the area is being asked to subsidize the coal industry to make it more competitive. It seems evident that coal mining will never provide employment to as many as it has in the past, and wages from employment is basically all the industry really provided. If the area is still producing a lot of coal but with fewer and fewer miners, if there is still as much now as we have mined in the past 100 years—even though more expensive to mine, is it fair to ask miners and mining communities to further subsidize an industry which has never paid the social costs of mining? . . .

We can never be completely *After Coal*. We have a legacy from mining. Mining has adversely affected the land. There are acres of slag, acid drainage, subsidence, damage to the water table, leveling of the mountains. . . .

What alternatives are we being offered? . . . The coalfields have . . . attracted and have welcomed new prisons. There are two state prisons and a federal prison planned for the region.

Breaks Interstate Park has become a white water rafting mecca. They are looking forward to tourism development tied to the new road, the Coalfields Expressway. . . .

Forest development is another alternative. Large forest operations are moving into East Kentucky, southwest Virginia, and West Virginia to harvest the new growth since the earlier pillage at the turn of the century. These are mainly chip mills, which can utilize hardwoods from three inches up. . . . It is the old story again of an extractive industry removing the resources. . . .

What are other alternatives? Over the past 30–40 years the development strategy in the region has been to recruit new industries to fill the void of closed industries. Competition is great between towns and counties and other rural areas. . . . Each place provides industrial parks, the magic carpets, which are supposed to attract another fly-away factory. Smokestack chasing has been prevalent, and the region had some early success as plants came down from the North looking for lower wages and fewer unions and fewer regulations and tax incentives. But the stampede is over, especially for rural areas without a skilled workforce, transportation, infrastructure and cultural amenities. Most states and regions offer many inducements and the costs are heavy. No one has done any careful cost-benefit analysis of this strategy.

A major problem in the coalfields for both recruiting industry and developing alternatives to coal is that the companies still own the land, timber, minerals, up to 80% in many counties. The coal or land companies still control the resources. Most companies have been very reluctant to sell or make land available to the communities. There are some hopeful signs of coal companies becoming better neighbors. . . . But the coal company's goal is not to provide jobs but to mine coal as efficiently as possible and make as much profit as possible. Every regulation for the safety of workers, health benefits, and environmental regulations had to be fought for. . . .

There is no doubt that the rest of the states and nation owe the coalfields a lot. They provided the energy for the industrial development and enrichment of other parts of this country and still provide most of our electricity. . . . Why not develop loan funds and access to capital so former miners and their families could become entrepreneurs, create new small and medium-sized businesses to boost employment? Make funds available for local business ownership and expansion, provide training in entrepreneurship, develop untapped local and regional markets for local products, use local resources both natural and people. Provide land for local development, recreation, and housing. There are some examples of worker-owned businesses, small flexible manufacturing networks, which provide support for small business development, cottage industries. Utilize historical, scenic, farm, forest, water resources. Jobs can be developed by providing services: housing, medical services, transportation, child care, education, vocational training, infrastructure rebuilding, reclamation and restoration of degraded and devastated land and communities. A major job could be repair and restoration of the region. . . .

What does the area have to offer? The coalfields are part of a beautiful region increasingly scarred by an industry that has never demonstrated respect for the land or its people. The loss of water and destruction of communities to strip mining has left an area in need of a lot of repair and restoration.

The people share a place and a history. Underground and in the camps, miners are bound by a sense of mutual obligation. Traditionally, they have pulled together in times of crisis, and they have endured. . . . It is an area and people deserving of better than outside garbage, returned coal ash, devastation of the remaining forest, a prison economy, more mining of dangerous thin seams of coal (probably at non-union, lower wages) or greater surface mining or recruitment of low wage industries. We need to imagine more creative development programs to rebuild communities and to repair and restore the region.

It is time to be creative, dream new dreams, and develop new models. Let us plan for resurrection, not designate the region as a further sacrifice area.

Working with Women and Participatory Research at Highlander

Working at Highlander in the '80s and the early '90s, I have worked most closely with rural communities seeking to revitalize their communities which have been devastated by mechanization, closing coal mines and runaway factories. There is something of a social movement led by women in these communities. In 1984, we developed a workshop of 30 women from ten communities who came together to share their work histories and those of their mothers and grandmothers in order to understand how women's work has changed and remained the same over recent generations. The stories were so powerful that we put them together in a booklet, Picking Up the Pieces: Women In and Out of Work in the Rural South. *A group of us from the workshop selected, edited and put it together. I wrote a brief conclusion called "Coming Forward and Taking Charge." ("My Life and Good Times in the Mountains; or, Life and Learning in Central Appalachia")*

from "Coming Forward and Taking Charge," in *Picking Up the Pieces: Women In and Out of Work in the Rural South* (1986)

These stories from one meeting of 30 Southern women present a perspective on rural women and their place in the economy. The stories were told by rural women, poor women, black women, Appalachian women, Native American women, and Southern women, who by class, sex, race and/or region are peripheral to the mainstream economic system. Yet from these stories about women and work in the rural South, there is something we can learn about the economic system and possibilities for change.

First, the work histories make clear that many women in the rural South have been working very hard and living in poverty for a long time. The work of rural women is strenuous, involving extremely long hours and a wide variety of tasks, which take enormous amounts of time and are essential to the survival of the family. Rural women have birthed and nurtured the young, cared for the old and sick and managed the household. Through gardening, canning and bartering work and goods with sisters, mothers and neighbors, women have been the source of livelihood for families. They stretched resources, "made do," saved and scraped by. Women have worked at low-paying, low-status domestic service and manual labor to feed families when the men were unable to find jobs. When men left the family or women left husbands, women have worked at two or three jobs to support themselves and their children and to provide education, decent clothing and health care for their families. They managed farms, did "man's work," whatever they had to do to survive.

Women have also been the main providers of social services. They have soothed and restored those damaged by economic crisis, cared for the victims, helped people migrate away and come back home. They have provided health care, midwifery and counseling. They have been the teachers passing on traditions, telling stories, singing songs, bringing joy in what otherwise could have been a tedious and dreary existence. . . .

Although poor women have been an essential part of the work force, the labor market has been open only in certain places, sectors and times. Much of it has been the extension of work previously performed within the home. . . . Today, women clean motels and condominiums or cook in the fast food restaurants. As some of women's work became very profitable and brought power and status to the performers, women were excluded from the jobs and lost their traditional work as midwives, healers, preparing the dead for burial and teaching. . . .

Women have experienced being both cheap labor and a surplus labor force available when needed, discharged and returned to the household when no longer needed. . . . In this way, women's labor is used as a safety valve to maintain the economic system through cycles of inflation and depression. Social programs can be cut because women are back home in the informal, "non-economic" economy feeding and maintaining family members. Their labor within the home is considered "non-work" since it is performed outside the market context, yet the men who work outside rely on women's work in the home to make their paid work possible. Industry relies on the unpaid services of the wife to cut labor costs and increase profits. . . .

In the coalfields, the labor participation rate of women has always been the lowest in the country, reflecting women's essential role in shoring up an industry. . . . The impacts of changing technology, consciousness and economic necessity have resulted in a greater range of occupations open to women. In recent years, women have struggled to enter the higher-paying "non-traditional" jobs. . . . Still today, the reality for most women in the mainstream economy is low-wage jobs, at the bottom of the system: the cheap and flexible labor force required by the demands of market forces.

In contrast to work in the mainstream economic system, the women's economy is life-sustaining, life-producing, family- and community-based. The term "livelihood" seems best to characterize it. It is an economy with long-range rather than short-range goals. Women reproduce and work for their children and their grandchildren to provide a better life or pass on a way of life. The domestic economy deals with actual people and their needs, treating people as human beings, not as raw material or commodities, not just a labor force for economic production. And women's personal experiences of being treated as property, as sex objects, and used for private sensations lead to a clear understanding of how people and resources can be exploited as raw material. . . .

In contrast to "planned obsolescence," women make things to last; place emphasis on durability, quality and economy. Preservation, not exploitation of resources, is women's style. As gardeners they understand the need to care for water and soil. . . .

Although much of women's work and production are basically useful and practical, they usually have time for the beautiful, the aesthetic. There are flowers in the garden, pleasing designs in the quilts, and songs when they work. . . . Women also pay attention to history, tradition, stories. . . . Education is also primary—not only in schools but learning from each other.

Women's community development projects typically draw from their experiences and values, and recognize both community and individual needs and combine education and development to link personal and community growth. Because much of women's work has been considered unimportant, it has given women a degree of freedom to experiment and develop non-traditional patterns. . . . As a result, women working in communities have had the freedom to develop innovative, experimental projects. Some women are working to develop community-owned businesses, worker-owned co-ops, self-help projects, and other subsistence and small income-generating projects. They have started community-controlled educational programs. The planning process tends to be democratic, more participatory, seeking to develop and use local skills and resources and to involve everyone. Their projects provide some models for community-based economic development, democratic planning and production, which meet the needs of families, communities and environment. . . .

Today the "de-industrialization" or restructuring of the economy is again expecting to use women in the same two ways as in the past: as cheap menial labor in mobile small manufacturing plants with sweatshop conditions, or in tourism and fast food industries; and as survivors and supporters of families. The needs are greater than ever. Because of cuts in wages and cuts in social services, families are expected to absorb the social costs of economic restructuring to make the economy more competitive. . . .

Women recognize that they do not have the resources and can no longer serve as back-up for a depressed economy. They cannot protect the family without land and resources, without more control over the economy. As shown by their stories, working and grassroots women are more aware of their own power and their history and are critical of both the dominant economy and patriarchy. They are emerging as leaders in the most creative and progressive groups in the country. They are looking for ways to deal with the economic changes which are posing a threat to them and their families and communities.

In times of family or community crisis, women are traditionally called on to "pick up the pieces," to help get everyone reorganized and functioning. Today, rural families and communities are in economic distress. Women are beginning to realize that to save them will require more than patching up the system, or gaining integration into the national and global economy. In the organizations these women are building in rural communities today, they are developing new structures, and new approaches to growing needs.

from "Participatory Research and Education for Social Change: Highlander Research and Education Center" (1999)

The term *Participatory Research* did not enter the vocabulary of Highlander staff until the 1970s. Communities which Highlander worked with had begun to organize around issues of environmental pollution and health problems, corporate ownership of land and minerals, taxation and occupational safety issues which required information often limited to professionals. People needed to gain control over knowledge and skills which were considered to be the monopoly of the experts. John Gaventa and Juliet Merrifield joined the staff of Highlander and developed the library into a resource center to provide research assistance to community groups and train citizens to do their own research and participate more effectively in public policy decisions. John Gaventa remembered in 1996, "I first heard the words 'participatory action-research' 20 years ago when I was working at Highlander. We met some folks, who after hearing about our work said, what you do is called participatory research. So we grasped it then because all of sudden, aha! We had something to call our own work."

One of the first Highlander projects which was called "Participatory Research" was a major collaborative Land Study Project developed at Highlander by John Gaventa and Billy Horton of the Appalachian Alliance. About 100 grassroots "researchers" were mobilized and trained to gather data from tax rolls and deed books in their home communities about land and mineral ownership throughout the coalmining region of Appalachia. They documented the absentee and corporate ownership of land and minerals of the region. The data became the tools of organized community groups working for fair taxation. The research became a means of popular action itself. When people began to see themselves as researchers, they developed many ingenious methods of gaining information. They also learned to use their own water sampling kits, video cameras, computers to get and compile the information they needed. Because those who are experiencing the problem were the ones researching it, they had many sources of information in the community, which were not available to the professional researcher.

Participatory action research became a major part of the Highlander curriculum. An economics education curriculum developed at Highlander taught community members how to assess community needs and resources to begin community-based development. Combined with the Highlander pedagogy of beginning with people's own experiences, community members used oral histories, their own and other members of the community, to analyze their past development history and family employment histories, to understand the economic changes which they had experienced. Asking questions of grandparents, parents and peers about their work and means of survival, and then charting those responses became a way of understanding broad economic changes through peoples' own experiences. They could then begin planning for development which would be more just and democratic or which could preserve some of the means of survival, which had been part of their community and family history.

Community surveys were developed by members of the community, and they interviewed several hundred people in each community. The survey was not only a way to gather data, but a way of mobilizing the community discussions and consideration of the problems. Collective analysis of survey results became a way of developing research skills and of stating and prioritizing problems to be addressed.

Community mapping and drawing, visual portrayals, became an important way for participants to describe current problems and relationships in the community, as well as to articulate visions for the future. Young people made photographs throughout the community and then drew their vision of changes they would like to see. Some communities developed elaborate maps of every street, house, business and other structures.

Community members then carried out decision-makers' interviews. After their own research on the changing economy and on community needs, they interviewed bankers. . . . The community definitions of needs usually contrasted dramatically with those of the power holders, so participants were then able to analyze the cultural components. . . . Some communities developed theater from the oral histories to tell the story of changes in the community and hopes for the future. People wrote poems and songs. In some communities, Bible studies were used to talk about the economy and analyze and understand community experiences and develop values and visions of what should be done. Some communities developed history books and museums in the community to tell their story. . . .

Highlander's tradition of using culture, acknowledging and respecting people's culture, remains in helping people to develop and recover their own knowledge through oral histories which have been denigrated or suppressed by dominant knowledge structures. Bumpass Cove and Yellow Creek both discovered that songs and poetry written about the pollution problems helped organize and educate around the problem. Communities used their cultural expressions in their gatherings and celebrations as an affirmation of their identity.

The process of people gaining control over knowledge and skills normally considered to be the monopoly of the experts is an empowering one, which produces much more than just the information in question.

When people begin to research their own problems, they begin to feel that they have some control over the information, some beginnings of a feeling of power vis-à-vis the experts. That feeling is strengthened when they confront the experts such as the health department or other government officials, and they discover that they knew what the scientists did not, and that they had a right to speak out on what they knew. . . .

Highlander and similar organizations have an important role to play in systematizing and giving validity to people's knowledge. Many Highlander projects have helped systematize and analyze their knowledge, while teaching people how to gain access to other information about problems that affect them. People learned how to carry out their own health surveys, to document problems they suspected and to give validity of numbers to what they already know. . . .

When people learned how to do their own research, they began to recognize that experts are not objective, unbiased, disinterested purveyors of truth. Instead, their use of "science" is often not accountable and responsible to the needs of ordinary people, but serves the power holders. Highlander was able in some cases to find scientists who would join with citizen or worker groups to address their problems. Physicians worked with communities to develop health surveys which would be accepted as legitimate. Scientists worked with communities to study water and air pollution. In these relationships between scientists and people in communities with the problem, these crucial questions have to be asked:

- Who determines the need for the research?
- Who controls the process of research and makes decisions along the way, which affects its outcome?
- Who controls the dissemination of results?
- Where does accountability lie?

Highlander tends to work most often without reliance on cooperative scientists—relying on people's knowledge and helping them systematize and analyze their knowledge. We find that this knowledge is closer to the "truth" than the theoretical scientific knowledge. . . . We need a science that begins to meet the needs of ordinary people rather than the power-holders, a constructive and humane science.

Economics Education and Community Development

Sue Thrasher and I were dreaming of what sort of things we would like to see Highlander do, and we wrote a proposal for an economics education program which was funded by the Fund for the Improvement of Post Secondary Education. . . . I had reached the conclusion that we couldn't do anything about schools, health or anything until we did something about the economy. Our idea was to develop some way of teaching economics at the grass-roots level that could empower people to begin to move and feel like they could handle it. . . . Sue and I took the Popular Education course at Amherst, which is an introductory radical economics course. . . . It was good for people like us, who never had enough college economics, but that kind of class was too far removed from people in small communities. You have to work through immediate problems about jobs: How would you start a business? What kind of business would you start?—and as you help answer those questions, you tie in an understanding of the economy as it works right now.

As part of the project, I developed a course called Community Development and the Economy, first with Bill Horton and the Dungannon students and then with John Gaventa and Mountain Women's Exchange at Jellico, Tennessee, in 1987. It is designed as a college course in community development for a community-based program. Later, I developed a six-week non-credit community-style workshop called "Economics Discussion" in Ivanhoe, Virginia. The Ivanhoe Civic League had organized to get industry and economic development to revitalize the town. They had tried to recruit industry and hadn't had much luck, so they were willing to discuss what they've been doing and why they aren't successful and what they will have to do to develop their community." ("You've Got to Be Converted: An Interview with Helen Lewis")

I began to develop a curriculum for courses and workshops, which would help communities assess and profile their communities, understand what the economy was doing, what their needs and resources are and how they might make changes and improve the quality of life. Part of that work was done in conjunction with Carson Newman through a class in Jellico and produced a small booklet, The Jellico Handbook, *from a class taught there by John Gaventa and me. Following that, I worked in Ivanhoe, Virginia, a community that has lost its industrial base. One of the community development projects was a participatory research project to write a history book. We ended up with two magnificent volumes of pictures, stories, poems, song, history* [Remembering Our Past, Building Our Future and Telling Our Stories, Sharing Our Lives]. *I wrote a short essay in the back on "What I Learned," which sets out a philosophy of community development, which is growing in popularity, a more holistic definition of economic development, which includes building "social capital." ("My Life and Good Times in the Mountains; or, Life and Learning in Central Appalachia")*

from Helen M. Lewis, "Notes on the Educational Methodology of the HEEP Curriculum" (1988)

The goals of the Highlander Economics Education Program are to help people in rural Appalachian communities understand the changing economy and be able to develop ways of dealing with the economy and community economic development. We have been trying to develop a curriculum to help people in rural communities to look at how larger economic forces affect them and to identify the possible options for affecting the local economy, to decide on the most desirable approaches, and to develop the possible strategies.

In developing the curriculum for the project, we followed the educational approach of participatory research, adult and popular education. We believe that courses for a community-based education program should be different from the educational approach of the traditional college-based classes. Most of the students are older than the usual college student and bring valuable experiences, which can be utilized in the learning process. More of the students are women who because of home, family and life style plan to remain in their rural communities. They want an education which will help them develop skills they can use to improve their lives and the community in which they live.

Participatory research and non-formal education combine research, education and action around issues considered important for a community and allow the students to define their issues, do most of their own research, educate each other and participate in collective activities to solve their problems. It is a collective or group process of education, where the teacher and students learn together, beginning with the concrete experience of the participants, leading to a reflection on that experience to bring about some action for personal or community change. . . .

Equally important with content of the curriculum is the method of education. A competency in learner-centered curriculum development involves more than designing course materials. It also requires a careful examination of teaching techniques and classroom organization. Methods and content of education should be compatible. There is often a contradiction between content and method. What is being taught, equality, democracy, active participation, is contradicted by how it is taught. The structure of the classroom is very important. Participants need to be seated so they can have a dialogue with each other. When they sit in a circle or in small groups, they can see each others' faces and speak and listen.

Characteristics of non-formal adult education:

- Everyone teaches; everyone learns
- The starting point is the concrete experience of the learner
- Involves a high level of participation
- Is a collective effort
- Is an on-going process, not limited to a class or workshop
- Leads to action for change
- Stresses the creation of new knowledge
- Causes us to reflect on what we've done to improve what we are going to do
- Strengthens the ability of people to organize themselves
- Links local experiences to historical and global processes

Non-formal education insists that education should not take place in isolation from the community, should not be separated from experience and learning by doing. Education should relate to real life, use knowledge to solve problems in the community. Rather than alienating students from their home and community, education can build a commitment to community, a sense of self-worth and dignity. It involves people acquiring the knowledge, skills and attitudes necessary for their community responsibilities.

Education should produce a fully developed individual who understands the forces of work in society, an individual desirous of total control of his/her natural and social environment. Proponents of this methodology assert that "only through knowing their past and present, only through understanding and analyzing their reality can people choose their future." Education should stress learning more than teaching. A basic tenet is that teachers act as facilitators and pose problems and give students the confidence to analyze their problems and plan ways of overcoming them. The students learn to speak out, take the lead, and make changes in their lives and in their communities. The teaching approach should strive to expand students' skills to critically think, make decisions, and act on those decisions in their own lives. Another important part of the teaching approach is to look for alternatives so that students look to changes in their own lives and in their community. . . .

The role of teacher as facilitator or animator:

- Creating a learning climate
- Posing problems
- Encouraging process of search for causes and solutions
- Assisting the group to discover as much as possible for themselves
- Planning action

This methodology is based on certain assumptions about adults and the way they learn. Adults have a wide experience and have learned much from life. They learn most from their peers. Adults are interested and learn quickly about those things that are relevant to their lives.

Adults have a sense of personal dignity and must be treated with respect at all times and never feel humiliated or laughed at before others. Adults need to discover answers and solutions for themselves. People remember the things they have said themselves best, so teachers should not speak too much. They need to give participants a chance to find solutions before adding important points the group has not mentioned.

- People remember 20% of what they hear,
- 40% of what they hear and see,
- 80% of what they discover for themselves.

Non-formal education is more flexible, more concrete and more subjective as compared with structured, abstract, objective formal education. Teachers are more facilitating, advising, and learners more active and responsible. Students are more cooperative, process-oriented. Decision making is shared.

The students in the community-based programs are active adults with rich experiences who have not been able to gain certain skills and knowledge. They bring to the classes their own history, experiences, strengths and potential which are invaluable in the education process.

A goal of curriculum development is to integrate teaching basic skills with content that reflects concerns and issues affecting students' daily lives. Skills include basics such as reading, writing and math and "critical" skills. Through a process of questioning, abstracting, analyzing and reformulating, students understand the social, economic and political background of their history. The community is a resource for learning. The students analyze their lives, their community and look for possibilities for change. Teachers and students are equal partners in an active learning process.

This methodology is not without problems and drawbacks. For many students, this approach represents a new way of learning. Most of the participants have been "schooled" and expect teacher-delivered information and answers. Some are shy to participate. As older, returning students, they may feel that they don't know much and so have little to contribute. Other participants such as teachers or speakers may feel threatened by the challenge to their traditional role as "expert."

Students in community-based classes also want assurance that their classes are academically sound, as good as those on the college campus. They do not want patronizing, less demanding courses and may equate the traditional style of presentation with high standards and quality. Once students understand the philosophy of the method, they usually respond positively to increased opportunities to participate and to come to some new understandings. The course also must be demanding, stretch the students to greater understanding and analysis. . . .

Many found this class had too many outside tasks, and the requirement to participate demanded students to attend regularly and to carry out the research, interviews, fact-finding, and observations. For the adult students with work and family responsibilities and classes every night, this type of class can be more demanding than the traditional academic course.

One may also encounter resistance to the analysis developed by the class. The resistance and conflict can be used constructively to help clarify positions and aid in learning.

Here are some of the ways in which we used the non-formal, participatory research approach:

1. The starting point is the experience and knowledge of the participant.

We began with what the students, all residents of the Jellico community, knew about their economy and the changes which had occurred in the community. Participants began to share what they knew: their work experiences, migration experiences, their family economic histories and their understanding about the economic structure of the community. They interviewed older members of their families and elders in the community to develop a history of the economy and changes which have occurred. This helps the student understand and place value on their own experiences and knowledge and places their knowledge in the arena for critical discussion. It helps the teacher-facilitators understand where people are at and what experiences and information they bring to share.

They studied the businesses, services, sources of employment through interviewing and collecting data from their own work places and the schools and other services which they use. Most of the students worked, and they were able to use their work, their knowledge of the businesses and industries they worked for into the discussion.

We used the students' experiences and knowledge to relate what's happening in the regional, national and international economy to people's lives, helping to identify similarities without minimizing the differences. We used a book of readings on the changing Appalachian economy and used news articles from local papers and local statistics to discuss issues.

2. The methods are participatory.

The techniques or activities were chosen both to meet specific objectives and to maximize participation. Exercises emphasized their roles as fact finders, discoverers within their own environment. Classes involved reports from students as individuals and as members of work groups. They were encouraged to share work, knowledge and experiences. The goal is to make learning more creative. This does not deny the use of a good lecture, speaker or film presentation, but it changes the way you use the speaker or film, adding more opportunities for participation.

3. The relationship with participants is based on mutual respect and shared responsibility.

The teacher doesn't have to know everything or be the expert on everything. You can say you don't know and suggest ways to find out. With the teachers being from outside the local communities, the students were the experts and taught us about their community. . . . We acted as facilitator-resource persons. We worked to find ways for participants to learn from each other through study and work groups.

Being a facilitator-coordinator is more demanding on the educator. You need to put a lot more effort into planning; and you have to be very well prepared, bringing reading materials, research materials, pictures, articles, materials to stimulate discussion. We found it much better to work with a partner, so you can back each other up. One can lead discussion, while the other makes notes or writes on board or newsprint. You can share critical reflection afterwards. If one is not picking up on some comments the other can interject, pose a problem or lead to a reflection on the experience.

4. The activities end up with action.

Many exercises included some opportunity for people to define action based upon what they'd learned. A discussion of the philosophy of *Small Is Beautiful* [by E. F. Schumacher] ended with suggestions on practical steps a community could take to become more self-sufficient. Based on the community needs survey, business plans were developed for possible enterprises which members of the class or the community might develop. At the end of the class, an economic development committee was formed, and a proposal was developed and sent to TVA [Tennessee Valley Authority] for funding to continue their planning.

People also get a chance to reflect on and evaluate the class experience. They evaluate their growth on how they have deepened their understanding of the situation. They critically evaluated all parts of the course and suggested changes in the content for future classes. They began to critically examine how they learn.

"No Ordinary Teacher: Helen Lewis of Highlander," by Patricia A. Gozemba

With the birth of the second wave of feminism . . . Lewis began to nourish the leadership skills of women, whose role she realized had been undervalued, ironically enough, in both the theoretical model of colonial exploitation and Highlander's community development work. . . . Candie Carawan, whose affiliation with Highlander over almost 40 years made her a colleague . . . notes that, "Helen felt that women were at the heart of many community struggles and had the stamina and skill to make a huge contribution to social change." Lewis created the space for women in what she jokes about as the "blue jeans macho days" of Highlander. . . .

Her feminism and fierce commitment to democratic pedagogy as well her long-standing alliance with and presence in rural communities distinguished her work. She constantly put her theory to the test. As Candie Carawan remarked, "Helen, perhaps more than anyone, was willing to spend time living and working in communities. She partici-

Helen leading an economics education workshop at Highlander, 1980s

Helen with women leaders (*left* to *right*): Pat Gozemba, Maxine Waller, Addie Davis, Helen Lewis, Frankie Patton Rutherford, 1980s

pated in community life and gave support to community members—particularly women just emerging to speak out and take on issues—in a deep and ongoing way."

At a time when most teachers pause to consider what they will do in retirement, and many of them dream of a more relaxed pace, Helen Lewis, between the ages of 63 and 73, embarked on an exemplary decade of teaching in and working with communities relegated to the margins of society. In her work with three community leaders and their local organizations—Maxine Waller and the Ivanhoe Civic League, from 1987 to 1989; Addie Davis and the McDowell County Economic Development Authority (EDA), from 1989 to 1992; and Franki Patton Rutherford and the McDowell County Action Network (MCCAN) and Big Creek People in Action, from 1996 to 1997—Lewis demonstrates how an imminently skilled democratic teacher forges increasingly more creative and effective strategies for developing community education programs, encouraging shared leadership, creating empowerment zones, forming alliances, and creating the conditions in which people can bring about social and political change for their community. (Eileen de los Reyes and Patricia A. Gozemba, eds., *Pockets of Hope: How Students and Teachers Change the World*)

from "Participatory Research in Community Development and Local Theology: Ivanhoe, Virginia, USA" (1997)

What happened to Ivanhoe is part of a larger economic crisis affecting not only Appalachian/Southern communities in the United States, but rural communities in many parts of the world. As plants close and economic growth bypasses rural areas, communities are not just being marginalized by the economic restructuring; they are responding to these changes in creative ways. . . . This is also the story of the collaboration of three women: a sociologist-community educator, who worked on an almost daily basis with the community for over two years; a feminist theologian and Catholic sister, who visited the community on numerous occasions and developed a series of Bible study sessions in an effort to explore the existent and evolving local theology; and a resident local community leader, who is the energetic, visionary organizer and interpreter of the experiences. Together, we documented the process from our different perspectives. We worked together over a five-year period, participating in an exciting on-going educational and development process, interviewing and being interviewed, discussing, arguing, crying, laughing, trying to understand and to pass on this understanding to others so that they might also learn from our experiences. We experimented with a number of participatory projects; a community history, economic discussions, Bible study and theological reflection, a puppet show and theater production based on oral histories from the community. The work is documented and recorded in the book *It Comes from the People: Community Development and Local Theology.*

The participatory research project began in June 1987, when I visited Ivanhoe as a community educator to help the year-old Ivanhoe Civic League assess their efforts and understand the economic changes of which they were part. My work was part of an economics education project of the Highlander Research and Education Center. . . . The series of economic discussions evolved into a collaborative, participatory research project involving the Highlander Center and the Glenmary Research Center of Atlanta, Georgia. . . . The Center asked me to make an in-depth case study of a rural community which had lost its industrial base, concentrating on how people are affected by and respond to these changes. . . . I asked the Ivanhoe Civic League to participate in the case study. They agreed to be active participants, but only if production of a community history book could be included in the process. . . .

Since Glenmary wanted the study to include a theological reflection piece as well as a case study, Mary Ann Hinsdale, IHM, a feminist theologian teaching at the College of the Holy Cross in Worcester, MA, was invited to join the project. . . . Because of my on-going education work in Ivanhoe, I suggested that the theological reflection also be participatory. Making the study participatory and involving the community in the research, analysis, and reflection (including the theological reflection) drastically changed the nature of the work, the time schedule, and the resulting product, the gradual uncovering and recognition by the community of its own "local theology." Approached from the perspective of liberation theology, Ivanhoe's faith and religious convictions—concepts which are often suspect in community organizing circles, since they are seen as dulling and prohibitive to the development process—helped to foster an emergence, from apathy and silence, of a community of outspoken, knowledgeable citizens who are demanding participation in the planning and direction of their community.

Maxine [Waller], as community leader, was central to the development process and to the documentation. To use the words of [Antonio] Gramsci and [Robert] Schreiter, Maxine is an "organic intellectual," a poet, preacher, and "local theologian." Maxine speaks with vigor and feeling from the community perspective and gives an analysis often missing from academic publications. We were also able to document her growth and change as a leader and her education as a community developer. . . .

The process of book publishing with the community brought to focus all the problems of being "fully participatory." The group was anxious to complete the project but still wanted to keep control over the final product. Others in the community wanted the book to be done and were putting pressure on the Civic League to produce the book. So we compromised and stopped the participatory process, and let it go to the experts to expedite the final production. . . .

A later conflict occurred after the books were published. Volume one was quickly sold out, and I was very anxious for this to be reprinted. It won the 1990 W. D. Weatherford Award for best book on Appalachia; and the community authors were invited to numerous conferences, asked to lead workshops and make presentations at a number of colleges and universities. Not only were these opportunities to make sales, but there was recognition and prestige for both the community and myself.

I had spent two and one-half years working with the community on the history and had considerable personal investment in the project. I began to push the Civic League to reprint the book. . . . Although the history committee agreed to reprint the books, . . . the cash flow of the organization was not adequate for reprinting. Maxine did not want to go into debt to reprint. . . . This resulted in Maxine feeling that my only interest was in the book and not the community. . . .

Three processes were always on-going in my work in Ivanhoe: 1) being a community educator and/or providing "technical assistance"; . . . 2) being a sociologist-anthropologist and documenting and observing the development process; and 3) being mentor, friend, and confidant to Maxine. All were part of my Highlander staff role, but number three was also personal as Maxine and I developed a strong friendship. . . .

Very early in the process, this book had centered on Maxine as the main narrator and interpreter of her own and the community's experience. She was interviewed frequently, studied and observed by us, and we wrote the chapters to which she could respond. Late in the process, she began to feel exploited and betrayed. In an . . . interview . . . she said: "I feel like a bug under a microscope. I mean it's fine to write a book that other people can do something with. . . . But, . . . I feel like a sacrificial lamb. I been laid up on the thing, and they are getting ready to burn me."

. . . A major goal of popular education and participatory research is to develop critical awareness, a critical consciousness, which enables the learners to recover their experience, reflect upon it, understand it and improve it. This requires the ability to be self-critical and to learn from the internal practices and organizational experiences, as well as analysis of the outside economic and political system or the specific problem which the group is seeking to change. Self-criticism—group criticism of the organizational structure and leadership practices—is frequently the most difficult thing for both grassroots groups and their leaders to do. Similarly, it is very difficult for social activist trainers, educators and facilitators. But it is essential for developing strong, viable groups as well as good leadership and democratic practices. Organization building requires the same type of analysis and action based on the research and reflection process, which the group uses to understand the social problem. . . .

But working together has to be learned. . . . For two years I had spent several days each week in Ivanhoe with Maxine and her family, . . . [and then] I . . . [became] involved in a series of workshops in West Virginia communities as part of my work. Maxine commented that I had "deserted" Ivanhoe. Although we both recognized that I could not remain as permanent volunteer staff in Ivanhoe, it was hard on both of us. We missed the working relationship we had developed. It is always tricky to avoid creating dependency and to maintain the friendships and develop on-going collaboration. . . .

It is hard to judge when to go, when the outside help is counter-productive. Outsiders need to make their own presence progressively unnecessary, so that the community can carry on alone the tasks which had been initiated without having to appeal to them as resource persons, except in special and extreme cases. . . . I was not a value-free, neutral observer. I pushed people, especially Maxine, concerning her leadership and management style. And she would respond, sometimes very forcefully. In a recent exchange, she responded: "Damn it, Helen! You drive me crazy! You have educated me too damn much!" . . .

In participatory research, everything is not always successful. There are ups and downs, sometimes quite serious, resulting from various crises and difficulties. There were "crises of perception" between myself and Maxine, and there were periods of fatigue when interest was lost in the interaction and organization. . . . The golden rule is to persist as far as possible in order to achieve the objectives of transformation. . . .

Most community groups go through stages. Ivanhoe was no exception. At the beginning, there was a movement based on the struggle for specific demands. If such demands are not met early on, many give up, drop out, and only the dedicated or "hard-headed" stay with the movement for the long haul. . . . And outside helpers need to rest sometimes too.

"On Community Leadership," by Maxine Waller

I think [each person] is a leader in their own right. . . . But can people be a leader like me? Is that the only kind of leadership there is? I don't think so. I think people can lead where they're at and grow as people. I feel like we got a lot of little leaders.

See, we've been an incubator for this to happen. And I've had to be out here, doing all the crazy things that I do, so that other people would have a space too. But people have styles of leadership. And I have my style. And right now there's not any other styles like me [in Ivanhoe]. But how many Martin Luther Kings was there? How many Jesse Jacksons are there?

Why, God almighty, I hid for thirty-eight years. You know, what if I had come out thirty-eight years ago, or twenty years ago? Think about it. So, hell, it took me thirty-eight years, so how can anybody expect people that's been oppressed and told what to do all their life, to become leaders overnight? Three years? I just now am seeing the fruits of the labor. Honest to God. All them nights and days that I sat in that office, and I worked. And it weren't so much trying to raise the money. I was just keeping up and keeping going, and I couldn't find nobody. . . . I kept thinking, even me, they ain't no leadership. But now, three years, I'm just seeing what leadership is. And it stops. And there ain't going to be no more of me. And why does anybody want to look for another leader? I mean, hell, *two* crazy people?

I been looking and studying people's leadership styles, and I'm trying to right some of the wrongs in leadership. And the reason that I'm doing this is because of my belief and my faith that all of this work that's been done in Ivanhoe was really, really God-intended. And that God intended for what's happening there to happen so that we would grow as people. (Mary Ann Hinsdale, Helen Matthews Lewis, and Maxine Waller, *It Comes from the People: Community Development and Local Theology*)

"Holding the Whole World in Her Hands," by Sue Thrasher

I never quite figured out how Helen Lewis could hold the whole world in her hands. At least that's what it seemed like to me. She is deeply at home in the southern mountains but has people across the globe she considers family. I first met Helen in the 1970s—but her reputation preceded her. I knew of her as the sociologist who gave up a college faculty position to work with community groups. The free spirit who hung out with nuns and other assorted radicals. The visionary who, with said nuns and assorted radicals, started a cooperative farm in such an out-of-the-way place that I, a rural Tennessean, was convinced the

Helen on her sixty-fifth birthday, in the Netherlands, 1989

road would pitch me off the side of the mountain when I first visited. The woman who likened Appalachia to a third world colony and brazenly called attention to the fact that its natural resources were being plundered with no regard for the people who lived there. The woman who helped define the new discipline of Appalachian studies. Later I came to know that this woman with the soft southern voice could also feed multitudes from a small garden or her pantry, depending on the season. I learned that she usually traveled with a retinue of the most interesting people on the planet. That she adored having company come to her red-roofed home overlooking the Clinch River. That sharing and giving were as much a part of her nature as the act of breathing.

Paulo Freire talks about the critical moment when we are able to "name" something as a necessary first step in taking action to change it. Helen's "naming" process about women's work and its role in the mainstream economy began with a women and economy workshop with more than thirty women from Appalachian, southern, and Native communities. After documenting and reflecting on the knowledge generated by that workshop in *Picking Up the Pieces,* she went on to de-

velop a curriculum for women and community development through
the Economics Education Project. Eventually, she made her way to
Ivanhoe for a five-year project that was utterly breathtaking in its risky,
creative exploration of women, work, leadership, community, and
spirituality. Participatory action research seems like too clinical a term
to describe her work there using oral history, theater, Bible study, and
economics education.

I remember Helen saying that women's work is often done "in the
cracks"—the small spaces that are little noticed, but where things can
grow. She argued that the result was more flexibility, more room to
deviate, more freedom to experiment. Perhaps it is that flexibility, that
willingness to experiment, that makes it possible for her to hold the
world in her hands. Perhaps. I don't really know; I just know that she
does it.

from "Paulo Freire at Highlander" (2010)

*In December 1987, Paulo Freire came to the Highlander Center . . . to "talk a book"
with Myles Horton, the founder of Highlander. They met at a conference in California
earlier that year and Paulo asked Myles to consider "speaking a book," a method
Paulo had used to develop some of his books. . . . Sue Thrasher of the Highlander staff
mobilized the staff and friends at the University of Tennessee who arranged for Paulo
to . . . meet with Myles at his home at the Highlander Center on the side of Bays
Mountain. . . .*

*Both men were great story tellers, so those of us who sat with them mostly listened
as they got to know each other, shared their experiences, questioned each other, compared their own development, exchanged ideas and educational philosophy. We also
observed two people, who had known about each other but had never really spent time
getting to know each other, develop a deep and lasting friendship. The conversations
were both relaxed and spontaneous and developed into what has been described as "a
dance between old companions accustomed to the subtle ideas and responses by one,
then the other." It was like watching two people discovering each other with feeling
and respect. They were excited and amazed at the many commonalities, how they both
came to similar analyses despite differences in cultural contexts. It was like watching
two old men falling in love.*

*During this visit, I was on staff at Highlander and working with rural communities
trying to rebuild their communities, which had lost their industrial base of mining. We*

invited some of these community leaders to come meet Paulo and talk with each other about their community development work. Paulo was excited to meet these grassroots leaders, mostly women, who with the help of Highlander educational programs had analyzed their experiences, developed their own understanding of the causes of their problems and had created some unique community programs. One of the exercises at the workshop with Paulo and Myles was drawing a picture of the relationship between their community and the Highlander Center. Maxine Waller from Ivanhoe, Virginia, drew a picture which included a goat on the hill looking down on the workshop at the Center. She explained that the goat was like Myles Horton, observing the educational process and occasionally butting in to push for more analysis. Paulo was delighted with this description of Myles' educational methodology for empowerment. . . .

The process of "talking a book" became intensely personal and therapeutic for both. It renewed their strength and gave them a new sense of possibility and hope. Myles was 82 years old, 16 years older than Paulo. . . .

Two years and one month after these conversations, in January 1990, Paulo returned to Highlander to visit Myles. The plan was for them to review the manuscript draft and possibly add or make revisions. Myles' cancer had reoccurred, and he was very ill. Myles had struggled to be alert and have enough energy to work with Paulo. They had several short conversations and agreed that the manuscript was almost ready. They together expressed pleasure with the form it had taken. But the situation was very emotional. When Paulo saw his friend, he said the work on the book was not the agenda for this meeting. It was to be with his friend in his last days. Myles relaxed and enjoyed Paulo's friendship and support. They ate together and looked out over the mountains and watched the birds in the feeder. Paulo commented: "It is sad, but dying is a necessary part of living. It is wonderful that Myles may die here . . . dying in the midst of life." It was their last conversation.

*Three days after Paulo left, Myles slipped into a coma and died on January 19, 1990. The book [*We Make the Road by Walking: Conversations on Education and Social Change, *edited by Brenda Bell, John Gaventa and John Peters] was published by Temple University Press later in the year.*

"Helen at Highlander," by Mary Thom Adams

I came to Highlander for the first time when I was ten years old. My father, Frank Adams, was writing a book with Myles and would soon become the director of Highlander. We were the first people to live on the site in New Market, and we lived in what is now the library.

In 1990, Helen and I both moved to live on the hill at Highlander. Myles had died, and Helen moved from the River Farm to live in Myles's house and be the director of the Horton Chair, a newly established program that allowed activists to come to Highlander for an extended period of time to write, rest, and share their experiences with the staff and community. I was hired to raise money for the Horton Chair and the other Highlander programs.

Since Helen and I both had a long history with Highlander, we shared a reverence for the history but also a bit of irreverence toward the creation of heroes. We embraced the opportunity to make the Horton House a place for people to come. To ensure Myles' continued presence at the house, we created a "shrine" in his honor, pictures from his travels, some trinkets that he had picked up along the way, and a few other artifacts we thought appropriate. Sometimes, we'd toast him with a martini or one of Helen's famous Old Fashioneds. Sometimes we'd share our frustration and anger at the imperfections we shared with him that make all organizations complicated.

A philodendron, reported to have been Zilphia Horton's, covered nearly a whole wall of the house. By the time Helen was living there, we thought the philodendron needed to be repotted. Even Helen, who can grow anything, approached this task with some trepidation. No one would ever want to be known as the one who killed Zilphia's plant. Helen called the farm manager, David Gann, and they began the task.

To all our amazement the plant, though thriving, had hardly any root structure to repot. That plant is now all over the country and probably the world because we piled pieces of stem and leaves in a bucket of water and started little plants to give to any and all who came for a visit. I think more than any other thing we did, this plant captured the importance of keeping history alive, spreading what you learn from it, but not taking it or yourself so seriously that you can't make room to grow and change.

Helen and I never ceased to be amazed by the people who came to Highlander. At any given time there might be a woman from Africa, a man from India, a coal miner from Southwest Virginia, a Native person from Washington or Hawaii, all sitting at the dining table. Their cultures, community struggles, and, of course, the good food we shared

Helen visiting indigenous community clinics in Chile, 1997

became a part of Highlander. We ate, played music, laughed, cried, railed against inequities, and never forgot what Emma Goldman said: "If I can't dance, I don't want to be part of your revolution."

Connecting with Communities around the World

Since I've gotten interested in the similarities Appalachia bears to the Third World, I am also thinking that we need to learn from them more about rural development. In May 1987 I was in Africa, and I discovered some books called Training for Transformation, *which are training manuals for community workers used in Kenya, India, and Zimbabwe. They're based on liberation theology and Freirian methods of education—bottom-up village-level training through education for transformation, changing, democratizing the whole society. It's the same thing I've been trying to do with Highlander and at places like Ivanhoe with the economics education project. . . .*

Last fall, I visited community education and economic development programs being run by and for women in Wales and Scotland and Holland and Belgium, and they were all similar to Dungannon and Mountain Women's Exchange. One was for Moroccan women, one was Turkish women, one was people on the Isle of Lewis, and one

Helen and Lewis Sinclair celebrating their seventieth and eightieth birthdays at Highlander, 1994

was Welsh coal-mining women, and the similarities were very striking. I saw the same thing in Zimbabwe and Botswana and Southern Africa, in the middle of Soweto. Those women sounded like the women of the Dungannon Development Commission; they've got that same energy. They're breaking forth; they're beginning to learn and develop self-confidence and are organizing things, like a little quilting co-op I saw in the middle of Soweto. They're learning things. They're having classes of various kinds. They have literacy programs going. They are growing and developing and learning. They have some of the same problems, family and husbands not liking it and not getting the respect from the total community and not being taken seriously. But they're such survivors, and they're such determined people, and they really work to build community. . . . In very different cultures, problems are so similar. Particularly with the Moroccan and Turkish women, they were having some of the same severe problems that some of our mountain women have with their husbands wanting them to stay home, beating them up and burning their textbooks. Yet rural and poor women are the vanguard of the new economic system. ("You Got to be Converted: An Interview with Helen Lewis")

from "African Journey, Some Notes and Reflections" (1993)

I was in South Africa, Namibia and Zimbabwe for a total of five weeks from March 2 until April 5. I had visited Zimbabwe, Botswana and South Africa in 1987, so I revisited several places but also added Namibia and some different groups and places in Zimbabwe and South Africa. Erica Kohl (Judy and Herb's daughter) traveled with me. Many of the people we visited had been to Highlander or knew about us and sent messages and greetings to the staff. Going and coming from Africa, I also visited in the Netherlands with Piet-Hein and his family and friends from Bergen Folk School, with which we have had long time connections.

In Africa, I mainly visited three organizations and other groups with whom they work: Wilgespruit Fellowship Centre near Johannesburg, South Africa; Community Development Resource Center, Cape Town, South Africa; and ORAP [Organization of Rural Associations for Progress] in Bulawayo, Zimbabwe. I paid a short visit to the Popular Education Centre in Harare, Zimbabwe. . . .

We have long ties with Wilgespruit. . . . The place is a former farm on the outskirts of a middle-class white African community, Roodepoort, and is now surrounded by fancy suburban housing and apartments. They are like an island, and the city would like to buy them out. . . . In the past, the Centre has been harassed and attacked by police and government for being integrated, "communist training school," a squatter and terrorist refuge, etc. (sound familiar?). They now find themselves being called on to help prepare for the new government. Some of their work in training community workers is country-wide, while other fieldwork is in Soweto, new communities of shack-dwellers nearer by. . . . Much time at the beginning is spent in human relations training so that they can talk and listen to each other. All the various programs of the Centre work with the course and develop sessions, workshops, facilitate sessions, etc. including Conflict Resolution/Negotiation training which is also carried out in townships and with populations who are fighting each other. . . .

Wilgespruit recently underwent a painful reorganization, with staff conflict over program direction and a number of staff left. . . . Although people feel good about the degree of integration, the reforms and openness, there is a lot of worry about preparing people to vote and operate the new government. Many feel that elections should be delayed and a massive education program instituted first. . . . We talked to various staff in the various programs and visited projects in Soweto, shack dwellers, sewing projects, and church twice in Soweto. . . .

Community Development Resource Center [CDRA]: . . . We visited two groups who work in the black townships and squatter communities, an education group, and we went to the mountains to visit co-ops in the Montagu region. . . . It is in the fruit and wine region of Cape Town. . . . Capacity building is the new key word rather than training or leadership development to assist organizations to survive and serve well. CDRA works with a number of organizations over a long time and also offers a training course "Facilitating Organization Development" for community leaders and facilitators. . . . Here are a few interesting sound-bites: Organizations like individuals need therapy, care. Organizations as living organisms go through phases, which should be understood. Look at identity and strategy and culture first; become conscious of organization history and criticize the myths. Most powerful organizations have charismatic leaders, but there comes a point when they are disadvantageous. The worst situation is when there is denial of power; rhetoric of flexible, highly democratic, etc, a denial of structure. There is a need for structures to protect everyone from wild, eccentric leaders. Leaders need to be nursed through depression. Some leaders don't know how not to be charismatic and instead be a facilitator, observer, receive feed-back. Need procedures to make organizations work: problem solving skills, decision-making skills, evaluation skills.

World University Services was a group we visited. The director Phumzile

Ngcuka talked about "capacity disempowerment," referring to outside experts who come and go and do not share skills or teach others and leave the organization disempowered. . . . Practitioners don't document enough. It is important to document what you do and then evaluate. Organizations need to be learning organizations with on-going reflection and documentation. Learn from your work.

Organization of Rural Associations for Progress in Bulawayo, Zimbabwe, was a four-day visit. . . . The women of the community met with us at one of their houses, sang songs about their work, danced, discussed the problems of structural adjustment in their communities and fed us watermelon, sugar cane and boiled corn. ORAP organizes family groups, which cluster into associations, with a resource center which serves as community center, training center, place to store grains for drought, use grist mill, blacksmith and carpentry shop, bake in ovens, community garden, etc. Associations have representatives on ORAP board, which meets every six weeks at Bulawayo center for board meetings, workshops, trainings, etc.

Bergen Folk School: I visited with Peter van Sutphin and Louie Kool of the folk school. Louie is now retired (early at 55) but still worked with Peter on international projects. He wrote a book about Highlander and Appalshop in the 60s. I attended a meeting with a group of women from northern Holland, who are initiating a program to encourage and support women entrepreneurs. They were brainstorming various possible types of businesses or services they might develop in their communities. I shared some stories from this region. They have a yearlong environmental and ecology training program for people on water boards, park service and other government agencies related to the issues. They have a program with Mexican and Dutch farmers around trade issues (GATT), etc. Louie has worked with lots of migrant groups (Turkish, Moroccan, and Spanish) who come to Netherlands to work. Bergen has only adult residential programs and has an on-going program with people being retired to deal with problems of retirement. . . .

Namibia was a visit with a young friend whom I met in South Africa in '87, and she came to the U.S. and just graduated from Berea. . . . Namibia is very American; the TV is almost all American (the latest) sit-coms. . . . Namibia is very modern but outside lots of the country in desert, desolate.

Some impressions about differences from 1987: Arrivals were simpler. Customs/papers simplified and open, no checking of baggage or any attention to where you are staying. A general openness in the airport and in the townships, fewer police presence or barricades. Still lots of gates, locks, razor wire, bars, car immobilizers. Lots of thievery from homeless, squatters, migrants, unemployed. More integrated in housing, schools, buses, trains, restaurants. Black professionals moving to white suburbs, buying country houses, lots of blacks on TV ads buying stuff and being trendy, modern, young and healthy. Lots of people overworked and overwrought in organizations we visited. People worried about inflation (especially Zimbabwe), recession, and unemployment. In Namibia, workers in copper mines and uranium exports, and these are their major exports. People in Zimbabwe upset that government is pushing and rationalizing and supporting the structural adjustment program. A government spokesperson was on TV saying transnationals will help consumers and lower prices. Inflation is bad. . . . Teachers and service workers need two jobs to meet costs. . . . People were more worried, overworked and depressed than in '87. We were there during a big celebration of Independence and there was lots of hope and optimism.

In Namibia, the policy has been to keep all former employees, civil service, etc. With independence, whites were encouraged to stay, no loss of jobs or land or farms. This leaves former combatants, exiles, those who fought for independence unemployed and unhappy. With recession and loss of more jobs, there are more complaints and criticisms of government policy. . . . The policy of the government has been reconciliation—forget the past—all start together anew. This also makes for ignoring history, forgetting past sacrifices and pushing modernization (mostly American style).

Visiting the organizations as an outside visitor made me more aware of how it can be a problem for staff who want to get on with their work, find it a burden to talk with you. Some, however, were very anxious to hear about Highlander and what we do and use the encounter for sharing and real dialogue. Some avoided or did a quick summary of their work and got you out as soon as possible. Some saw it as a way to build networks, learn from the visitors, reflect and share their work. Some were very willing to take us with them on their field visits, some invited us to their homes for dinner, and some probably found us to be a pain in their neck.

"Reflections on My Time with Helen in Pre-Mandela South Africa, Namibia, and Zimbabwe," by Erica Kohl-Arenas

In 1993, only months before South Africa's first democratic election and the nomination of Nelson Mandela, I traveled to South Africa, Namibia, and Zimbabwe with Helen. We arrived in South Africa during a time when whites were told not to stop at stop signs and to be careful of which highways they took, for fear of the frequent racial shootings. Only two months after we returned to the United States, white American student Amy Beihl was killed by a mob in Cape Town. So this was a difficult time in South Africa. It was during this trip that I realized that in addition to Helen's quiet and graceful facilitation and sharp intellect, it is her vibrant sense of humor and playfulness that makes her such an amazing popular educator and human being.

During our travels to the Wilgespruit Fellowship Centre in Transvaal South Africa, churches and community centers in Soweto, and the homes of progressive advocates and leaders, we learned that despite the hope brought by the coming democratic elections, the people of South Africa, black and white, were fearful of what was to come. One way the deep internal sadness and suffering was managed was through humor and celebration. This was perhaps my deepest learning while traveling.

After sitting with a family in their earth and grass home, a women's group in a church, or an organizer's office in Cape Town, Helen would pull out her suitcase full of Dolly Parton and Carter Family CDs to gift our hosts. Every time joyous laughs and thanks would follow. For the hardworking grandmother, Helen would reach into her bag, with a sneaky smile and her generous Georgia charm, and pull out a bottle of southern whiskey to gift. Always followed by more laughs and joy. Helen danced and sang with the community groups that welcomed us to their villages, asked appreciative and honoring questions of everyone we met along the way, and told the Highlander story slowly and openly, always comparing Highlander's achievements to the struggles and strategies of the people in the circle.

After several weeks of traveling, Helen insisted that we take a mini-vacation. We chose to visit Victoria Falls in Zimbabwe. After taking a champagne cruise on the Zambezi River, we returned to our hotel to find five monkeys rummaging through our suitcases and wallets! In all of our travels, this was the only time I saw a hint of hesitation or fear in her eyes! And even then, Helen belted out a warm laugh. Watching the almost three-foot-tall monkeys escape out of the transom windows,

Helen proposed, "Let's follow these rascals to see where they stash everyone's things! I bet they've found some good stuff."

It has always been a true joy and honor to travel and learn with Helen. I will forever remember and attempt to embody her sense of humor, joy, and love of humanity (and monkeys) in good and in difficult times. As a friend at the Wilgespruit Fellowship Centre told us then, "Living in times and places like these, once you lose your sense of humor you are finished." While I listened with wide eyes, Helen nodded and smiled.

At a conference in Toronto, I heard Reg Crowshoe of the Peigan Nation talk about the role of the medicine bundles in the Blackfoot culture. Many of these bundles are now in museums and the tribe had to petition for the return of the bundles, so that they could revive the Sun Dance and revitalize their culture. Reg explained: "Our strength is in these bundles that we need today to keep our culture alive." The bundle belongs to the Creator, but requires each keeper to take all the tribe as his or her children. The keeper encourages broad participation in the cultural life of the community. Through the strength of the bundle, the Peigan people are reclaiming a heritage that was almost lost as a result of the reservation system and residential schools. After hearing this talk by Reg Crowshoe, I reflected on our attempts to preserve and revitalize Appalachian culture and communities. ("My Life and Good Times in the Mountains; or, Life and Learning in Central Appalachia")

Where Are Our Medicine Bundles?

Where are our medicine bundles?
In what museum?
Buried in a landfill?
Floating in space in a satellite?
In a safe deposit box of a bank in New York City?

Was it
Lost on a Greyhound bus on the way to Detroit?
Packaged and sold in breakfast cereal?
Thrown out the window of a pick-up truck?

Where are our Elders?
Rocking on the porch?

In a nursing home?
Homeless on the streets?
Living in Florida?
Playing Bingo in Cherokee?
In prison?

Where have our communities gone?
Stripped away by a D-9 Dozer?
Moved to a free export zone?
Covered over by the shopping mall?

How do we find our bundles?
Reclaim our Elders?
Rebuild our Communities?

CHAPTER 5

Telling Our Stories, 1999–2010

Bill J. Leonard

Stories build connections between people, provide ways to share knowledge, strengthen civic networks, provide the tools to rebuild communities, and produce the infrastructure, the social capital, which is essential in democratic community-based development. You need to get people talking, planning, dreaming. As people begin telling stories of individuals and local places, they share work histories, listen to stories from the elders who recall the good old days and the bad old days. On these stories, community is rebuilt, pride develops, a sense of identity and roots are established.

—Helen Matthews Lewis, "Rebuilding Communities: A Twelve-Step Recovery Program"

In May 2000, Helen Lewis joined Frederick Buechner, the well-known Presbyterian minister and author, in receiving an honorary doctorate from Wake Forest University. Buechner was named Doctor of Humane Letters in recognition of his distinguished literary contribution. Helen was both delighted and amazed that she, not Buechner, was given the degree Doctor of Divinity! It was no fluke. Any survey of Helen's life as teacher, scholar, and writer cannot overlook the impact and implications of her work for religious communities, particularly those doing ministry through churches and community agencies in the Appalachian region.

The sources cited here give clear evidence of Helen's response to the importance of faith, in whatever ways it may be expressed. Her own spirituality was born in southern Protestant churches where persons got "saved hard" in struggles with sin and salvation in seasonal revival meetings that raised the rafters with shaped-note singing and southern gospel. One of my great memories is standing around the piano in the parlor of a Berea College dorm, singing harmony with assorted students as Helen played gospel hymns. Helen understands and takes seriously the distinctive strains of religious life, old and new. Indeed, she has long been a bridge among religious groups, conservative and liberal, from Pentecostal to Roman Catholic, Primitive Baptist to post-modern Buddhist.

After serving as interim director of the Appalachian Center at Berea College, from 1993 through 1995, she returned to the Highlander Center staff. In 1995 she published *It Comes from the People: Community Development and Local Theology.* Her coauthors for that volume linking religious traditions and community organizing in Ivanhoe, Virginia, were Mary Ann Hinsdale, a Catholic sister, and Maxine Waller, who identifies herself as a "shouting Methodist." Chapter 9 of that book explores the spirituality of the community-organizing program called "Hands across Ivanhoe." It begins with a quote from Maxine Waller that sums up the book—and perhaps Helen's own view of Christian faith. Waller comments: "I believe Jesus is alive today. I don't believe he's in heaven. I believe he's down here with the poor people."

Even as she celebrates the depth, diversity, and quirkiness of Appalachian spirituality, Helen Lewis insists, with prophetic determination, that true religion must involve both faith and praxis, particularly when it comes to justice for persons on the margins. Nowhere is that more evident than in her work with students from seminaries and divinity schools across the nation.

I met Helen Lewis in Berea, Kentucky, in 1988 when I joined the summer faculty of the Appalachian Ministries Educational Resource Center [AMERC], a seminary-based consortium that she helped found with Mary Lee Daugherty to provide experiential learning in churches and community agencies throughout the region. From that time on, she became my teacher and my friend, guiding all of us, faculty and students alike, toward a deeper understanding of Appalachia and the ways in which religious institutions both promote and inhibit justice. I have watched her energize students, not only with her knowledge of Appalachian studies but with their calling to address issues of poverty, the environment, women's studies, and overall injustice, not simply in Appalachia, but wherever they might pursue ministry.

One summer in the early 1990s, Helen had to return to Virginia for a court hearing after she and others had been arrested for protesting with the Pittston coal miners. We thought we might need to raise bail money to get her out of jail! Helen loved the fact—reported in this section—that during the protests a local Pentecostal minister drove the participants to the mine and then picked them up at the jail after they had been arrested. Helen saw that action as one example of the way in which "enthusiastical" Pentecostal religion united with a Christian "witness" on the margins of the public square.

With students, Helen is an invaluable bridge, introducing them to multiple networks in the region, including the Appalachian Studies Association, Appalachian centers at educational institutions, bibliography from across multiple decades, and innumerable individuals she has worked with throughout her career. The years immediately before her "retirement" illustrate the extent of her networks and areas of teaching and research. Returning to Highlander from Berea in 1995, she taught and worked with the Community Partnership Center at the University of Tennessee and also continued work in McDowell County, West Virginia. She was invited to serve as an advisor for the Kellogg International Leadership Program, for which she traveled to Africa in 1997, another of the numerous trips that took her abroad as an advisor and resource person.

Also in 1997, she left the staff of the Highlander Center and retired to north Georgia. That move brought her into contact with Fred Craddock, one of the best-known preachers and preaching professors in the country. Craddock, recently retired from Emory's Candler School of Theology, was founding pastor of the Cherry Log Christian Church near Helen's new home. She joined that congregation, and it was the setting for the excerpts from the sermon provided here. Her friendship with Fred Craddock and his appreciation for her work led him to begin the Helen Lewis Lecture at the Craddock Center in Cherry Log, Georgia, in 2005.

During these years, Helen also collaborated with Monica Appleby for a significant work entitled *Mountain Sisters: From Convent to Community in Appalachia*, published in 2003. Helen continues to be a resource for schools and organizations throughout the region. In 2005 she served as an adjunct professor at the Wake Forest University Divinity School, coteaching the course "Fierce Landscapes: Listening to the Land and the People of Appalachia," with Reverend Pauline Cheek of Mars Hill, North Carolina.

Her research never ends. In fact, Helen's curiosity for new areas of research seems insatiable. Most recently she is working with Sandra Godwin on a new book dealing with the impact of the Young Women's Christian Association on the social and community consciousness of females at women's colleges in the South during the 1920s and 1930s. Helen cites her own "radicalization" by female professors at Georgia State College for Women in Milledgeville (now Georgia College and State University). At age eighty-six, Helen Lewis continues to pursue the radical nature of faith and its implications for radical action in the world.

[Working at Highlander], in just a short time I went from primary health care clinics to environmental waste dumps to economics education. I wanted to be involved in work that created the most change for people, and I saw that looking at the economic system was the best place for that. When Sue [Thrasher] and I were working on this curriculum. . . . we wanted to look at the whole host of development alternatives available to people. Instead of running out and recruiting any business that would come into the community, we asked people to look at what jobs they really enjoyed doing. And this brought up all kinds of great conversations where people were asking each other questions like what resources are available? What social capital is available? What do we want to see preserved in the community? What are we willing to give up? Do we want our rivers to be polluted? Exploring these questions gives people a sense that they know something. ("Interview with Helen Lewis")

Community Development as Ministry

Helen's response to faith commitment is unceasingly pragmatic. Across the years, especially in her work with the Appalachian Ministries Educational Resource Center, one of the most enduring seminary experiential learning consortiums in the country, she challenged seminarians to begin their ministries by carrying themselves and their congregations into some type of community action and then gave them guidance in how to do just that. For Helen, as with the book of James, those who claim to be Christians should be "doers of the word, and not hearers only, deceiving your own selves" (James 1:22 [KJV]). This lecture, given at Samford University, illustrates the fact that Helen continually "preached at preachers" the need for community engagement and their calling to listen to grassroots theologians in their midst (especially women) who had already discovered that ministry and mission. Yet she did not simply hold up an ideal of community development; she gave concrete methods for actualizing it.

from "Community Development as Ministry" (1995)

I am pleased and somewhat awed to be invited to speak as a woman in ministry or woman theologian. Basically, I have identified myself as a teacher/educator/activist, but I have taught emerging ministers, preached at preachers and worked with theologians in rural communities. I have tried to convince ministers and church workers that community development should be part of their work. It is a form of ministry and there are some incredible, strong women doing community development who are local theologians, grassroots ministers. The community groups they develop often serve as church for the community. Many of them are doing work which the rural churches could and should be doing.

I am not alone in writing and speaking about the importance of community development work; the need to build, rebuild, preserve and create *community*. Many link the loss and destruction of communities to many of today's problems and feel the most important work of the next several decades will be rebuilding community.

We have seen the erosion and destruction of communities, some deliberate through so-called development programs: the building of dams throughout the TVA, sports arenas, urban renewal, interstate road corridors, World Fairs, Olympic games, spurred on by our great faith in industrial progress; we have seen towns destroyed in the name of progress. Some of the so-called progressive choices we have made, such as consolidation of schools and building of new roads which cut through neighborhoods, have led to loss of community. We have seen the mom-and-pop grocery stores, which were local gathering places, cafes and filling stations replaced by smart, modern, outside-of-town outposts of distant firms. I have been told that for every new WalMart, 21 small stores close. Most of our communities have suffered not only a loss of gathering places, participation, and involvement, but cooperative caring and mutual aid. . . .

For some of these reasons, I preach to preachers to join a social movement to rebuild community. In many communities, the post office and the churches are the only viable institutions left where people can come together and talk. So the space is there for churches to bring people together and rebuild community. Unfortunately churches tend to divide people by race, class, family, and that helps separate communities. So they must also come together as churches. . . .

Based on this recognition of the importance of social infrastructure, there has evolved a new model for economic development which is *community-based development*. In the past, economic development has relied on recruitment of industries through building physical infrastructure: roads, sewage, water, developing the community for the industry. Many dollars have built industrial parks to coax factories to relocate in your community. Much like the cargo cults of the South Pacific, where natives built airstrips in the jungle and lit torches to magically call down the planes which left after World War II, our industrial parks sit like magic carpets hoping to attract a flying factory.

For a while, industrial recruitment schemes worked for the rural South. Along with the industrial park, we offered tax incentives, low wages, a non-union labor force, and lots of exploitable resources with few restrictions and low taxes. We offered up our coal, timber, water, air and people's labor and their health. But soon, greener pastures in the form of new industrial parks beckoned from other places, desperate for jobs and willing to offer lower wages, fewer environmental restraints and untapped resources. Most of these were further south in developing countries. The communication revolution and use of computers for management helped make this possible.

Despite these changes, we continue to rely on industrial recruitment as a main strategy for economic development. We continue to build industrial parks and shell buildings to attract an industry on its way further south. Our reliance on the industrial recruitment model seems almost like an addiction—to the degree that I felt we needed a 12-step program similar to an AA recovery program to recover from this addictive and co-dependent behavior.

This *12-Step Recovery Program* grew out of my work with rural mountain communities where I have spent much of the last 20 years working. Most of these communities had lost their economic base: mining, timbering, agriculture, manufacturing. They were usually on the backside of the mountain and the backside of the county, ignored by the county seat and bypassed by whatever development came down the interstates. They were peripheral, marginalized, "left out" of all the traditional economic development activity that was going on. Mines had closed or were mechanized so that they no longer provided much employment; the resource of timber or minerals had been exploited and used up or badly damaged; the factories had closed and moved further south to Mexico, Brazil, Indonesia.

In many of these declining rural communities, groups of people, usually led by women, formed community development groups to try to rebuild their communities and their economies from the bottom up. They call it the "trickle up" theory of economic development. They say the trickle down never reached them and doesn't work. The *12-Step Recovery Program* is drawn from their work. So if you want to take up the challenge of trying to rebuild our communities, to develop socially responsible, democratic, sustainable communities, here is what these communities have been doing in places like Ivanhoe, Virginia; McDowell County, West Virginia; Owsley County, Kentucky; and Letcher County, Kentucky.

The 12 steps are not a straightforward staircase to community revitalization. It is more like dance steps. Sometimes you go two steps forward and one step back to repeat number one. You tap dance for the funders, foxtrot around the local authorities and slow waltz into some of your projects. The metaphors are endless: you can rock and roll, do the twist, tango or do a dip. Sometimes you go in circles, sometimes individuals come up with a creative improvisation and you keep repeating the steps.

There are some basic values and assumptions underlying this model, such as *sustainability,* which basically means development which uses resources today so there will still be resources in the future. It stresses the welfare of future generations. We don't trade the soil, water or people for BAD jobs, polluting industries. This is exploitation, not development, and we need to stop recruiting and subsidizing folks to come in and exploit us. It stresses people development; people gaining skills, education, using and encouraging their creativity and culture. It is inclusive, not limited to one elite group, one gender, those who already have and have always run things. We start with local resources and look at the cup half full rather than half empty. We aim to help build a just economy, a moral economy.

from "Rebuilding Communities: A Twelve-Step Recovery Program" (2007)

1. Understand your history—share memories. . . . Recalling past development histories is a way to begin planning and developing an understanding of the economic system and what has happened to produce current problems. When mines close or factories move, often the people feel they have failed, have caused the problems and are not worthy people. Understanding the reasons for the moves, the economic benefits of leaving or closing, frees people to make changes. As communities regain their histories, they also develop an understanding of the community's role in the larger history of region, nation, and world.

2. Mobilize/organize/revive community. You need unifying events. Meetings, reunions, festivals, parades, discussions, study groups, and cel-

ebrations are ways to make community building fun. Music, dancing, and food bring people together and revive the spirit.

3. Profile and assess your local community. Survey and map community resources and needs. Catalog "people resources": skills, gifts, talents, and local expertise. Survey land resources: water, soil, timber, minerals, and beauty. Draw on the resources rather than emphasizing deficiencies and needs. Look to businesses and organizations which are already in place. Do a study of the various groups, networks, and social capital. . . .

4. Analyze and envision alternatives. Talk and plan together; share dreams and hopes and visions in study groups, bible study, civic group meetings. Determine what the community wants to preserve and to change. Visit other communities, look for models, alternatives, new ways of development, and analyze strategies for change. Concentrate on the potential and resources.

5. Educate the community. Personal transformation and community transformation should occur together. To develop new and better businesses, people need to develop new skills. The community organization needs to develop a leadership program—and people need to rethink leadership styles to allow for greater participation and use of many skills and talents.

   The process of education allows a community to develop understanding, which can be used to plan, control, and monitor change. The questions become not only about which development policies will shape the region, but also about who will participate in shaping the policies in the first place, and how to define success. Ask questions like "development for whose interests?" and "development by whom?" and "toward what ends?"

6. Build confidence and pride. Communities that have been dominated by one industry have a history of dependency and attitudes which must be changed. Regaining community history through oral histories, music, and theater helps build identity and pride. As the community rebuilds, people's work and the group's accomplishments should be recognized and celebrated.

7. Develop local projects. As the group begins a planning process, they can link needs and resources and develop projects to bring them together: a volunteer child care center, tutoring for children after school, a craft

cooperative, a recreation area, a park, activities like cleaning up the town, repainting, planting flowers or trees, honoring the ancestors. Community-wide and small group projects increase participation and involve new and different groups in the community.

8. Strengthen your organization. The community organization group needs care and nurturing. Although many communities have very strong charismatic leaders who get the process started, they can't rely on one charismatic leader. . . . Leadership development and staff training are important, and training is needed for special skills such as fiscal management, bookkeeping, and fund raising. Everyone needs to be involved in strategic planning and evaluation.

9. Collaborate and build coalitions. Community groups need to make linkages and form networks and partnerships with other groups to gain strength, share resources, and learn from each other's efforts, successes, and failures. Small isolated community groups can become marginalized, be labeled as "trouble makers," and ignored. A coalition of groups can form a power base to influence or control local government. . . . With a coalition of groups, it is more difficult for the established power structure and decision makers to ignore them or marginalize them. You can't develop alone.

10. Take political power. Political activity becomes essential to challenge and change policies to redirect resources to the community. Community groups can encourage and support members of the community to run for political office. They can begin civic education, voter registration, facilitate participation, develop a local monitoring program, attend all council/commission/board meetings, and get members on all the boards. Advocacy skills can be taught, and members can lobby elected officials, bring them to your community, recognize them when they make progressive moves, and educate them about community needs.

11. Initiate economic activity. Community groups can encourage and begin development of home-grown businesses. They can seek capital for local projects, develop a revolving loan fund, establish a mini-grants program, and work with local banks to invest in community businesses. Groups can work to make policy changes in banks and economic development agencies. . . . Through the education program, they can develop local job training and business development educational programs. Communities can establish an incubator for small local businesses. They

can work with young people in the schools to develop entrepreneurial training and encourage small business development as a career.

12. Enter local/regional/national/international planning processes. Communities must recognize that they are part of a regional, national and international economy, so they need to understand how the global economy impacts the local community. They can join international movements, which will help small communities worldwide. They can make international linkages with other grassroots community groups and rural communities. They can be a part of an international movement to develop a moral, just economy. In a global economy, communities must also organize globally to make structural changes. . . .

While grassroots community groups have succeeded in developing many creative, innovative programs, they cannot become completely self-sufficient within the present system. It is almost as if they find a steel ceiling which limits how far they can develop. For some the ceiling seems higher, depending upon their resources and ability to manipulate the larger system, but for some of the poorest communities with the fewest resources, the ceiling is very low. The more capacity and social capital they have developed, the more resources they can access, and the higher their ceiling.

Rural communities find that they can develop community services, rebuild community spirit, and develop educational programs, but they still lack access to capital and other resources needed for substantial economic development. They are still outside the mainstream economy. Major changes in development policies, distribution of development money and resources must occur before rural communities can really develop economic security and substantially improve their income and economic well-being. . . .

Rural communities are still part of national and international economies, the agendas of which do not include preserving or reviving small rural communities. Until the needs and agendas of these communities are included in national and international development plans, community efforts will be stalled and short-circuited. Rural communities will continue to be disposable, and the creativity and participation which these grassroots movements encourage and develop will be ignored. That is why communities must also enter the policy arena, change development policies so that this vigor, energy, and social capital can be used to develop socially responsible, democratic, and sustainable communities throughout the world.

Helen's Recipe for Ratatouille or Garden Vegetable Stew

Great food for bringing people together

Heat a deep skillet or Dutch oven, preferably black iron.
Add:
>   3 Tbl olive oil
>   2–4 cloves of garlic, minced
>   2 cups onion in strips
>   2 bell peppers in strips

Sauté 5 minutes
Add:
>   1 medium eggplant or 3 small Japanese eggplants cubed, salt,
>   and a handful of fresh basil and oregano or marjoram or 1 tsp
>   dried.

Sauté about 10–15 minutes, until tender.
Add:
>   1 medium zucchini, sliced
>   4–6 plum tomatoes, chopped
>   black pepper

Cook 5–19 minutes, until zucchini is tender. Top with parsley and
serve with rice.

(Unpublished correspondence with Judith Jennings, 2010)

Telling Appalachia's Story

I've been doing oral histories with the local history group, a bunch of storytellers, mainly, who are wanting to get good stories to tell for storytelling, and also working with the Fannin County, Georgia, group collecting oral histories. We've been trying to find the oldest people and get their stories. Actually, you know, North Georgia was the last of the Appalachian range of mountains to be really settled by white settlers. So it's fairly close to when some of those folks came in, and they know those great-grandfathers who came in. And they're the fine old elite families of the region. And there is a sense of how did you get your land? What stories have you been told about how you got this land? "Well, the Cherokees were there, and the Army came in and ran them off. . . . We waited in the county right over from there until that happened, and then we moved right in. We had their crops, and we had their corn. We had their houses, and we had their peach trees."

Some of those stories make me think of historical trauma. I almost feel like that process needs to go on throughout America, so that we can be critical of our own histories and understand that we haven't always been this pure and innocent and great, you know, that we are today. There are some dark sides to our history, so I'm really interested in this whole remembrance and this trauma, historical trauma, and the importance of reconciliation and . . . understanding, some of our own history. ("Whose Development? Whose Movement? What Justice? What Sustainability? Perspectives from Latin America and Appalachia")

from "Telling Our Appalachian Stories, Changes over Time" (1993)

Why am I here What is my story? Which story do I tell?

Everybody and every community, place, and region needs stories, narratives, tales, and theories to serve as moral and intellectual frameworks. Without a "story," a framework, we don't know what things mean. I have been thinking a lot about stories. I get tired of the sound of my own voice. The story is stale. I need a new story. . . .

Countries, towns, nations, as well as people, require stories and may die for lack of a believable one. The U.S. has been saying for 200 years that our experiment in government was history's plan, and for seventy years their story transported them into a position of worldwide importance. They no longer believe that story and are desperately working to develop another story. Many in the U.S. no longer believe the U.S. story. But they need a story to provide themselves with a sense of continuity or identity.

But even more, a story is an organizing framework. We are swamped by the volume of our own experience, adrift in a sea of facts. A story gives us a direction, a kind of theory of how the world works and how it needs to work if we are to survive. Without a theory, we have no idea what to do with all the information.

Occasionally people rise up and try to tell, construct a new story for a changing world. We need a new story for the problems we face today. We can reconstruct old stories, reread tales in the light of new problems. Many no longer believe the stories of industrial progress, technology which will produce a paradise through bigger and better machines. The Yuppie story that being a consumer is life's greatest goal leads to cynicism and hopelessness.

Science is being questioned. People no longer believe science can save us. To such questions as "where did we come from?" science answers, "it was an accident;" and "how will it all end?" technology answers, "probably by an accident." Is accidental life worth living? . . .

The early stories of Appalachia—and many continue today—are a good example of life developing from someone else's script. The people of Appalachia, at least those who did not adopt the outside story and join the ranks of the modernizers, were unable to articulate their story or were not able to get their story heard. (They had no access to the media. We still have that problem).

Yet in the past 25 years there have been a growing number of Appalachians who have articulated a different story. Writers, musicians, poets, scholars and researchers have rewritten much of the history from the viewpoint of the people who grew up here and lived the history. We are no longer a poor, helpless, ignorant lot who willingly gave away our minerals. We have set some of the record straight. There was an organized invasion of financiers and lawyers who took over power and stole the wealth. In the past few years, Appalachian culture has been redefined and celebrated and added to.

We have tried to redefine ourselves, take pride in our culture, and tell our own stories but we have not been able to transform the economy to gain sufficient control of resources and power to have control over our futures. Changes in the past 10 to 15 years have further devastated the economy, the environment, and communities of Appalachia—and in our fight for survival we have not been able to keep up with the outside stories coming down on us.

And the degree of modernization, which helped devastate, has continued:

Remember the first K-Mart? The first Hardee's? The first WalMart? We have floated local bond issues to support them. Who told us that would help?

We still need to take back our stories, compose our lives, and compose our communities from our own experiences, understanding, and analysis.

from "From the Gold Mines to the Coal Mines and the Other Way Round," with George Reynolds (comments here from Helen M. Lewis) (1996)

Appalachian studies have played an important part in uncovering lost history, reconstructing, and revising older history. Those of us who romanticized traditional Appalachian culture in order to criticize the destruction and exploitation of industrialization have been taken to task for our inattention to earlier signs of capitalist development and class difference. [Mary Beth] Pudup, [Dwight] Billings, [Sally Ward] Maggard and others looked at class and gender differences in the region and found earlier home-grown capitalists and exploiters. Today, there is another generation of young scholars and some recent revising of history by anthropologists, historians, and sociologists pointing to greater diversity in the region than has been acknowledged. . . .

We have long blamed local color writers for establishing the stereotype of Appalachia as white European, Anglo-Saxon, which denied the ethnic complexity. As Cratis Williams had to confront that stereotype and establish the importance of Scotch-Irish in the history, the new revisionists are reminding us of lost and forgotten history, of the formation of significant mixtures of people in the region—the mestizo nature of the Appalachian population. They are not only re-looking at the early influence of Spanish, French, Turkish, and Portuguese settlements, which predated northern European settlements, but they are looking at the history of the creating of whiteness and the delineation of all people in the mountains as either white or people of color (some free and some enslaved). This definition erased most ethnic identities and denied all mixtures. Brent Kennedy in his controversial but very important research into Melungeon families [*The Melungeons: The Resurrection of a Proud People*] calls it a case of ethnic cleansing. . . .

What the Appalachian studies movement, Foxfire, and Appalshop have done is play a role in this process of denial of diversity. As newly defined Appalachians in the '60s rewriting our history, we inadvertently ignored the diversity. We were largely white scholars (probably Scotch-Irish), and we ignored class differences to put a positive slant, wanting to be more egalitarian than we were. We paid token attention to both Native Americans and African Americans and talked some about Southern European immigrants to the coalfields. But we got tied up in trying to define and identify *Appalachia* and find an Appalachian ethnicity or identity. And we did this for many good political reasons. . . .

Where are these latest revisions taking us? What will recognizing the multicultural heritage of Appalachia do to our sense of Appalachian identity? Can we all join the movement to claim an identity as Maroons? Perhaps if we could admit nationally the arbitrariness and reasons for the invention and definitions of what it means to be white, it could be a liberation, a transforming shift of understanding. If we all recognized the wonderful mixtures we all are, wouldn't that be fun? There are many changes in the mountains. Despite our resistance to modernization, it has happened. How do we identify ourselves with these changes?

[George Reynolds and I] both now live and work at Highlander Center, which also plays a role in trying to preserve, uncover, and propagate the resistance and social movement history of the region. Highlander also has a history, which takes on the semblance of myth at certain points and makes it hard for those of us who work there to live up to.

We also live a few miles from Gatlinburg, Cades Cove, and an Appalachian theme park, Dollywood. I am very fond of Dolly Parton, and I like most of her theme park. She has a great roller coaster (called mountain railroad), a replica of the cabin in which she was born, a museum housing souvenirs of her life and career. She has provided jobs for all her relatives and lots of commercial establishments selling Appalachian crafts. It is sometimes hard to sort out the bits of traditional culture from the Hollywood, popular, consumer, and mass culture. The uses of traditional culture and regional history to boost tourism have been growing. One of the rides at Dollywood shows the way such uses cannot only trivialize history but inverts the whole message. It is a ride through a mine in a boat through dark tunnels where explosions, cave-ins, fires, and other mayhem blow up, drown, and injure miners, all dressed in convict clothes. Knowing the history of Coal Creek, the use of prison labor in Tennessee, and the rebellion of the coal miners who freed the convicts who were used as scabs to break their strike, I found the uses of such history as funny, amusing, scary, and entertainment to be a desecration. I came out of the tunnel nauseous and very sad. Probably most who went on the ride did not know the stories of Coal Creek, which was renamed Lake City, which is another way to erase resistance history. . . .

I guess our last word is stories are important. It's important who names people and places, who tells the story, who constructs the history, who uses it and why, and how important it is that we keep revising, inventing, constructing, and deconstructing our history for our own survival.

from "Appalachian Studies: Telling the Truth or Preserving the Myths" (2007)

I have been called the Mother and now Grandmother of Appalachian studies, but there were earlier Mothers and Fathers of Appalachian studies. . . . We can go back to the local color writers who discovered the quaint, peculiar people of the mountains at the turn of the century. . . . Along with the industrialists came educators and missionaries to pick up the pieces, rescue the perishing.

They tried to save some of the traditional culture, meet the needs of the new population, and train people to work and serve the new order. They were the forerunners of current-day Appalachian studies. Emma Bell Miles, an outsider who married into a mountain family, published *The Spirit of the Mountains* in 1905. . . . Helen Dingman, a sociologist and Presbyterian church worker at Berea [College], encouraged government research and intervention into the problems of the region, and the U.S. Dept. of Agriculture published a first and important *Survey of Economic and Social Problems and Conditions of the Southern Appalachians* in 1935. . . .

It was not until the mid-1950s that another major study of the region was organized by the Ford Foundation and headed by President [Willis D.] Weatherford of Berea. Tom Ford of the University of Kentucky organized the research and wrote the final report, and the survey was published in 1962. In the meantime, several scholars and writers had emerged and were active in studying, teaching and writing about the region: Cratis Williams at Appalachian State Teachers College taught an Appalachian ballads and songs course. He had written his dissertation, *The Southern Mountaineer in Fact and Fiction.* James Still published *River of Earth,* the classic novel about the coal region. Richard Drake developed an Appalachian history course at Berea. Richard Chase collected locally and published the *Grandfather Tales.* Harriette Arnow wrote *The Dollmaker* about urban migrations. James Brown wrote his Harvard dissertation on the Beech Creek Community in Clay County, Kentucky. Tom and Pat Gish bought and began publishing *the Mountain Eagle* [in Whitesburg, Kentucky]. . . .

These were some of the forerunners of modern Appalachian studies.

Appalachian studies as we know it today grew out of the social movements of the 1960s, largely in the Central Appalachian coal fields. . . . . It was heady times and exciting times for teachers. Beginning an Appalachian studies program was considered a radical action, and many colleges were reluctant to do it because it was considered too activist oriented. . . .

We painted a somewhat mythical romantic view of the region as brave pioneers, who were cooperative, non-competitive, [living] in self-sufficient communities, lovers and preservers of the land. These brave pioneers were exploited by the invasion of outside colonizers, who wrongly developed and destroyed the land and the people. But the pioneers resisted, and there were courageous survivors with a rich culture, enriching the American culture with music, crafts and life style for a post-industrial world. I think these were helpful myths at the time in efforts to confront stereotypical images of the region, which were devised and developed to justify exploitation and modernization.

I wrote an article which was published in *Mountain Life and Work* in 1970 titled "Fatalism or the Coal Industry" to counter the "culture of poverty" explanation which blamed the victim. I laid out the Colonialism Model instead. . . . This turned out to be a useful rewriting of history and influenced many young scholars and researchers and activists at the time, who continued the process to rethink, reinterpret, redefine the region. Instead of colonialism, they pointed to the global history of capitalism, the uses and abuses of peripheral regions, and brought a more truthful analysis to bear on the problems of the region. They explored diversity and racism in the region and brought greater truths to light. I think there is still some usefulness to the Colonialism Model, a good metaphor to explain the exploitation of the region, but not the whole truth and nothing but the truth.

So we need to think about what are the truths and also the myths we need to tell today, and why and what is the role of Appalachian studies in that process. And we must be willing to accept when our truths are declared myths and are no longer useful to describe reality as we see it now. . . .

My original vision of Appalachian studies required a change in academic structure, teaching methods, curricula design and learning about and from the region, which leads to action. But this type of action through Appalachian studies was very hard to do and led to my leaving academe. I went to work at the Highlander Center and then became a circuit-riding sociologist, practicing Appalachian studies with community groups in the region, teaching in community college outreach programs and working with Appalshop and AMERC at Berea. . . .

Getting students out of the classroom and into the community, and using the expertise of community people in the classroom, are most difficult to fit the schedule and require a redefinition of expertise and upset the power relationships. So Appalachian studies folk develop programs around the edges, hoping to influence or evade some of the structures. In this process, they sometimes become marginalized or get in trouble with the Academic Culture Bearers, who feel they are subverting the system. [But] there is a positive side. There's more freedom. They can also develop experimental programs and sometimes influence the larger structure. . . .

There has been enormous growth of [Appalachian] Centers. . . . Today there are 14 Centers in ten states, which are part of a Teaching Project, an ARC [Appalachian Regional Commission] collaborative on how to sustain Appalachian communities. The recent collaboration of writers, artists, media, environmentalists, Appalachian studies students and faculty in stopping Mountain Top Removal is a hopeful sign of a growing ability of groups to work together for needed social change. The group "Just Connections" is providing a model of colleges developing long-term relationships with community groups to provide services and work together for social justice. Finally, there seems to have been a change in focus of Appalachian studies from classroom to community. If we look back on the 40 years of Appalachian studies, we can see considerable changes.

There has been a cultural revival in Appalachia of which Appalachian studies has been part, a great increase in novels, poetry, music, art and an observable increase in or admission of pride in being Appalachian; pride in the history, traditions, music, literature of the region, music festivals and concerts. We have some outspoken professional "hillbillies" who speak with nationalistic fervor about the region, especially challenging the stereotypes, which still emerge in films, theater, books, and now blogs. . . .

There is a generation of young people who have remained in the area and developed some creative ways to live, work and enjoy the region as filmmakers, artists in the schools, musicians, craft persons, farmers, writers. We have developed a much more sophisticated social and economic analysis of the region. We have regained some history and developed considerable knowledge of the problems. There have been many good research papers, articles, books and dissertations published. Appalachian studies has influenced regional studies in other parts of the country. It has provided a critique of modern society. Appalachia is still in some ways a resistance culture—resistant to assimilation into Middle America—however WalMart, McDonalds, television have made massive changes in life style. The international global economy has always been part of Appalachia, but the new global economy has had enormous impacts on textiles, coal and chemicals and has brought new immigrants to the region. The new immigrants are changing the region, enriching the culture and challenging us to make the region a more pluralistic culture. International projects to compare and contrast and collaborate with rural mountain communities in other parts of the world are part of some of the programs. . . .

In summary: What is the basic nature of Appalachian studies that makes it different from other parts of the curriculum?

It is different in that it is interdisciplinary—including geology, biology, political economy, anthropology, sociology, ecology, humanities, literature, music, art, history—it is holistic and integrative. It promotes collaborative research between different departments within the university. It involves study of and with the local community and brings in local knowledge and expertise. It involves field trips, internships, service learning. It promotes collaboration between the university and grassroots groups, as well as regional agencies, and with other Appalachian programs in other colleges and universities. It is problem-solving in focus and provides a platform for student research and professional development. The ASA [Appalachian Studies Association] encourages student papers and participation. It promotes community-based or participatory research and involves community leaders as teachers and supervisors and consultants for student projects. The community becomes the classroom when the students, faculty and community research and study together. . . .

There are difficulties in balancing the agendas of academia, policy makers and the community. It requires long-term involvement, which does not fit easily with time lines, contracts, academic schedules. The community has another very different time line. The community needs a stable connection with follow up. Colleges can develop centers or outposts who continue the relationship and support. Colleges can help people gain access to information about problems that affect them and help them to interpret and present their results. . . .

Appalachian studies can be a resource for positive social change in the region, but it requires a commitment from the institution to provide services to the region and to collaborate with communities to deal with social and economic problems of the region. . . . They can help communities create new or innovative programs, strategies or organizations which tackle the major problems of the region. Communities, in turn, can reinvigorate universities and provide incredible learning experiences for students and faculty.

Foremothers and Sisters

Well, finally there has been a big interest in looking at class and gender in the mountains, and race. I think a lot of stereotypical beliefs about race relations in the mountains are disappearing. I think there has been some—finally—study of women's roles and also diversity. ("Unruly Woman: An Interview with Helen Lewis")

Helen presiding at the Appalachian Studies Association meeting, Unicoi, Georgia, 2002

from "Appalachian Foremothers: A Celebration of Mountain Women" (2001)

It seems women in our society are used to playing extreme, even contradictory roles. In Appalachia, we have had the screamers—the Carrie Nations, the Bessie Smiths a while back and more recently Lois Scott of the Harlan County Brookside Strike. We have had the Pillars of Society, the protectors of status quo, the President of the DAR, the caricature of the matron with the four-orchid bosom waving the American flag. But none of these roles are quite respectable. To be overly religious may be offensive to someone and hurt your business, for example. To scream for change and try to stop coal trucks will get men in trouble. So let the women do it.

The men come in when it is safe. Women pave the way. Women are bell-wethers. Run them up the flagpole, and see if someone shoots them down.

There is also lots of work to be done in society which is not very profitable, but necessary, like nursing, teaching, helping, serving. So let the women do that. Women are placed in jobs which are not profitable and more monotonous, menial, and the lowest paying, like fast food, hospital workers, home health nursing, cooking, cleaning and child care. Women have been used as a low-paid menial labor pool, a surplus worker pool, a reserve army of labor to be mobilized in times of need. Look at Rosie the Riveter in World War II or part-time seasonal workers now. They can be laid off or sent back home during slack periods. When the mines close, the women will take the low-pay sewing, cleaning, serving jobs to feed the family. They take the non-glamorous jobs, fetching and toting, cleaning, serving and nursing. But these jobs are really basic, close to survival skills. This is important work but not compensated as important and not given credit or appreciation. Women pick up the pieces. They clean up the messes. Their own domestic work is meeting essential survival needs, such as caring for children, feeding the family, raising gardens, nursing the sick.

Often women begin to speak out for the children, for the family, for the needs of the community, family and community maintenance. Community building is left to the women. When a grassroots community group gets some money, the men come in to handle the finances.

. . . But, being marginal to the economy and to the political system, women are often freer to act. They are not tied into the system.

How do we account for the many strong women leaders and activists in the mountains?

With the beginning of industrialization, interesting women came into the mountains. I don't know of any women land buyers or Philadelphia lawyers or exploiters, probably there were some. But many women came as wives of lawyers and speculators, and they tried to add a bit of urban or tidewater culture. Later, women followed to pick up the pieces: missionaries, settlement schoolteachers, frontier nurses, deaconesses. [Coming in from outside the region,] they were called "fotched on" women. They have been criticized as exploiting and destroying the culture, but they also brought needed services and provided care for women and children. They preserved and appreciated much of the work and creations of women, like their quilts, songs, and stories. Women began to sell their crafts and get a little spending money. Near here, the Pine Mountain Settlement School developed outreach health clinics, which provided the first "secret" family planning clinics, and women walked miles to learn the "secret."

In coal camp life, women lived close to the industry, and they were controlled in their houses and shopping. There are lots of lost stories of women and their actions to improve [coal camp] life. Women marched against the

[mine] superintendent to improve the housing and lower prices in the [company] stores. Hungarian women forced the [mine] owners to build ovens for their bread. Women also wrote a lot of the songs. Some of these women have become well known. Florence Reece, Sara Ogan Gunning, and Aunt Molly Jackson here in Harlan County wrote songs which live today as part of the history of the [labor] struggles.

On the other side, there were also women who were wives and daughters of the [mine] owners. These women grew up as Little Princesses of the coal camp. They started literary clubs to bring in civilization and establish control, social and cultural control, as well as economic. Class distinctions were blatant and kept women apart. But some broke those barriers such as [Mary] Breckenridge, [a wealthy woman] who developed the frontier nursing service.

The coalfields produced an amazing number of strong women activists. Widow [Ollie] Combs, at age 61, lay down in front of a bulldozer to stop strip mining on her land. Despite her age and gender, she was drug off to jail. Her action inspired and began the anti-strip mining movements all over the mountains. Another woman elder, Granny [Frances] Hager, organized roving pickets, made up of groups of disabled miners, to fight for compensation for black lung, and she worked for UMWA reform.

Wives, sisters, mothers, and daughters have always been active in union organizing, and during strikes the participation of the women has been particularly crucial. They were a militant component in the strikes, and they have been beaten, jailed, shot, and killed. During the strikes at Brookside, Stearns and Jericho in Kentucky, and later in Virginia in the Pittston strike, the women's clubs played a crucial role. They organized rallies and benefits, fed the strikers and families, confronted the scabs and state troopers, and along with their children spent time in jail.

Women fought for the right to work in the mines. In 1980 there were 4,000 women working in the coalmines. There are very few now, as they were first fired when mechanization and mine closures cut the labor force.

Women today are facing the challenge of developing alternative economies, and they are taking the lead in developing Appalachia "After Coal." They have enrolled in great numbers in the community colleges and training programs. They started many grassroots community development groups, seeking to develop jobs and services [to replace those] which have disappeared in the community. They worked for school reform to develop relevant education. They fought against environmentally destructive industries and sought to repair the devastation which mining has already caused. Concerned about the health of their children and the quality of life in their communities, they are no longer bellwethers, but the bell ringers.

It is time to celebrate women in the mountains.

"Three Generations of Women Friends," by Beth Bingman and daughter Amelia Kirby

Beth: I met Helen when I was eight or nine. My family moved to Wise, where she lived in an apartment in an old house with big high-ceilinged rooms and a menacing Siamese cat. My parents [Fred and Mary Bingman] became close friends with Helen and her husband, Judd. I remember being on the sidelines as my parents and Helen, Judd, and other friends gathered for what they called the "Chowder and Marching Society," regular gatherings for dinner, beer, talking, and laughter.

Helen was an advocate and support for my decision to skip my senior year in high school and enroll at Clinch Valley College. Sociology classes with Helen and her friend Mackey Hamilton brought new ideas like "cultures" and "roles." She also expected that we would be getting out into communities and looking carefully at what was going on.

I went on a college trip with her to New York. After an all-night bus trip, we woke up in the city. We spent a week learning about and from the Puerto Rican community there. We did get to do some sightseeing, and we made it up to the top of the Empire State Building. We also met with members of the Young Lords party in the church they were occupying in East Harlem. We were able to talk to them, recognizing the differences and similarities in our communities.

Another time, I spent Christmas with Helen at the Rose and Crown in Wales. Again, our group was welcomed in yet another of Helen's communities. We enjoyed confounding men in the pub when we talked to each other in "Appalachian" that they could not understand.

Rich [Kirby] and I moved to Scott County [Virginia], where Helen and the Applebys [Monica and her husband, Michael] had bought the River Farm. We had endless meetings while we figured out how to make it work. We talked through how to live with each other and all of our cats and dogs. We discussed how to work together on planting, harvesting, putting up all the food we grew. There were many, many meals with many different people around Helen's table. Helen brought people together from wherever she met them, down the road in Dungannon or from the other side of the world. She welcomed them all. She welcomed us, and she welcomed any cat and at least one small dog.

Amelia: When I was a little girl, the most wonderful thing in the world to me was to walk across the farm to my friend Helen's house for a visit. A cozy, magic house full of art and music and food and work. Office flowing into kitchen into living room into porch. A wall of LPs for dancing, a shelf filled with jars of dried herbs from the garden for tea with honey, art and artifacts from her life of travel and activism for imagining.

When I was eight years old, Helen took me on a grand road trip— DC, Philadelphia, and New York City. We loaded up her pickup truck and meandered up the East Coast, visiting friends, exploring places new to me. It made me feel independent, grown up, proud to be a friend to someone like Helen.

After my grandfather died, my grandma and I spent a week with Helen at her home in Georgia. Stories and meals flowed as they reminisced about the days of living side by side in Wise, of the raising of my mom and aunts, of the early days of the River Farm. At the nearby folk school, we took an Indian cooking class that week. Helen scandalized our fellow students, well-heeled ladies from the Atlanta suburbs, by declaring the unctuous slime of okra "erotic."

I remember recording Christmas dedications with Helen to all of our friends for our community radio station at Appalshop. We played Eartha Kitt's *Santa Baby* over and over as we kept remembering just a couple more people we cared about that needed a holiday greeting.

I remember endless meals around the table at the River Farm, bowls brimming with food from the garden, homemade chowchow, highballs of Old Fashioneds, with heady conversation from family, neighbors, international guests, newfound strangers on the verge of becoming old friends. One of Helen's greatest abilities is her way of bringing people together to find commonality and friendship. . . .

Thinking over the times I have spent with Helen, the ideas and people that she has led me to, and then reading from this collection of her writings, particularly from the earlier and the most recent pieces that were not as familiar to me, has been a bit like rereading a well-loved book after many years or revisiting a place that was once very familiar. Not only am I reminded of what I knew, saw, learned at various points, I learn new things, gain new understandings not only of Helen and her life, but of the issues we deal with as women, as concerned citizens, as engaged scholars. Her life and writings serve now, as they have served in the past, as a guide to reflection and pondering on the complexities of living a life that is both rich and useful, rewarding and challenging, enough and not too much.

Beth and Amelia: From the viewpoint of home and community, one main thing we've learned from Helen is the importance of sharing food as a means to build community. She has taught us that simple, sustaining joys like cooking and gardening and good conversation are the foundation that holds up the work of radical activism. She showed us that radical activism itself takes many forms, and plays out on many arcs of time. She helped us see that Appalachia is a home worth fighting for. With Helen, there is always another project, story, piece of work, fascinating person on the horizon or around the corner. She helps us remember that building and sustaining intersecting commitments to each other, to place, to culture, and to justice is the most important work we can do.

I'm also writing this story called "Changing Habits" about a group of nuns who came to Appalachia, the Glenmary Sisters. All 70 of them left the order together en masse in '67 because they were making changes. They were following Vatican II and trying to be involved in the life of the community, and they had gotten radicalized by the mountains. So the Cardinal put a priest in charge of their order, and they left. But they formed a secular organization called FOCIS (Federation of Communities in Service), and they've stayed in the mountains. They have done incredible community development work, and they've set the pattern for community-based development all over the region. One of them started the Hot Spring Clinic, which turned out to be the model for all the primary care in North Carolina. They started the first community development corporations in Appalachia, in Dungannon, Virginia, and in Clairfield, Tennessee. I've got all the oral histories, and I've got a rough draft of a book. I'm trying to find a publisher. ("Unruly Woman: An Interview with Helen Lewis")

The book *Mountain Sisters: From Convent to Community in Appalachia* illustrates the breadth and depth of Helen's work in the region. It traces the journey of a group of Glenmary Sisters as they moved inside and outside the Catholic Church. An early chapter of the book, written by Monica Appleby, was published in *Christianity in Appalachia: Profiles in Regional Pluralism,* a book dedicated to Helen Lewis. The sisters were sent to Big Stone Gap, Virginia, in the 1960s, just as Vatican Council II was getting under way. Their progressive response to the documents of the Council, symbolized in the modification of their traditional dress codes, created controversy with their bishop, who proposed to move them from the region. In response, numerous sisters left the order, refusing to leave the people of Appalachia and founding a community service organization known as FOCIS. Helen's engagement with them reflects her wide networks of friendship, her strong commitment to the role and voice of women, and her appreciation for the social consciousness and action that the women fostered within and without the Catholic Church. Their efforts and their differences with the Catholic hierarchy demonstrate another aspect of Helen's life and thought: the reality that community development inevitably involves challenge to the status quo and may be costly for those who work for social and religious transformation. Helen herself is no stranger to the "cost of discipleship."

from *Mountain Sisters: From Convent to Community in Appalachia,* with Monica Appleby (2003)

Twelve years of research, reflection, and writing have produced this book, a collective participatory process led by Monica Appleby, a Glenmary Sister from 1955 to 1967 and the first president of the Federation of Communities in Service (FOCIS). . . .

Several members of FOCIS formed a study group in 1991 and began telling their stories. That same year, Rachel Anne Goodman, a radio producer with WMMT, the community radio of Appalshop Media Center in Whitesburg, Kentucky, became interested in these former Glenmary Sisters who had left the order in 1967 to continue their work in the mountains without the encumbrances of the church hierarchy. She carried out interviews and developed a radio program, *Changing Habits: Catholic Sisters and Social Change in Appalachia,* which was aired by Horizons of Public Radio International (PRI) in 1992 on 140 stations.

Monica Appleby, fellow FOCIS member Anne Leibig, and Appalachian sociologist and activist Helen Lewis began to talk about publishing the stories in a book, believing it was important to document the history of Glenmary/

FOCIS and the group of women who had played very important roles in the social movement in the Appalachian Region. The original theology study group became the FOCIS History Book Committee, and they decided to collect oral histories from the members. . . .

FOCIS celebrated its twenty-five years in Appalachia with a Festival of Friends in 1993. The festival's storytelling sessions and reflections on their quarter-century together allowed the book to become a collective FOCIS project. . . . In 1996, Helen Lewis took on the task of compiling the material and writing the book. By 1998 rough drafts of thirteen chapters were sent to all FOCIS members who had been interviewed and who were willing to read them and come together to reflect on their experiences and the stories of their colleagues.

By reading one another's stories, sharing experiences, and reflecting on the meaning and impact of their work, the FOCIS women composed a collective story that helped them understand what they had experienced, what was important, and what they could now ignore. The book became a structure for their perceptions and a way to make sense out of the facts and events of their lives. . . .

The year 2000 was a year of rewriting, revising, and reorganizing. Monica and Helen worked closely together to rewrite and reorganize the chapters. They felt at times as if they were snipping lives apart and piecing them together again, selecting from all the stories to make a collective story. . . .

Initially many Sisters were resistant to the process of remembering and reflecting on their experiences. In the discussions, both guilt for leaving Glenmary and anger at the church's actions surfaced. The metaphor of divorce was used. The twelve years of writing and meeting have offered some the opportunity to express their feeling and hopefully to come to peace. The project had also allowed FOCIS members to document their contributions to Appalachia and understand more fully the influence they have had in the region—and the impact the region has had on their lives and work. . . .

This story is part of several larger stories. It is part of the history of the post–Vatican II revolution in Catholic religious life in America. It is part of the story of the sweeping change in private and public values that occurred in the 1960s. It is part of the story of what is now called the women's movement. It is part of the history of American movements for social change and part of the history of a troubled region. But above all in these pages is the story of one remarkable group of individuals who came together, first as members of the Glenmary Home Mission Sisters of America, and later as creators of a new community to support their continued service to the people of Appalachia. . . .

This group of creative, dedicated women has lived and worked primarily in the mountains of central Appalachia since the 1960s. There they have upheld their motto: "Honor and Trespass Boundaries as Love and Justice Demand." Although they live in different communities, they maintain a remarkable network of communication and support. In 1966 they were a part of a group of one hundred Glenmary Sisters living in a communal life under the directives of the church. Today they are wives, mothers, educators, artists, and community workers living independent of church control but still following their commitment to service. . . .

Pope John XXIII's historic 1962 proclamation was revolutionary for all religious orders in the United States. The decree endorsed sweeping changes in traditional practices and rules once considered written in stone. While some changes were endorsed by Rome, the hierarchy of priests over nuns remained intact. Although they outranked priests in numbers and education, Sisters had little power within the church even in the post–Vatican II world. Even so, the Second Vatican Council (1962–1965) resulted in dramatic changes in all aspects of Catholic life. In particular, the changes enacted by the Council had significant effects on the lives of women religious, who were encouraged to reexamine all aspects of their constitution and practices in light of contemporary needs and issues. The Glenmary Sisters took the directives to modernize and renew the church seriously, and they began to make changes to better serve the poor. With the permission of local bishops they became an experimental community, and they believed the directives of the Second Vatican Council condoned and encouraged their attempts to make their order fit the modern world.

However, their efforts to modernize their order's governing rules were not universally accepted in the institutional church, and their negotiations with the bishops, cardinals, and priests went without success. The changes in the habit became a hot issue in the church, and their struggle with the male hierarchy over their experimental short habit led to an impasse. Discouraged, some Sisters began to "slip away" from the Home Mission Sisters of America.

In 1967 seventy Glenmary Sisters left the order. Of these, forty-four decided to form a secular, non-profit organization, the Federation of Communities in Services (FOCIS). These young women chose to continue their work with Appalachian families in rural Appalachia and in the urban center with Appalachian migrants.

The forty-four Glenmary Sisters who left to form FOCIS and the thirty women who left individually were at the forefront of the exodus of women from religious orders in the United States in the 1960s. The effects of that exodus are still reverberating through the religious world. . . .

Living and working in the Appalachian Mountains, where they had "sided" with the poor, greatly influenced the Glenmary Sisters. They visited and listened to the people up the hollows of West Virginia, Tennessee, and southwest Virginia. They interviewed the families who became refugees to Detroit, Chicago, and Cincinnati. Instead of converting the mountain people to Catholicism, the Sisters were evangelized by the mountain families. The Sisters had carried out a "religious survey" asking questions of mountain men and women about their beliefs and their faith. They were reeducated by mountain theologians and were "baptized" in the mountains, "converted" by Appalachia. Theirs is a story about a change from missionaries to community. In it they describe how they influenced and were influenced by the incredible economic and social changes that are part of the Appalachian story. . . .

As FOCIS women, the former Sisters developed a new way of working in communities, in partnership with the poor. In 1968 they stated their mission: "FOCIS members live in local communities as inside-outsiders, residents of Appalachia who have come from other places. With this identity they live as neighbor, friend, interested citizen, professional worker, and community participant. . . .

Their stories document the evolution of women religious (Catholic Sisters), the development of Appalachian communities, and the tenacity of relationships between women committed to a region and to one another.

"Mountain Sisters," by Monica Appleby

Most often when Helen introduces me to someone, she says, "Monica and I bought the River Farm together." And we did that in 1972, with Michael Appleby and eventually with friends, who were active in mountain resistance and trying to create alternatives to the mainstream.

We have worked together on many projects created from ideas that came up from the experience of living in Wise and Scott counties in southwest Virginia since the mid-'50s, from other parts of central Appalachia, and actually expanded to global coal and energy issues. It all kept getting larger and larger, including Southern Africa.

We wrote the book *Mountain Sisters: From Convent to Community in Appalachia.*

So, we have done a lot together.

But we are also sisters. Helen is sister to many women and men, a mountain sister, at that. "Sistering" means more than doing things together, as important or challenging as they may be.

A mountain sister remembers to write a note or call during a family crisis. She is hospitable and opens her home as a place to stay. Stay awhile. Helen creates delicious food out of the garden or freezer. All are welcome at the table. She is gracious and kindly in conversation. Sitting awhile. Helen is always connecting people, she knows so many, building relationships and forging networks. She is a community gardener and cook, who brews up, stirs up, and hunts up something to combine anew. She includes vegetables, flowers, herbs, and so-called weeds in her garden patches. She cans and preserves, telling stories all the while. She collaborates with others in her writing projects. She is a community worker. I actually don't think of her as someone that important or above me. It is a pleasure to be with her at her side through the years.

Helen Lewis is surely a mountain sister.

Returning Home to Georgia

I decided to retire and go back and live near my sister, which is the only real close family I have. She's got four kids and 12 grandkids, so there are 30 of us around the table when we all get together. So I ended up going back to Gwinnett County. By the time I got there, they moved to Blue Ridge, Georgia, so I followed them there. If they move again, I guess I'd better get the message that I need to leave. ("Unruly Woman: An Interview with Helen Lewis")

[My sister] said, "If you want to come up we'll give you a piece of land and you can build a house." So I decided to do that. I drew out a house plan on a piece of paper and stuck it on that pine tree out in the front yard. This neighbor guy who was a builder happened to be free just at that moment. He said, "If you want to build it right now, I can." So he built this place in two months. . . .

So I moved here in 1998. Right after I moved here, I had this horrible automobile accident. I broke my femur, and it's messed up my walking ever since. So that was the bad part of it. I went up to Appalachian State and taught for a few years. Kind of a long commute! Those were some good classes. Pat Beaver and I taught a joint class in Appalachian Culture. ("Interview with Helen Lewis")

from "North Georgia: Is It Southern, Appalachian, or Hillbilly Chic?" (2007)

After 50 years living in Virginia, Kentucky, and East Tennessee, I returned to North Georgia ten years ago and supposedly retired. I have been trying to catch up on what happened in Georgia while I was gone. . . . Since I have been in Fannin County, I have been reading local histories and getting reacquainted with the region, collecting oral histories, and I thought I would share with you some of my observations about changes in North Georgia. . . . I ask the question: North Georgia—is it Southern, Appalachian, or Hillbilly Chic?

First, when you come into Fannin or Union Counties, which are the northern-most Georgia counties, bordering Tennessee and North Carolina, the rivers no longer flow south. They flow to the north, draining the north side of the Tennessee Valley Divide. And we get radio and news and most of our weather from Tennessee and North Carolina. When the rest of Georgians were Southern Democrats, the voters here were Lincoln Republicans. During the Civil War, they voted against secession and many joined the Union Army. . . .

North Georgia was the last part of the mountain states to be settled by Europeans, for this part of Georgia remained Indian Territory longer than the other states. It was Cherokee Nation until the 1830s. In some of our oral histories we have collected, we heard stories of grandfathers and their families camping out on the mountain tops waiting for the soldiers to remove the Cherokee families from their homes so they could move in and take over their farms, houses, gardens, and peach trees. . . .

So is North Georgia part of the South? Of course it is south of the Mason Dixon Line, but is that enough? Don't forget the Civil War. People fought on both sides. And in the mountains there were few slaves, no large plantations, and they developed a different culture in the mountains from that of lowland, coastal plantation Georgia. We are living in the folded mountains made by the crashing of the continents. We are the last of or the beginning of the Blue Ridge part of the Appalachian chain, which goes from Nova Scotia to north Georgia and Alabama. Some 13 states have parts in this Appalachian chain. . . .

So we are in the South but with a different history and geography from the plantation South. . . . Mountain people became named Appalachian in the 1960s, when the Appalachian Regional Commission defined and classified the region. North Georgia became classified as part of Southern Appalachia. . . . The mountain counties in each state are less powerful and less prosperous, but with resources others needed and wanted: land, minerals, timber, water, landscape, cooler temperatures, trees, fish, and wildlife.

So where does the term "hillbilly chic" come in? . . . They are advertising in Kentucky their gentrified, transformed tobacco barns and old tobacco factories which have become trendy condos and apartments, artists' studios, for the emerging creative class and calling them *hillbilly chic*. . . . This developer says he is launching his cosmopolitan art, design, and lifestyle company for the 21st-century urbanites.

Actually, he seems to be trying to latch onto, rename, and market what has actually been happening throughout the mountains. The region has been changing with the growth of a tourist economy, which includes retirement villages, gated communities, and second homes to escape heat or cold weather, retreats for artists and refugees from urban sprawl seeking better places to live and work. It is sort of a "back to the land" for the upper middle class rather than the hippies of the '60s. We now have a tourist economy, part of the national consumer society. We now have in north Georgia artists, writers, and entrepreneurs marketing the environment, water, clean air, beauty, ecotourism, and selling the mountains.

This has some positive and some negative results. There is some strain and conflict between locals and newcomers but also some collaboration. Locals have learned how to survive by exploiting the newcomers. They provide land, now called real estate, log cabins with beautiful views from ridge tops or a lot by a clear bubbling stream. Always with a hot tub. And the urban refugees seek this solitude and beauty, but they want the urban amenities: good services, roads, cell phone service, dependable electricity, and water. Locals have answered some of these needs: lots for sale, and providing landscaping, housekeeping, garbage collecting, road clearing, and pet grooming. All are new jobs which locals have developed. There is some resentment and feeling that the newcomers want all the amenities of urban life without the bad problems of traffic, more concrete and streetlights. They put up no trespassing signs, fences and gates, which prevent their participation, assimilation and acceptance of the rural lifestyle. The urban refugees wear their denims, plaid jackets, cowboy hats, and drive their four wheelers and maybe raise a garden and learn to weave or play a banjo. We don't call it hillbilly chic. . . .

But the newcomers have brought skills needed for the schools and community. They are artists and writers and business owners and community leaders. There is considerable sharing and changes of values on both sides. A slower pace for the overachieving, manic urban dweller learning to live a simpler lifestyle. They also bring new ideas and challenges to the political powers, and they have brought interesting new houses, shops, and food. Add to these changes the other new immigrants—Latino workers who provide needed labor and a new cultural influence and interesting new vegetables in the supermarket, restaurants with good food, music, and art. They bring a challenge for the schools, churches, and social services, and a work ethic and ambition and family support which is inspiring.

So, who are we today?

Today, North Georgia is all of these things. Southern. We share a history: rural, pre-industrial, even plantation and slavery, which pushed many early settlers to the mountains, the Civil War, and a climate, a geography and political ties.

We are Appalachian. The mountains have made us different from the rest of the South. We have maintained more of the rural, traditional values and developed a rich culture. We have experiences of exploitation of rich resources and survival through hard times. We live with a growing diversity with both Latino immigration and hillbilly chic changing the culture and the image of mountain communities. . . . Our problem is to preserve the best of the mountains, and mountain values and lifestyle, while incorporating the new creativity, which comes with the newcomers.

I will end this with my latest writing: poetry. It probably is not good poetry, but it is my way of dealing with some of the contradiction which these changes bring.

The first would be my protest against Bradford Pear trees, which is a protest against hillbilly chic and developers who produce quick beauty to sell by destroying good trees and planting Bradford Pears, so the urban cowboy in the hot tub has early blossoms to enjoy.

Bradford Pears—A Lament

Presumptuous Newcomer
Bursting forth in white profusion
Advertised as Chanticleer—proclaiming Spring's arrival.

False harbinger of spring
You announce the warmth of spring too early,
Encouraging the apples to blossom too soon,

You are a flamboyant scene-stealer,
Upstaging the shy service tree
Quietly calling forth the hidden arbutus.

But you are a magical sight
Growing upward as perfect pyramids
Producing an autumn blaze of purple, orange, and red.

Pretty, seductive deceiver
You provide showy, fast, drive-through beauty
For instant gratification.

You are a decorative militia.
Marching down the median of the polluted highways
Drinking the Carbon Dioxide soup.

An invasive carpetbagger pushing out the natives,
Replacing sturdy oaks, tall poplars, and maples,
Decorating the mountain tops and creek sides.

Guarding the gated communities,
Lining the driveways to million-dollar fortresses,
Protecting stages for sunset viewings.

You come in drag as back-combed silver-haired matrons,
But you are the landscape goats of greedy developers
Serving rich refugees from urban sprawl.

But you get your comeuppance.
You stink to high heaven,
With a sickly, sweet smell foretelling early death,

With weak limbs and fragile crotches,
You break to wind and snow
Bearing bitter fruit and deformed thorny saplings.

I am not fooled by your clever pronouncement.
I wait for oak leaves the size of squirrel ears
Before planting my garden.

And watch my fruitful pear tree,
Limbs heaving with a heavy load of fruit
And prepare the jars for pear preserves.

Helen's Recipe for Ginger Pear Preserves

8 lbs pears
6 lbs sugar
1 cup water
4 lemons (juice and rind)
1/8 lb ginger root

Take coarse and firm pears, peel, core, and cut into thin strips. Add sugar, water, juice, and rind of lemons cut in thin strips and ginger root cut in pieces. Simmer to 220° F. Pack into hot jars and seal immediately. Optional: Process in hot water bath 15 minutes. You may choose to use Sure-Jell and follow recipe on the Sure-Jell package.

(Unpublished correspondence with Judith Jennings, 2010)

When I moved back to North Georgia, I joined the Disciples church. I have worked to develop a social justice program in the church, but I have found it to be very difficult. The congregation includes Democrats and Republicans, liberals and conservatives. Some consider taking a stand or working for social programs, such as health care for the uninsured or programs dealing with hunger and poverty, to be partisan issues instead of human rights or Christian concerns. Members do much social service work, such as supporting the food pantry or sending help to Haiti, but they view advocating or supporting any type of legislation or government program to be a Republican or Democrat issue. I argue that these are Christian and human rights or civil rights issues and that Jesus taught about and did social justice work. I have tried to move the church to the next step from charity to social justice. I was allowed to preach a sermon when we were in between ministers, and I delivered the sermon on civil disobedience that I had prepared for chapel at Wake Forest. I based the sermon on a text from Exodus, the story of Puah and Shophrah, the midwives who disobeyed Pharaoh's order to kill the Israelite male babies. They not only refused to obey this law, but they also lied about it to Pharaoh, but God blessed them for it. (Unpublished correspondence with Judith Jennings, 2011)

from "Cherry Log Sermon" (2007)

Some of you know my history or reputation as an activist who broke some laws. I never intentionally went forth to be a rebel or an activist, but sometimes you are in the right place at the right time to take a stand for what you believe to be right and you end up breaking a law.

My experiences as an activist began in 1942 when I heard Clarence Jordan, a young Baptist preacher, speak. . . . I heard him tell the story of the Good Samaritan, the Cotton Patch version (he rewrote all the Gospels in the language of the South at that time). . . . It was an "Ah ha" experience. I had never connected my Sunday School Bible stories with the social problems of the day: with segregation, discrimination. It was a true conversion experience; there was no turning back. After that, I became a Civil Rights activist in the 1940s before it was called the Civil Rights Movement. . . . When you are in such a place and feel that you are doing the right thing, it is a great feeling, and it may change your life.

Today, how can we deal with unjust laws, with institutions, with policies that are harmful to people and to God's creation?

We live in a global economy where powerful corporations and conglomerates can impose policies for their interests and escape controls established by countries and states. This is threatening the natural environment and increasing global inequality. We live in a world in which thousands of children die each day and many more live in poverty. We have a few with great wealth and prosperity, and the largest gap ever between the poor and the rich.

Paul spoke of the powers and principalities as Cosmic, Nameless, Faceless, Controlling: a good description of transnational corporations.

This is where we need the belt of truth around our waist to speak the truth to power. What is the truth? The way I understand it: Free trade has brought prosperity to some and benefits to others. There are discount stores everywhere. We can buy shirts and sweaters cheaper due to sweatshops and child labor in other countries—the poor in underdeveloped countries are being provided with jobs, so it's only $.54 an hour; she lives in a tin shack and chemical water runs through the yard. So NAFTA provided a market for U.S.

agricultural products and enriched firms like Archer Daniels Midland, which we subsidize. As a result, impoverished Mexican farmers migrate to the U.S. to pick our crops as day laborers. We blame them for the problem, and build a fence to try and keep them out. We need to study, seek the truth and deal with the problem, not blame the victims.

On an individual level we vote, but voting is not enough. Democratic participation requires eternal vigilance, monitoring, petitioning our leaders, and being willing to run for office, uncovering corruption. Voting can make changes locally. But voting and the usual democratic participation do not reach the faceless cosmic powers. What strategies can we learn from Jesus' ministry? From the beginning of his ministry, he was in conflict with the authorities: remember he was living in an occupied land, controlled and dominated by the mighty Roman Empire, and many local institutions including the church were collaborators. He spoke out.

His stories and parables were critiques of economic exploitation and political oppression of the poor. (For example, the story of the widow's mite is not just a sweet story about a poor old woman who gives her last penny, but a story of an unjust economic system which produces such inequality.) The Good Samaritan indicted the religious leaders for their indifference and lack of care for the injured members of the community. Jesus also developed alternative ways of meeting the needs of the people. His ministry was an alternative to the established, inadequate ways of dealing with health problems. He developed what I would describe as shade tree clinics, and alternative ways of dealing with the poor and hungry by sharing food in the countryside. Our closest equivalents are our free clinics for AIDS victims, soup kitchens for the homeless, and food pantries.

I am reminded of Eula Hall, a woman from Mud Creek, Kentucky, who developed an alternative health clinic because the health needs were not being met in Mud Creek. When the clinic, which was established in her home, was burned, she reopened the clinic under the trees in the yard.

Jesus set up an alternative social system with different rules; the Discipleship community, which demonstrated God's reign, redefined family and kinship to form new bonds of family with outsiders. He demonstrated new forms of table fellowship, friendships, hospitality, defying the segregation and purity laws and codes. The new community was non-hierarchical and non-patriarchal, inclusive, and demonstrated servanthood and equality. It was a community in which the goods of the Earth were shared, and all were assured enough. The rich young man was invited to join, to participate in this new economy, a community of Disciples drawn from the working and marginalized classes, and he taught them to heal, exorcise, forgive, and to challenge a corrupt system.

Why did Jesus' healing, casting out of demons and forgiving evoke such hostility from the authorities? Healing a leper was an act of social subversion. Jesus broke segregation laws, purity codes, rigid Sabbath rules, and he sent the healed back into the community to confront the community and the priests, as witnesses against these laws and rules and to tell the good news. Jesus does not counsel passivity in the face of injustice, but he offers strategic ways of nonviolent resistance. How to take on the system in a way that shows its essential cruelty and burlesques its pretensions to justice, law and order.

But what are the costs of non-violent resistance? When you break the law, you must be willing to undergo the penalty. . . .

I think of the 61-year old Widow [Ollie] Combs who sat down in front of a bulldozer in Kentucky and was carried off the strip mine site and spent Thanksgiving Day in jail for obstructing the mining operation on her land. Uncle Dan Gibson, an 80-year-old Old Regular Baptist preacher, sat up on the hill with a rifle and prevented the bulldozers from strip mining the land. These two started a movement called "Save the Land and People," which resulted in the first Reclamation Laws signed by President Carter in 1977.

Non-violent resistance is not the final objective; it is one strategy. Building alternative institutions is another, changing the oppressor, making the enemy live up to their own rules is another. Resistance may evoke violence of the oppressive system, and there are casualties, pain, suffering. Jesus gave us examples of violence and suffering. His own angry outburst in the temple: he overturned tables, ran out the moneychangers, released all of the animals. One wonders who paid for all of the damages? Jesus' ministry was a model of long-term social struggle. He was a threat to the authorities because he destroyed their credibility and exposed their wrongness. He also used some performance theatre, devised a demonstration to mock their grandiose parades and show of power. Marcus Borg and Fr. Crossan, in their recent book [*The Last Week: A Day-by-Day Account of Jesus's Final Week in Jerusalem*, 2007] describing Easter Week, portray Jesus' entry into Jerusalem as a deliberate guerilla theatre performance demonstration: entering on a donkey with followers with palm branches shouting Hosanna, in contrast to the Roman parade on the other side of town with chariots, soldiers with swords and flashy uniforms and

Roman rulers displaying their power. When Jesus and his crowd used terms such as the Kingdom of God, he was proclaiming that the real power was with God and not with Rome. He prayed, "Thy kingdom come," and we repeat this every Sunday. But Jesus was a threat to the authorities, he destroyed their credibility, exposed their wrongness, and finally his resistance led to his arrest and death.

But Jesus further challenged people to love their enemies; don't just out-wit the enemy, but oppose them in a way that the enemy can reform, become just. Pray for the enemy, work for transformation; they are also victims of the Principalities and Powers. Provide space for transformation. There are good people in bad systems. Lovingly challenge the powers to change.

I think of the example of South Africa and the Reconciliation and Forgive-ness of oppressors, to form a new system, after years of incredible violence and oppression. A new society made up of both the oppressors and the op-pressed, and the incredible process they have gone through to reconcile and forgive. The verses from Ephesians give us the armor to deal with cosmic powers: Truth, Righteousness and Faith as a shield, Salvation, The Word of God. Keep alert, never give up, pray for all God's people and speak boldly. Hold your ground. I would also add Vision and Hope to the armor. . . .

This is the Power of Hope and Vision, without which we would perish, and lose our soul.

Our goal is a new creation, transformation, the reign of God, the beloved community, and we need a clear vision of what that can be. There is a gospel song which goes, "There is a Land that is fairer than day, and by faith you can see it after." Many sing it thinking of heaven after death. I think we need to dream of a Land that is fairer than Day in this world. . . .

My last time to be arrested was in the last big coal mine strike in the Appalachian coalfield, in Southwest Virginia on the picket line in the Pittston strike. Miners went on strike to protest the company's decision to drop the health and retirement benefits of the retired miners. Many were disabled and suffering from black lung disease. The company thought the young miners would not stand up for their fathers and grandfathers. A large part of the community supported the strike. Daily, miners, their wives and children and kinfolks and preachers and teachers and friends from all over the country would come to the picket line and sit down in the middle of the road to stop the large coal trucks from hauling the coal into the processing plant. The governor supported the company and sent the state police with injunctions against stopping traffic; those who sat in the road, about 50 each day, were picked up by the police and carried to a prison about 15 miles away on top of the mountain. A woman friend [Sue Massek], a musician who was playing songs on the picket line, and I sat down one day with about 40 coal miners. At the prison, we were all ticketed and released. A Pentecostal preacher driving an old blue school bus called the *Blue Goose* daily picked up the released prisoners and returned them to their cars at the foot of the mountain. Later we had to go to court, both State and Federal, for breaking the laws. Each time it was like a homecoming; we were proud and celebrated what we had done. This strike was the first in which non-violent civil disobedience was the practice and whole communities participated, and they won the strike. The miners had been inspired by the Civil Rights Movement and the preaching of Martin Luther King.

We don't all have to be protestors, but let us remember those who have confronted pharaohs, governors, county commissioners, corporations, and unjust laws. [Let us remember] those who broke the law to do the right thing, and those who are developing alternatives, and building and rebuilding communities.

Let us remember Rosa Parks, who defied the segregation laws of Alabama, sat down in the front of the bus and started a social movement for justice. Let us remember Dietrich Bonheoffer, who spoke the truth to the Nazis and was killed by hanging. Let's remember those who are whistleblowers, like Lois Gibbs at Love Canal. And those who speak the truth to power, those who go to stockholder meetings and urge corporations to change policies which are destroying the environment and leaving communities without an economic base.

Let us remember our members who work each week with the food pantry to feed those in need, our members who work as hospice volunteers to give help to caregivers of the dying, those who visit the sick, the lonely, those who work for policies in their companies and governments to help the poor, children in need, who are sick and homeless. Those who take stories and music to Head Start children, those who call or write to our Congress people or write letters to the editor to encourage just policies and legislation.

I am no longer sitting down in front of coal trucks; and if I did, I would need the police or someone to help me up. But there are many in the mountains today trying to stop the devastation caused by mountain top removal coal mining. This includes writers, artists, church groups, as well as the communities in West Virginia, Virginia and Kentucky, suffering from the problem. What

I can do is write. So I wrote a poem about it. And I would like to close with my latest form of protest: poetry. I am letting the trees and flowers speak up for me, as a gentler protest.

With fall coming on here is a poem about the Queen of the Meadow, also known as Joe Pye Weed, which is blooming along the roadways now.

Queen of the Meadow (Joe Pye Weed)

In late summer, The Queen of the Meadow, a stately matron
Rises and sways above the goldenrod, daisies and asters,
With a plume of lavender for a tiara
And whorls of lance shaped leaves as her regal dress.
She nods graciously to her subjects
And gives a royal wave to all who pass.

A seer and prophet
She foretells the coming of Fall,
And bids goodbye to katydids and hummingbirds
She welcomes the bright turning of the Sourwood leaves
And makes room for her regal cohort Ironweed.
A sister clad in deep purple
Who pronounces Summer's End.

An ancient healer
Called kidney root, and gravel root
She relieves kidney and gall stone problems, breaks high fevers and repels
    flies.
Tea from her flowers, roots and leaves have cured typhus,
Indians claimed her potions were aphrodisiac.
She taught Indian medicine man Joe Pye her secret powers
And joined his name to her many titles.

She is a refugee, running from her enemies
Seeking refuge in ditches and rocky edges
As the weed eaters and bush hogs search her out.
Clearing the meadows, shaving the fields,
They eliminate diversity and creative spontaneity

Landscaping grassy fields to produce order and predictability
The community is mowed down.

Who is left to close the season?
To warn of cold nights, frosty mornings?
And who can heal our world,
Provide the secret powers for earth's renewal,
Give us energy to rebuild diversity,
While waving gently,
Promising another year of survival?

Shaping the Future

I really think that that's the next big extractive industry, taking the water out of the region. You see it now with all these companies that are making bottled water. . . . I think it's part of a whole international problem. It's not just Appalachia. I think water resources are a problem everywhere, because not only have we polluted the water, and polluted the ocean, but we've also dropped the water table in many places. To get really pure water, to get enough water anymore, is really difficult.

When strip mining first started in Appalachia, I saw areas within Wise County and that area of southwest Virginia lose their water. People had to start going to the mountains and springs and filling up plastic jugs and hauling those back. Most of the mountain counties now are really struggling with trying to develop water systems to serve the whole county. It's because the water table has dropped so from all the mining. . . .

I really see it as an extractive industry on which there is no severance tax. Again you've got the same problem as coal going out by the trainloads and no tax left. So they're taking all the water out of Fannin County and putting it in bottles and selling it somewhere and making money, but there's no tax on it at all. It seems to me that's an issue somebody's going to grab onto and do something about. Maybe we will wait until it's too late when everybody's out of water and trying to figure out where to get water. (Interview in Jamie Ross, Appalachia: A History of Mountains and People)

from "The Highlander Center: Working for Justice and a Moral Economy" (2008)

I would like to begin by reading a paragraph from a book I have been reading:

The consequence of the war in this country has been not only the stabilization of capitalism but also the strengthening of its vices. Never in the story of mankind has any nation made as much money with as little consideration for moral values and social consequences as the United States in the last decade. This fact and what it means for the future of this people, especially for the part they will play in relation to economic developments in the rest of the world, must determine the course of those among us who discuss the economic problem from the standpoint of ethics and religion.

The quote is from a 1929 book by Harry Ward. The book is called *Our Economic Morality and the Ethic of Jesus.* Harry Ward was a theologian at Union Theological Seminary. . . . I have been thinking about how the 1928–32 period and today are similar—so much so that Harry Ward's description of the 1920s sounds like today. . . . Today we are in another time of economic and environmental crisis. The growing poverty, unemployment, declining health care, and increasing environmental problems threaten not only our quality of life, but also the existence of life on the planet. Many are seeing the American dream eroding or unreachable. We are overwhelmed by fear of worldwide terrorism, so much so that we give up our freedom and human rights. . . .

I began going to Highlander for workshops in 1969, and was on staff off and on from 1977 to 1997. First, I worked with communities in the coal fields of West Virginia, developing community health clinics. The newly elected reform president of the United Mine Workers asked us to help miners and their families develop the clinics and run the clinics. We recruited progressive health providers, trained local community boards and developed health rather than medical clinics—clinics which dealt with occupational and community health problems. Unfortunately, the UMWA lost their health and welfare program in contract negotiations and many of the clinics closed. We continued to work with remaining community clinics throughout the region as they tried to develop alternative health care systems. We became concerned about occupational and environmental health issues and developed a series of Science for Citizens forums throughout Appalachia dealing with health issues related to coal, chemicals and toxic waste problems. . . .

We realized that so many of the problems communities were dealing with were related to the economic system, and if we could not reform the economy—develop a moral economy, one which serves all the people—we could not solve health, education, environmental problems. We began more specific workshops studying the economy. We developed classes through local community colleges on popular economics and organized workshops with communities trying to develop local economic development. . . . We used the pedagogy of Highlander, which is using the experiences and knowledge of the people to plan and develop alternatives to the exploitive, outside industries they were seeking to replace.

. . . It is a pedagogy that insists that for institutional change to be effective solutions must come from the people experiencing the problem and those who will be directly affected by the action taken. Grassroots leadership is developed through an educational process that allows people to analyze their problems, test their ideas, and learn from the experience of others. The uses of culture for vision, hope and spiritual renewal when combined with the critical analysis of people's experiences produces a pedagogy which is trans-formative. The song "We Shall Overcome," which developed at Highlander, evolved into the Civil Rights Anthem and is sung in social movements all over the world. . . .

We need more Highlanders today—grassroots organizing of those who are being marginalized, underserved by mainstream programs. We need Democracy Schools or more civic education: discussions about the democratic process, the bill of rights, the constitution, voting, economic democracy, political democracy, proportional representation, environmental democracy, human rights. We need to come together to discuss common ground, positive visions, and participation that affirms and learns from diversity not divisiveness. . . .

We also need a new ideological base. The social gospel as a basis of discourse has largely disappeared from the seminaries and churches. Christian socialism is not a respectable field. Liberalism and populist politics have become dangerous words. The right-wing conservative elements in all the denominations have struck fear into many a liberal theologian. . . . Critiques of capitalism are hard to find. The story is that "Capitalism Won." The alternatives: socialism, communism, cooperatives scarcely exist. The right wing built a social movement using traditional values of "family," rugged individualism, "hard work and self-reliance" and distrust of big outside federal government. It has destroyed caring for your neighbor, community concern, social responsibility for those in need, thus leaving a divisive, punitive agenda which favors large corporations and the rich at a time when we have the greatest inequality, the greatest gap between rich and poor in our history. Free enterprise and market economy becomes equated with democracy and freedom. The reality is that the profit motive is the governing force in the global economy.

In this new phase of capitalist expansion, we find that Appalachia and rural America become like third world economies and share their problems, high unemployment, lower wages, environmental degradation, community destruction, increasing poverty. Structural adjustment policies imposed on third world countries took the form in this country of welfare reform, lowering wages and cutting social services in order to compete in the world economy. There has been a decline in democracy, growing distrust in and alienation from government and less participation in civic affairs. In the '30s when the social contract of the New Deal was being formed, people looked to the government to provide some protection and security from the failures of the economic system. This is now questioned. Public schools and social security are in danger of being privatized. For some the government is an enemy to be destroyed.

I am seeing the beginnings of a new social movement of students and young people questioning the status quo and asking for a new social order. There are many community grassroots groups trying to rebuild their communities, deal with environmental problems, develop coalitions. Many women have emerged as leaders trying to rebuild communities. But people seem less confident of what to do about the many problems. The inaccessibility of economic decisions leaves people feeling both frustrated and very vulnerable.

We need something today to bring people together to deal with the destruction of our communities, degradation of the environment, growing poverty, economic distress and alienation and not just in our country but worldwide. We cannot hide from the fact that we are part of a global economy, but we can work to be cooperative, helpful and not exploitive. We live on a fragile planet—we are all spinning around together and need to come together to save us all.

from "A Clean Glass of Water for Every Appalachian Child" (2010)

Appalachia contains the headwaters of many important rivers and streams that supply water to much of the eastern seaboard. . . . It is estimated that Mountain Top Removal has buried nearly 2,000 miles of streams [in Appalachia]. The number . . . does not include the ephemeral streams, which flow sporadically throughout the year. . . . Mountain Top Removal mining in the coal regions of West Virginia, Virginia and Kentucky and Tennessee not only destroys water sources for local communities but threatens the water sources of neighboring states. . . .

Other polluting industries (paper mills, chemicals, tanneries) in the region have poisoned the streams and water sources for both animals and humans living on the streams. . . . Carcinogens have been found in tap water and unsafe chemicals in drinking water from wells. . . .

The water sources throughout Appalachia have been badly abused, used as garbage dumps, sewage systems, waste disposal sites and recklessly exploited for recreation, energy production, industrial development, transportation routes and bottled water sales. They have been damaged by landscaping for home development, urban development and road building. They have been over-used to water golf courses, lawns, irrigation farming and recreational water parks.

Modern lifestyles and urban living have alienated people from nature, from the sources of their water. When they turn on the faucet and water comes out, few know or check out the source. One step in the recovery and protection of our water sources will be education and reeducation of everyone not only as to the source of their water but also the importance of water to their health and well-being and ways to protect and restore this resource. School curricular development, adult education programs and public policy development are needed to bring about this reeducation and awareness and civic engagement to restore water resources. . . .

There are a growing number of community groups concerned with environmental problems. Many of these concentrate on river systems: river watchers, river clean up groups, etc. National environmental groups have joined with Appalachian community groups to fight Mountain Top Removal and to work with organizations to preserve rivers and streams from pollution and devastation. Among these are Nature Conservancy, Environmental Defense Fund, Sierra Club, and Summer Justice student groups.

Some colleges and universities have developed environmental studies programs and joined with community groups and regional and national environmental groups in researching water quality of streams and rivers, studying salamanders, fresh water mussels, and other indicators of stream health. They train and work with community groups to monitor water quality. . . .

The challenges confronting the Appalachian communities and watersheds are immense. Restoring them will require years of sustained effort to provide clean water for every child. . . . To restore some watersheds will require major work projects. Models of conversation include past national projects of reforestation, the Civilian Conservation Corps' work to restore land and develop recreation facilities, WPA projects to build infrastructure, the conservation work of the Job Corps and Agricultural Extension programs to change farming practices. Projects can provide work for the unemployed as they restore the watersheds, rebuild community water and sewage systems, change agricultural practices, rebuild communities destroyed by mining, deal with left-over pollution from mining, deal with ash and sludge from coal generating plants and help remediate damages from other industrial operations such as chemical plants, paper producing industries, tourism, and transportation. The task seems overwhelming, but the restoration of water resources in Central Appalachia could serve as a model for national and international recovery programs. . . .

The right to clean water must be included in the rights of individuals and all living organisms. The goal is to provide clean water for all and do away with inequity.

"Redbud Trees (Flowering Judas)" (2009)

In Early Spring,
Forming a tunnel of blossoms along the road to War, West Virginia,
The redbud trees burst forth with knots of red, rosy, purple flowers on
    naked branches,
Circling the trunk like the red kerchiefs worn by coal miners who fought
    on Blair Mountain.

Clinging perilously to mountainsides, they make a shrouded gateway to
    the Billion Dollar Coalfield.
But the Billion Dollars left the coalfields.
Each Spring, the redbuds tell that story and point to the destruction just
    over the hill.

The mountains have provided a place of refuge for people, animals, trees
    and flowers,
A home place in which to settle, work, live, for a diversity of people, wild
    flowers and grouse.

A sanctuary, a haven for mussels, salamanders, Baptists, wood thrush and
   pileated woodpeckers.

Now scavengers are removing the mountains to dig out the coal.
Giant machines turn forested hills to moonscapes,
Cover streams and valleys with "overburden," reduce the mountains to
   rubble.

Holding fast in the arms of the mountains,
Wearing their red badge of courage,
The redbuds resist their removal and protest the devastation of their living
   place.

They are also called Judas trees.
Named for the Judas who hung himself in shame from a redbud tree
And dangled the blood money from the branches.
The Flowering Judases blush with shame.

They shout "Shame" to the Judases destroying God's creation.
As the blossoms fade, the heart-shaped leaves wave to passersby,
Crying out for the wilderness:
Wake up, the earth is being destroyed.
Change your ways of thinking, acting, being.
You are part of all living creatures.

Recognize your kinship, interdependence.
Listen—put your ear to the ground.
Listen to the voices from the mountains.
Listen to the prophets, the hemlocks, the dogwoods, fish in the streams,
   the bacteria in the soil,
All living things.

The mountains have provided a fortress: support and strength to survive,
For immigrants, moonshiners, Indians, copperheads, escaped slaves and
   servants.
A safe place—"A place to rest your eyes."

Helen at the Seedtime on the Cumberlands Festival, Whitesburg, Kentucky, 2010

When the mountains are gone where do we get our strength?
Where do we find the rock to hide behind or beneath?
Where do we find solace and rest for our eyes?

Put a sign in your yard—Obey the Laws of Nature.

The Final Word

After reading Helen's influential writings, innovative ideas, and world-travel stories, coeditors Pat Beaver and Judi Jennings invited her to meet with them to discuss her thoughts and reflections on more than eighty years of living social justice. Steve Fisher was then working on the introduction, and he wanted to participate, too, because he had a few questions to ask Helen. The four of us gathered at the annual homecoming weekend at the Highlander Center on September 6, 2010. We all agreed that Helen should have the final word in this book, so what follows are the highlights of what she said that day in response to the questions we asked.

Pat: What advice do you have for young people today? Where is the hope and courage?

Helen: In 1946, when I graduated from college, the United Nations and World Court were just coming into being. I remember giving talks to Kiwanis Clubs, speaking about my hopes for the world and for world peace. The U.S. had just won the Second World War, and I had the feeling that personally I could do anything I wanted and that the world was opening up to me. Young people today may not have that feeling, but they may be more realistic.

Graduating from a women's college with a lot of suffragette teachers, I believed that women could do anything. I thought women could do anything until the 1950s started pushing women back into the kitchen. That's when women started facing discrimination in the workplace.

Today's youth understand the environment in ways we did not

Helen at the Highlander homecoming weekend, 2010 (*left* to *right*): Pat Beaver, Helen Lewis, Judi Jennings, and Steve Fisher

because we were still into being master over the earth. Today, many young people have good educations, more experience in the world, and tools we didn't have.

Young people today are facing a whole different world from what I was facing. We are at a real turning point in environmental and economic conditions in the world. Big changes are going to have to happen. Opportunities for cleaning up the environment and economy are enormous.

I want to tell young people to be creative and take risks. Don't get settled into a secure job. Create changes, take chances, follow your passion. They understand greening and global economic systems. They know all about the world. They have a great opportunity to develop some creative solutions.

Judi: Do you think unions will still be active players, fighting for social justice?

Helen: Unions were the grassroots organizing groups when I came out of college. I wanted to be an organizer for the CIO [Congress of Industrial Organizations], work for an Atlanta newspaper, and become a correspondent in Washington, D.C. Then, I would buy a county newspaper and run for governor. Politics, union organizing, and journalism were my three big interests. Instead, I became a teacher and ended up organizing students. My pedagogy was getting the students involved.

The Pittston Coal Strike [in 1989–90 in southwestern Virginia] is a wonderful example of a community solidarity union. Everyone pulled together: teachers and high school kids and college teachers and ex-nuns. The whole community was dealing with the health care of retired miners. Nothing is pulling together diverse groups in the communities anymore. Now middle-class people have concerns about aging and retirement, and young people can't get jobs of any kind.

Churches are one of the few places that can still make a difference, if they can do it. Some of us are working to push social justice issues at the congregational level, for example, showing that health care is not about Republicans or Democrats but a human rights issue. But sometimes retired conservatives with good pensions have a hard time making that move. So I try to worm my way into situations where I can have some influence and try to make a change and get them working on certain issues.

My church is feeding Honduran and Guatemalan kids in the trailer courts. By doing that, we are forming relationships and changing minds about the people as a result. We can look at service work and push it further. Service relationships can develop deeper relationships, and then folks can see why people are in the situation they are in and look for root causes, look behind the causes we are serving. That can cause people to get excited. Then, they can let other people in the congregation know. But sometimes the churches are unable to move. You just have to worm your way in around the edges. Just keep doing it.

The River Farm is exciting now. We bought the farm in 1972. People have stuck with it through the years. It's a good location because it's in between Highlander and Appalshop. That became a route for people from all over the world. People at the farm combined media, popular education, living on the land. I was a link between Highlander and Appalshop because I worked in both places.

Another generation is coming on now. It's more of a real organic farm. Some of the dreams I had are coming true. Folks there are getting certified organic, looking at their carbon footprint, getting funding for saving the forests, monitoring the water.

Looking back, I can see that I preached taking risks, so obviously I had to do it, too. I could have stayed at Clinch Valley College. But it was the year of the snake, and I shed my skin and dropped out of academic life. I had a reputation for being a radical, even though I didn't feel like I was doing anything that radical. So I was taking a big risk in leaving. I didn't have any real income. I took a job at Highlander and lived on the River Farm and started working with health clinics.

I always told social work students: Don't be afraid to lose your job. It can be a great opportunity. Stand up for what is right. Criticize what is wrong, even if you lose your job. Don't just accept things.

I always knew that I had friends with sofas that I could sleep on. Since I didn't have children, it was just me. I always thought it was important to do and be who I am. I have been a risk taker.

Young people today don't have permanent jobs anymore. You can't count on working in a factory and getting a pension. The challenge is to keep learning, keep searching and reading and talking and finding ways to keep learning. Take a class, join a reading club, start a book club, keep reading and thinking and talking and sharing ideas with people. Travel.

When I travel, I don't try to acculturate but assimilate. It's not easy to acculturate, but it is easy to assimilate. It's important to be who you are but also able to participate in other people's lifestyles. You don't have to change and go native, just appreciate and live with the people you meet. Developing relationships is the most important thing about working in different cultures and environments.

Steve: In one piece in this book, you say your proudest achievement was helping build the Library at Wise. Why do you think that?

Helen: I used what I had learned working in politics in Georgia. Ellis Arnall had created a safe space for progressives in Georgia when I was in college. Eighteen-year-olds were given the right to vote. The League of Women Voters started forming student leagues. GSCW was the first. I learned how county politics worked in that election [of 1946].

At Wise, I had students in every part of the county. County leaders didn't want to fund the library, so they didn't want to do the [library] demonstration project. So I used the skills I had learned from politics in Georgia to make the library happen in Wise.

We asked women's groups in every community in the county to support the library. Some of the women were wives of coal operators. We made a film showing the bookmobile going to the feeder schools, showing kids piling out of schools and going into the bookmobile. All the women's clubs came when the vote for the library happened. The leaders had to vote for it. They didn't have a choice. All the women and the women's clubs worked together. It was not the most radical thing, but it's a great success story. I am proud of it. It's still a great library now, one of the best in the state. The library has made a difference.

Steve: What are some of your other proud moments, your legacies?

Helen: Well, I am not really the grandmother of Appalachian studies. I really developed my ideas through Paulo Freire's influence. I was trying to develop a curriculum that was activist learning about the region, getting the students engaged to learn about the region.

I am proud about doing the article on colonialism ["Fatalism or the Coal Industry?"]. But what I do is take other people's ideas and make them popular, readable. Harry Caudill used the term "colonialism" [in his book *Night Comes to the Cumberlands*]. So I used it, and then other people started popularizing the colonialism model. I am more of a popularizer in my writing. I have more of a journalism style than a detailed researcher.

I pull things from other people and make it fit the current situation. For example, that piece I wrote about "A Clean Glass of Water." That idea came from George Brosi [of Berea]. I heard him mention it, and I thought it was a good idea, so I used it. I like to take ideas and make them fit what is going on.

Steve: You have the ability to see things others don't see and apply them.

Helen: I see connections, the big picture rather than the details. I try to tell the story. Even if something is against your idea, you can still see the big picture.

Judi: You really went out there and talked and wrote about your ideas. You didn't just have ideas and stay in the library.

Helen: I helped other colleges and universities start Appalachian studies programs. I would take Jack Wright, who was my student, and he would play music. John Tiller, a local coal miner, would come, too, and he would talk. We went to Virginia Polytechnic Institute [in Blacksburg], for example, where a group of students were trying to start an Appalachian studies program. We went to many colleges. East Tennessee State had a meeting about Appalachian studies, and we were there.

Judi: So you took ideas and planted them in other places.

Helen: Yes, I took ideas other times, too, to Berea College and Lees [Junior] College in [Jackson, Kentucky]. There were many people moving in several different directions throughout the region, but I was a spark there at Clinch Valley. For example, Bill Best brought the Council of Southern Mountains group to Clinch Valley to talk about Appalachian studies.

Another achievement I am proud of is restarting the interest in economy at Highlander with Sue Thrasher. "Picking Up the Pieces" was the best workshop I ever did. We invited three women from ten different women's organizations, so we heard these incredible stories from grandmothers, mothers, and daughters. We put the stories together to write *Picking Up the Pieces,* and it became influential in a lot of ways.

As did the Science for Citizens forums on the environment throughout the region. That helped strengthen the environmental movement. These forums initiated something that grew into the environmental program at Highlander. We started looking at Kingsport, [Tennessee], looking at the pollutants in the chemical industry there, and also at Charleston, [West Virginia]. We were the first ones to look at the chemical industry. That really stirred the waters. We did a lot of workshops.

What we did was to show up when things started boiling up in a community, like Bumpass Cove [in eastern Tennessee]. We went to places where things were stirring, like Pigeon River [in eastern Tennessee] and Yellow Creek [in eastern Kentucky]. We would get them to ask us to get involved. Highlander had perpetuated the image that we were not organizers, just educators. The work that I did made it more acceptable for Highlander to organize or start something. Organizing is not as bad a word now as it used to be. I didn't do the organizing but helped stimulate it. I saw that health problems needed to include environmental problems at the same time, like at Bumpass Cove.

Judi: So you were working with others "at the right time," pushing them to the next steps.

Helen: Working on the environmental problems led us to the economics, the need to understand economics. So we put together *The Jellico Handbook.* We used the pedagogy of popular education, pulling together a lot of information from other places, making it fit local situations, looking at root causes.

Steve: In one of your talks, you said: "This is the time to celebrate women in the mountains." Do you think that is a legacy?

Helen: I fought battles for being hired and for equal treatment for myself. Then when I began working with community groups, I saw that the women were the major movers and shakers; maybe it has something to do with them having Cherokee matrilineal ancestry. The mountains have a lot of activist women and grassroots organizations run by women. It's partly because the men were in the mines. The women had to manage things outside. The men were underground; they couldn't do things in the day. They had to turn over management to their wives. That's what I found out in my dissertation. I found out about women's roles in the mountains. Women are doing the leadership in the grassroots groups. Look at Eula Hall [founder of the Mud Creek Clinic in Kentucky], Maxine Waller [in Ivanhoe, Virginia], Addie Davis and Frankie Patton [in McDowell County, West Virginia]. They are really strong women.

When I was a child, people used to say if you can kiss your elbow, you can turn into a boy. As a child, I resented the inequality of women. Girls couldn't do what boys could do. They didn't want to be considered masculine. My father used to say he was being punished by having to live with all women. He was a Boy Scout leader. He would take them on trips. We always had Boy Scouts around the house.

But my mother said my father should pay more attention to his daughters and teach them, too. So he tried and took a special interest in teaching me how to drive. He wanted me to be independent. Neither parent ever tried to keep me at home. When I wanted to take part in the YWCA Students in Industry Project in Hartford, Connecticut, in 1945, they let me go. They pushed me to do things, even as a girl. My father made a big thing of being a Matthews.

The feminist stuff was in me since the beginning, an insistence on being myself and showing who I am. I'm not sure I know who I am right now though. I am still learning how to be an elder. Now that I am in the end-of-life phase, I am thinking about how do you spend your last years? What is your role? I have some writing I want to do if I can keep my mind together.

I still want to write the story of Vicki, my mother's mother, who never married and lived as a recluse, smoking Asthmadore cigarettes. I would need to take more time to learn about the turn of the century and what women were like in the 1890s. I would need to know more about rural Georgia. I am thinking about the book by Linda Tate, *Power in the Blood,* an enlarged family history, as a possible model.

I want to know more about the history of the Harris family coming into Georgia. My mother never talked to me about her family because she was embarrassed by Vicki's story. But my mother did tell me, "Your father never held it against me."

Vicki lived with us when I was a little girl, but she mostly stayed in her room and didn't take meals with us. One time when I was sick, Vicki gave me tea made out of chicken droppings. My mother had a fit and told her never to do it again. I remember when Vicki died. I was five or six. I saw buzzards flying around, and I thought they were angels.

I wasn't told the whole story about Vicki until I was a teenager. My mother called me and my younger sister JoAnn together to tell us the story as a warning. My mother didn't ever tell us her father's name, so I still wonder who my grandfather was.

I gained a new understanding about Vicki when I was in my twenties or thirties and smelled pot for the first time. I immediately recognized it as the smell of my grandmother's room and those Asthmadore cigarettes she smoked. Now that I am back in Georgia, I think of Vicki every day. She haunts me. She is in me. I have her picture on my wall at home. I have other pictures of her, too, but she is not smiling in any of them.

Judi: I hope you will write Vicki's story. I wanted to know more about her when I was working on chapter 1. It is important for us today to know about women like her who were silenced and isolated for not following sexual and social mores. It is important to understand what long-term impact that silencing had on their families.

Helen: I don't feel like I have a family anymore, but one of my talents is making friends, so there was no place in Appalachia where I couldn't find a sofa if my car broke down. Appalshop and the River Farm are at the center of the universe for the region. I felt out of touch in Lexington at the University of Kentucky. I still read the *Mountain Eagle* [the Whitesburg, Kentucky, weekly newspaper].

Judi: I like how you have fun being an activist.

Helen: I miss the community groups in central Appalachia. I enjoy the struggle. You've got to enjoy it. I like what Emma Goldman said: "If I can't dance, I don't want to be part of your revolution." I enjoy the conflict to some extent. Myles Horton always said, "The best way to know someone is to know who their enemies are."

Steve: I never could understand why the coal operators were so threatened by aging college professors like us.

Helen: My teaching philosophy was, "If you can't change them or make them learn, you can confuse them or make their lives miserable." Confusion can make them start thinking. Make folks confront their ideas, throw stuff at them. Ask them questions, keep asking why why why?

Steve: Looking back now, do you have any regrets?

Helen: I used to regret not going to Chapel Hill instead of Duke. I was invited by Howard Odum to come to Chapel Hill. Sometimes I think I should not have married. I did not want to get married, but that's what you did, and everyone wanted me to get married. But then getting married put me into all the great things that happened to me. It led to a situation that is really good. I had real choices. What would have happened if I didn't marry? Maybe I would have stayed in Georgia? Gotten into politics? But Gene Talmadge got reelected, and everyone I worked with in that campaign left the state. I wouldn't have gone to the Appalachia coalfields if I hadn't married. People ask me about why I got so interested in coal. I say, if I was living in the cotton fields, I'd be writing about cotton.

You just have to look for opportunities where you can to create a little trouble, to make changes where you are. I am at the point of thinking about where I want to go next. Where you are, you dig in and do what you can.

Chronology

1924	Born in Nicholson, Georgia, to Hugh and Maurie Harris Matthews
1934	Moves with family to Cumming, Georgia
1941	Graduates from Forsyth County High School, Cumming
1941	Attends Bessie Tift College, Forsyth, Georgia
1942	Works for insurance company in Atlanta
1942	Works as secretary to Forsyth County school superintendent in Cumming
1943–46	Attends Georgia State College for Women in Milledgeville; works in library; plays leading roles on yearbook staff her junior and senior years
1945	Participates in YWCA "Students in Industry" project, Hartford, Connecticut
1946	Graduates from Georgia State College for Women with a BA in social science
1946	Codirects "Students for Good Government" campaign for Jimmy Carmichael, candidate for governor of Georgia; lives in hotel campaign headquarters, Atlanta
1946–47	Enters graduate school, studying sociology and anthropology at Duke University; meets Judd Lewis of Virginia
1947	Returns to Atlanta to become a speechwriter for Governor Melvin Thompson; marries Judd Lewis
1948	Leaves governor's office to work with student YWCA regional office; is arrested for participating in interracial meetings organized by the YWCA; moves to Virginia with Judd

1948	Enters the graduate program at the University of Virginia School of Sociology and Anthropology; becomes a Phelps-Stokes fellow
1948	Serves as the director of the Bureau of Population and Economic Research, studying the impact of manufacturing on road use for the Bureau of Roads
1949	Receives her MA in sociology from the University of Virginia, writing a thesis entitled "The Woman Movement and the Negro Movement: Parallel Struggles for Rights"
1952–55	Serves as a social worker with the American Red Cross, Richmond, Virginia
1955	Accepts job at Clinch Valley College, a new branch of the University of Virginia in Wise, as a librarian and lecturer in sociology
1959	Works as a summer lecturer in sociology, University of Virginia, Charlottesville
1962	Receives a National Science Foundation Summer Institute grant and studies anthropology at the University of California, Berkeley
1964	Spends six months in Paris studying French
1964	Receives a National Science Foundation faculty award and enters graduate programs in sociology and anthropology at the University of Kentucky
1966	Lectures at the University of Kentucky
1966	Travels to the Yucatan, visiting Mayan ruins
1967–69	Receives Bureau of Mines grants for coal mining research; studies effects of mechanization on coal miners and families and conducts comparative study of zinc mining
1967	Becomes an assistant professor of sociology and anthropology at East Tennessee State University, creating an MA program in sociology
1969	Is fired by East Tennessee State University
1969	Rejoins the faculty at Clinch Valley College; develops rural social work program and launches Appalachian studies and urban sociology courses
1970	Earns her PhD in sociology from the University of Kentucky, writing a dissertation entitled "Occupational Roles and Family Roles: A Study of Coal Mining Families in the Southern Appalachians"

1972	Copurchases the River Farm on the Clinch River in Dungannon, Virginia
1974	Is divorced from Judd Lewis; moves to River Farm
1975	Receives a National Science Foundation postdoctoral fellowship to study coal mining in Wales; lives in Brynamman, Wales; works with Miners Library at University of Wales-Swansea, serving as a lecturer with the Extramural Program, University College
1976	Arranges and leads field trip in Wales for a group of West Virginia miners
1977	Resigns from Clinch Valley College
1977	Joins Highlander Research and Education Center staff; works with health programs and community clinics in Central Appalachian region
1978–79	Serves as acting director of Highlander Center
1978	Directs study and produces a report entitled "Coal Productivity and Community: The Impact of the National Energy Plan in the Eastern Coalfields" for the U.S. Department of Energy
1978	Coedits, with Linda Johnson and Donald Askins, *Colonialism in Modern America: The Appalachian Case*
1978	Delivers the Distinguished Alumni Lecture, University of Kentucky
1979	Organizes a series of forums on environmental health problems in Appalachia, funded by the National Science Foundation Science for Citizens Program
1979	Organizes and leads a three-week cultural visit of six Welsh coal miners to Appalachia
1979	Attends the international Congress of Folk Medicine in Peru
1980	Works as a visiting professor in anthropology and Appalachian studies for the National Collegiate Honors Semester in Appalachian Culture, Appalachian State University
1980	Arranges and leads a field trip to Wales for American women coal miners
1980	Attends an international conference on adult education and participatory research in Yugoslavia
1980–84	Serves as the project director for the "History of Appalachia" film series at Appalshop, resulting in *Strangers and Kin* and *Long Journey Home*

1980–81	Becomes a member of the National Academy of Sciences, the National Research Council, and the Committee on Underground Coal Mine Safety; works on a study of mine safety in underground coal mines
1981	Receives the Appalachian Leadership Award at Mars Hill College
1985–90	Working part-time, develops the Highlander Economic Education Program and curriculum materials for the Fund for the Improvement of Post-Secondary Education
1985	Travels to Nicaragua, visiting education programs and community groups
1986	Receives award in community education from the Clinch River Educational Center
1986	Organizes workshop for women on economics with Sue Thrasher at the Highlander Center; coedits the resulting booklet, *Picking Up the Pieces: Women In and Out of Work in the Rural South*
1986	Travels in Great Britain, Holland, Belgium, and France, visiting community groups and popular education programs
1986	Begins teaching in the summer term for seminarians at the Appalachian Ministries Resource Center in Berea, Kentucky
1987	Travels in Botswana, Zimbabwe, and South Africa, visiting community groups
1987–90	Works on local history project in Ivanhoe, Virginia, for Highlander Economics Education and Glenmary Research Center
1988	Returns to Nicaragua
1990	Coedits a two-volume history of Ivanhoe, *Remembering Our Past, Building Our Future,* and *Telling Our Stories, Sharing Our Lives.* Volume 1 wins the Weatherford Award.
1990–97	Leaves River Farm to live in the Myles Horton House at Highlander and direct the Myles and Zilphia Horton Chair of Education for Social Change
1990–92	Works with McDowell County Economic Development Agency in West Virginia and Highlander Center to develop workshops on community-based development
1991	Participates in workshop on Cultural Factors in Rural Development, East-West Center, Honolulu, Hawaii
1993	Makes a second visit to Zimbabwe, Namibia, and South Africa

1993–95	Serves as interim director of the Appalachian Center, Berea College
1994	Receives the Appalachian Educational Service Award from Carson-Newman College
1995–97	Teaches sociology course on collaborative research; works with Community Partnership Center on participatory evaluation project, University of Tennessee; serves as regional researcher with learning team, McDowell County
1995	Cowrites *It Comes from the People: Community Development and Local Theology,* with Mary Ann Hinsdale and Maxine Waller
1996	Travels to Cuba for International Education Conference
1996	Receives the Cratis D. Williams Service Award of the Appalachian Studies Association
1997	Attends the World Congress of Participatory Action Research, Cartagena, Colombia; presents paper on her community-based work at Ivanhoe
1997	Retires from Highlander Center and moves to north Georgia
1997	Receives the Laurel Leaves Award from Appalachian Consortium, Mountain Association for Community Economic Development in Berea; establishes the Helen Lewis Community Leadership Award
1997–2000	Serves as an advisor to the Kellogg Foundation International Leadership Program; visits Africa, South America, and England
1999	Receives an Honorary Doctor of Letters from Emory and Henry College
1999	Serves as a visiting faculty member in the Appalachian Studies Graduate Program, Appalachian State University
2000	Receives the honorary degree Doctor of Divinity from Wake Forest University
2000	Teaches at the Institute for Continuing Learning, Young Harris College, Georgia
2001	Develops and coleads summer course with Pat Beaver on "South Wales after Coal" in Wales and at Appalachian State University
2002	Teaches January short course at Berea College
2002	Serves as president of the Appalachian Studies Association. At its annual conference in Unicoi, Georgia, the ASA creates the Helen Lewis Community Service Award.

2002   Receives a commendation from the Kentucky State Legislature. Berea College develops the Helen Lewis Semester.

2003   Cowrites *Mountain Sisters: From Convent to Community in Appalachia,* with Monica Appleby

2003–7   Teaches at Toccoa Falls College, Epworth campus, Georgia

2004   Helen Lewis Lecture Series established by the Craddock Center, Cherry Log, Georgia

2004   Teaches January graduate seminar "Studies with Helen Lewis" at Appalachian State University; conducts the oral history workshop "Remembering Byron Herbert Reece," with Bettie Sellers, at the Institute for Continuing Learning, Young Harris College

2004   Delivers the Inaugural Alumni Lecture at the inauguration of Dorothy Leland as president of Georgia College and State University.

2005   Receives Alumni Achievement Award, Georgia College and State University

2006   Teaches at the Wake Forest University Divinity School; leads the Appalachian Ministries Travel Seminar, Valle Crucis, North Carolina

2006   Receives Service Award from Berea College

2009   Appears in the PBS film series *Appalachia: A History of Mountains and People*

2010   Receives honorary doctorate from Berea College; presents commencement lecture

Bibliography

Works by Helen Matthews Lewis

Manuscript and/or digital copies of all manuscript works listed in the bibliography can be found in the Helen Matthews Lewis Papers, W. L. Eury Appalachian Collection, Special Collections, Appalachian State University, Boone, NC.

Lewis, Helen Matthews. "African Journey, Some Notes and Reflections." April 17, 1993.

———. "Afterword." In *Down to Earth, People of Appalachia,* ed. Kenneth Murray. Boone, NC: Appalachian Consortium Press, 1974.

———. "Appalachian Foremothers: A Celebration of Mountain Women." Paper presented at Southeast Community College, Cumberland, KY, January 2001.

———. "Appalachian Studies as a Model of Education for Social Change and Regional Stewardship." Paper presented at Ohio University, Athens, 2007.

———. "Appalachian Studies: Telling the Truth or Preserving the Myths." Paper presented at Morehead University, Morehead, KY, 2007.

———. "Appalachian Studies—The Next Step." *Appalachian Journal* 9 [a special issue on the state of regional studies], nos. 2–3 (1982): 162–71.

———. "Appalachian Women and Social Action." Paper presented at Symposium on Women in Appalachia, Mars Hill College, Mars Hill, NC, 1977.

———. "Appalshop and the History of Appalachia." *Appalachian Journal* 11, no. 4 (1984): 410–25.

———. "Appalshop: Preserving, Participating in, and Creating Southern Mountain Culture." In *Cultural Heritage Conservation in the American South,* ed. Benita Howell. Athens: University of Georgia Press, 1990.

———. "*Are* They Old Enough to Vote—Georgia's Youth Take Up the Ballot." Typescript submitted to *Independent Woman,* June 1945. Shorter version published in *Intercollegiate,* 1945.

————, producer-narrator. *Artus Moser of Buckeye Cove, N.C.* Film. Dir. Anne Lewis. Appalshop Films, 1985.

————. "Backwoods Rebels—Resistance in the Appalachian Mountains." In *Conflict and Peacemaking in Appalachia.* Amesville, OH: Coalition for Appalachian Ministry, 1987.

————, consultant. *Beyond Measure: Appalachian Culture and Economy.* DVD. Dir. Herb E. Smith. Appalshop Films, 1994.

————. "Bright Lights and Bright Morning Star: Bicultural Appalachians." Paper presented at the Conference on Appalachians in Urban Areas, Academy for Contemporary Problems, Columbus, OH, 1974.

————, consultant-narrator. *Buffalo Creek Revisited.* Film. Dir. Mimi Pickering. Appalshop Films, 1984.

————. "Byron Herbert Reece and Don West—Two North Georgia Poets: Same Time, Same Place, Divergent Paths." Paper presented at meeting of the Byron Herbert Reece Society, Young Harris, GA, 2010.

————. "The Changing Coal Communities in the Southern Appalachian Coal Fields." Paper presented at the International Seminar on Social Change in the Mining Community, West Virginia University, Morgantown, 1967.

————. "Cherry Log Sermon." Sermon presented at the Cherry Log Christian Church, GA, August 12, 2007.

————. "A Clean Glass of Water for Every Appalachian Child." Paper presented at the Appalachian Transition Initiative, University of Colorado, Denver, 2010.

————. "Coal and After Coal." Paper presented at Virginia Polytechnic University, Blacksburg, 1996.

————. "Coal Miners' Peer Groups and Family Roles." Paper presented at the American Anthropological Association, San Diego, 1970.

————. "Coal Mining Communities of South Wales." Paper presented at the Appalachian Studies Conference, Berea, KY, 1985.

————, consultant-narrator. *Coalmining Women.* Film. Dir. Elizabeth Barret. Appalshop Films, 1982.

————. "Community Development as Ministry." Dotson Nelson Lecture on Religion in Life, presented at Samford University, Birmingham, AL, October 10, 1995.

————. "Community Diagnosis—Environmental Health Problems in Appalachia." Paper presented at the Primary Health Conference, Indiana University School of Nursing, 1981.

————. "Community History." *Magazine of History* 11, no. 3 (1997): 20–22.

————. "Community Studies: Writing with the Community." Paper presented at the John B. Stephenson Center for Appalachian and Comparative Highland Studies, Lees McRae College, Banner Elk, NC, 2001.

————. "Controversy over Proposed Federal Regulations of Surface Mining of Coal, a Statement." *Congressional Digest* 53 (May 1974): 156, 158.

————. "Dealing with Powers and Principalities." Paper presented at Wake Forest Seminary, Winston-Salem, NC, 2000.

————. "Delivery of Services in Appalachia: Some Comments on Health Care and Community Development." Statement before the Presidential Reorganization Staff, Washington, DC, 1977.

————. "Doing Sociology in Appalachia." Paper presented at the Plenary Session, Southern Sociology Association, Atlanta, 1994.

————. "Explorations in Kinship Analysis: A Study of Appalachian Kinship Systems." Paper presented at the Southern Sociological Association, Atlanta, 1967.

————. "Fatalism or the Coal Industry? Contrasting Views of Appalachian Problems." *Mountain Life and Work* (1970). Reprinted in *Appalachia: Social Context Past and Present,* ed. Bruce Ergood and Bruce Kuhre. Dubuque, IA: Kendall/Hunt Publishing Co., 1976.

————. "From Kingdom Come to Chestatee: The Importance of Learning History." Keynote address presented at the Appalachian Studies Conference, Unicoi, GA, 1984.

————. "A Funeral for Appalachia." In *Proceedings of Energy Crisis and Strip Mining Hearing.* Wise, VA: Interfaith Council on Corporate Responsibility, Clinch Valley College, 1974.

————. "The Future of Appalachian Studies." Symposium honoring Loyal Jones, Berea College, Berea, KY, 1993.

————. "GSCW in the 1940s: Mary Flannery Was There, Too." *Flannery O'Connor Review* 3 (2005): 49–54.

————. "The Highlander Center: Working for Justice and a Moral Economy." Paper presented on the seventy-fifth anniversary of the Highlander Center, University of Georgia, Richard B. Russell Gallery, Athens, 2008.

————. "The History of the Beginning of the Wise County Library—As I Remember It. Talk presented at the fortieth celebration of the Lonesome Pine Regional Library, November 22, 1998.

————. "The Impact of a New Manufacturing Plant upon the Socio-Economic Characteristics and Travel Habits of the People in Charlotte County, Virginia." Charlottesville: University of Virginia, Bureau of Population and Economic Research, 1951.

————. "Industrialization, Class and Regional Consciousness in Two Highland Societies: Wales and Appalachia." In *Cultural Adaptation to Mountain Environments,* ed. Patricia D. Beaver and Burton L. Purrington. Athens: University of Georgia Press, 1984.

————. "Industrialism, Class, and Regional Consciousness in Two Peripheral Regions, Wales and Appalachia." Paper presented at the British Sociological Association, Cardiff, Wales, 1983. Reprinted in *Reshaping the Image of Appalachia,* ed. Loyal Jones. Berea, KY: Berea College Appalachian Center, 1986.

————, consultant-interviewee. *Interweaving Patterns.* Video. Dir. Susan Spaulding. Virginia Humanities Project, 1989.

————, narrator. *In the Shadow of Power.* Video. Dir. Jean L. Donohue. Media Working Group, 1991.

————. "Introduction." In *Images of Appalachian Coalfields,* by Builder Levy. Philadelphia: Temple University Press, 1989.

————. "Introduction." In *The Long Haul: An Autobiography,* by Miles Horton, with Herbert Kohl and Judith Kohl. New York: Doubleday, 1990.

————. "It Has to Come from the People." In *Communities in Economic Crisis,* ed. John Gaventa. Philadelphia: Temple University Press, 1990.

————. "'It Shakes You Up'—The Social and Psychological Effects of Surface Mine Blasting." Paper presented at the Surface Mine Blasting and Public Policy Workshop, Cumberland Falls, KY, 1978.

————, project director. *Long Journey Home.* Film. Dir. Elizabeth Barret. Appalshop Films, 1987.

————, researcher-consultant. *Mabel Parker Hardison Smith.* Film. Dir. Anne Lewis Johnson. Appalshop Films, 1985.

————. "Mary Flannery O'Connor at Georgia State College for Women." Gallery talk presented at the Archives Opening, Georgia College and State University, Milledgeville, 2005.

————. "Maxine Waller: The Making of a Community Organizer." *Now and Then: The Appalachian Magazine* 7, no. 1 (1990): 12–14.

————. "Medicos and Mountaineers: The Meeting of Two Cultures." Talk given at Appalachian Regional Hospital's Spring Scientific Session, Bristol, VA, April 22, 1971.

————. "The Missionary Movement in the Southern Mountains: A Case Study of the Episcopal Church in Southwest Virginia." Paper presented at the Society for Religion in Higher Education, Maryville, TN, 1974.

————. "My Life and Good Times in the Mountains; or, Life and Learning in Central Appalachia." Carson-Newman Studies. Reprint, New Market, TN: Highlander Research and Education Center, 1994.

————. "My Life as an Activist." Paper presented at Appalachian State University, Judaic, Holocaust and Peace Studies, Boone, NC, 2007.

————. "North Georgia: Is It Southern, Appalachian or Hillbilly Chic?" Paper presented at the Georgia Literary Festival, Blue Ridge, 2007.

————. "Notes on the Educational Methodology of the HEEP Curriculum." 1988. Typescript notes on the Highlander Economic Education Project.

————. "Occupational Roles and Family Roles: A Study of Coal Mining Families in the Southern Appalachians." PhD diss., University of Kentucky, 1970.

————. "On Conserving the Nation's Human Resources." *Christian Index,* March 2, 1944, 3–4.

————. "Oral History, Spoken History: Why and How." Paper presented at the Oral History Workshop, Writers Conference, Blue Ridge, GA, 2006.

————. "Participatory Research and Education for Social Change: Highlander Research and Education Center." In *Handbook of Action Research,* ed. Peter Reason and Hilary Bradbury. Thousand Oaks, CA: Sage Publications, 1999.

————. "Participatory Research in Community Development and Local Theology: Ivanhoe, Virginia, USA." Paper presented at the World Congress on Participatory Action Research, Cartagena, Colombia, 1997.

———. "Participatory Research Theory and Methodology." Paper presented at the Southern Sociological Society, Knoxville, TN, 1983.

———. "Paulo Freire at Highlander." In *Memories of Paulo,* ed. Tom Wilson, Peter Park, and Anaida Colon-Muniz. Rotterdam, The Netherlands: Sense Publications, 2010.

———. "Preparing Appalachian Communities for Changing Environmental and Occupational Health Needs." Final report to the National Science Foundation, July 15, 1980.

———. "Proposal for a Severance Tax on Coal, Wise, Virginia." 1960.

———. "Queen of the Meadow (Joe Pye Weed)." *Appalachian Heritage* 35, no. 4 (2007): 100–101.

———. "Rebuilding Communities: A Twelve-Step Recovery Program." Paper presented at Appalachian State University, Boone, NC, 2001. Reprinted in *Appalachian Journal* 34, nos. 3–4 (2007): 316–25, and in *Participatory Development in Appalachia,* ed. Susan E. Keefe. Knoxville: University of Tennessee Press, 2009.

———. "Rebuilding Communities: Collaborative Research—College and Community." Paper presented at Berea College, Berea, KY, 2002.

———. "Redbud Trees (Flowering Judas)." *Appalachian Heritage* 37, no. 3 (2009): 68–69.

———. "Remarks Made to Energy Crisis and Strip Mining Hearing, Interfaith Council on Corporate Responsibility." Clinch Valley College of the University of Virginia, Wise. March 14, 1974.

———. "Report on Summer Experience in Campaign Headquarters for Governor of Georgia, 1946." Typescript.

———. "Response to the Region: The Role of a Small State-Supported College in Central Appalachia." Paper presented at the Southern Sociological Society, Atlanta, 1977.

———. "Risky Business: The Coal Industry in Appalachia." Paper presented at the Coal Institute, Lexington, 1987.

———, consultant and narrator. *Rough Side of the Mountain.* Video. Dir. Anne Lewis. Appalshop Films, 1997.

———. "Rural Families: Maintaining a Lifestyle." *Graduate Woman* 76, no. 2 (1981): 30, 44.

———. "Rural Healthcare in Appalachia." *Highlander Reports,* Newmarket, TN, December 1977.

———, consultant-narrator. *Sara Ogan Gunning.* Video. Dir. Mimi Pickering. Appalshop Films, 1988.

———. "Social Impact—Ignored or Mistreated Component in Environmental Impact Research." *Human Services in the Rural Environment* (1980): 12–16.

———. "Social Impact of Environmental Research." *Human Services in the Rural Environment* 5, no. 2 (1980): 12–16.

———. "Sociologist as Film Maker: Dealing with the Images of Appalachia, Community and Appalachian Sociology." Paper presented at symposium in honor of Willis A. Sutton Jr. and James S. Brown, University of Kentucky, Lexington, 1982.

———. "State College: The Clinch Valley Experience." *Mountain Review* 2, no. 4 (1978): 30–34.

———. *Strangers and Kin: A History of the Hillbilly Image—Notes on the Making of the Film on the History of Images about Appalachia.* Whitesburg, KY: Appalshop Films, 1984.

———, consultant-narrator. *Strip Mining, Energy, Environment, and Economics.* Film. Appalshop Films, 1979.

———. "The Subcultures of the Southern Appalachians: Their Origins and Boundary Maintenance." *Virginia Geographer,* no. 3 (spring 1968): 2–8.

———. "Telling Our Appalachian Stories, Changes over Time." Keynote address presented at Conference on the Influence of Southern Appalachian Culture on Mental Health and Substance Abuse Treatment, Lake Junaluska Assembly, NC, 1993.

———. "Testimony Presented at Hearings of Joint Subcommittees, Mines and Mining and Environment of the Interior and Insular Affairs Committee of the U.S. House of Representatives." Typescript notes, April 19, 1973.

———. "Toward Safer Underground Coal Mines." Committee on Underground Mine Safety, National Academy of Sciences. Washington, DC: National Academy Press, 1982.

———. "Tradition and Change: Lessons from the 40s." Inaugural lecture presented at Georgia College and State University, Milledgeville, 2004.

———. "Using Culture in Rural Development: Ivanhoe, Virginia." Workshop on Cultural Factors in Rural Development, East West Center, Honolulu, 1990.

———. "Using Participatory Research to Rebuild Communities." Paper presented at the Action Research Symposium, Fielding Institute, Alexandria, VA, 2001.

———. "Wales and Appalachia—Coal Mining, Culture and Conflict." *Appalachian Journal* 10, no. 4 (1982): 350–57.

———. "Wales and Appalachia: Today and the Future—Lessons to Learn from Each Other." Paper presented at the University of Wales Conference, Banwen Education Center, Onllyn, Wales, 1997.

———, researcher-consultant. *War on Poverty: Twenty Years Later.* Television documentary series. Appalshop Films, 1984–85.

———. "We Are Giving Birth to a New Way of Life: An Interview with Maxine Waller." *Anthropology and Humanism Quarterly* 13, no. 4 (1988): 119–26.

———. "Welsh Miners in the American Coal Fields—Culture Shock and Response." Unpublished report, 1979. Typescript notes.

———. "We're Tired of Being Guinea Pigs: A Handbook for Citizens on Environmental Health in Appalachia." New Market, TN: Highlander Research and Education Center, Health Project Committee, 1980.

———. "Whose Development? Whose Movement? What Justice? What Sustainability?

Perspectives from Latin America and Appalachia." Paper presented at symposium at Appalachian State University, Boone, NC, 2004.

————. "The Woman Movement and the Negro Movement: Parallel Struggles for Rights." MA thesis, University of Virginia, 1949.

————. *The Woman Movement and the Negro Movement: Parallel Struggles for Rights.* Phelps-Stokes Fellowship Paper No. 19. Charlottesville: University of Virginia Press, 1949.

————. "Women and Community Development: Growing Individuals and Communities." *Mountain Promise, Newsletter of the Brushy Fork Institute* 6 (winter 1996): 1–2.

————. "Women Have Always Been." Liner notes for *Coal Mining Women,* CD. Rounder Records, 1997.

————. "Women in the Coalfields." Paper presented at the conference of the National Women in Mining, St. Louis, 1993.

————. "Women of Change." In *Women of Coal,* ed. Randall Norris and Jean-Philippe Cypres. Lexington: University Press of Kentucky, 1996.

Works by Helen Matthews Lewis and Others

Beaver, Patricia, and Helen Matthews Lewis. "'A Cold Day in Hell'—An Interview with Jerry Williamson." *Appalachian Journal* 28, no. 1 (2000): 78–115.

————. "Uncovering the Trail of Ethnic Denial: Ethnicity in Appalachia." In *Cultural Diversity in the U.S. South,* ed. Carole E. Hill and Patricia D. Beaver. Athens: University of Georgia Press, 1998.

Gaventa, John, Helen Matthews Lewis, and Susan Williams. "Disposable Communities." *Dollars and Sense* 174 (March 1992): 12–16.

Hinsdale, Mary Ann, Helen Matthews Lewis, and Maxine Waller. *It Comes from the People: Community Development and Local Theology.* Philadelphia: Temple University Press, 1995.

Hornell, Hart, Marian Bessent, and Helen V. Matthews. "Comparative Standards of Social Science Periodicals." *American Sociological Review* 12, no. 4 (1947): 444–47.

Lewis, Helen Matthews, and Monica Appleby. *Mountain Sisters: From Convent to Community in Appalachia.* Lexington: University Press of Kentucky, 2003.

Lewis, Helen Matthews, and associates. "Coal Productivity and Community: The Impact of the National Energy Plan in the Eastern Coalfields." Washington, DC: U.S. Department of Energy. Reprint, Boone, NC: Appalachian State University, Center for Appalachian Studies, 1978.

Lewis, Helen Matthews, and John Gaventa. *Case Study of Community Based Learning in Jellico, Tennessee.* New Market, TN: Highlander Research and Education Center, 1988.

————. *The Jellico Handbook: A Teacher's Guide to Community-Based Economics.* New Market, TN: Highlander Center, 1988.

————. *Participatory Education and Grassroots Development: The Case of Rural Appalachia.* London: International Institute for Environment and Development, 1991.

Lewis, Helen Matthews, John Gaventa, and Richard Greatrex. *The Welsh Tapes, 1974–1981.* New Market, TN: Highlander Research and Education Center. Archived and digitized in the W. L. Eury Appalachian Collection, Appalachian State University, Boone, NC.

Lewis, Helen Matthews, and Laurel Horton. *Come All You Coal Miners.* Slide/tape production on coal mining music. East Tennessee State University, Archive of Appalachia, 1980.

Lewis, Helen Matthews, and Myles Horton. "Transnational Corporations and the Migration of Industries in Latin America and Appalachia." In *Appalachia/America,* ed. Wilson Somerville. Johnson City, TN: Appalachian Consortium Press, 1980, pp. 22–23.

Lewis, Helen Matthews, Linda Johnson, and Don Askins. *Colonialism in Modern America: The Appalachian Case.* Boone, NC: Appalachian Consortium Press, 1978.

Lewis, Helen Matthews, with Kingsport Study Group. "It Smells Like Money." *Southern Exposure* 6, no. 2 (1978): 59–66.

Lewis, Helen Matthews, and Rich Kirby. "All That Is Native and Still Undefined: A Response to David Whisnant." In *Appalachia Inside Out,* ed. Robert J. Higgs, Ambrose N. Manning, and Jim Wayne Miller. Knoxville: University of Tennessee Press, 1995.

Lewis, Helen Matthews, and Edward E. Knipe. "Attitudes of Selected Zinc Miners and Their Wives in Tennessee." Washington, DC: Bureau of Mines, 1968–69.

———. "The Colonialism Model: The Appalachian Case." In *Colonialism in Modern America: The Appalachian Case,* ed. Helen Matthews Lewis, Linda Johnson, and Don Askins. Boone, NC: Appalachian Consortium Press, 1978.

———. "The Impact of Coal Mining on the Traditional Mountain Subculture: A Case of Peasantry Gained and Peasantry Lost." In *The Not So Solid South,* ed. Kenneth Morland. Athens: University of Georgia Press, 1971. Reprinted in *Social Change in Mining Communities,* ed. Hans Joachim Kornadt. Saarbrucken: University of Saar, 1970.

———. "The Sociological Impact of Mechanization on Coal Miners and Their Families." Washington, DC: Bureau of Mines, 1968–69.

———. "Toward a Methodology of Studying Coal Mining." Washington, DC: Bureau of Mines, 1968. Reprinted in *Social Change in Mining Communities,* ed. Hans Joachim Kornadt. Saarbrucken: University of Saar, 1970.

Lewis, Helen Matthews, Sue Easterling Kobak, and Linda Johnson. "Kinship, Religion and Colonialism in Southern Appalachia; or, Bury My Rifle at Big Stone Gap." In *Growing Up Country,* ed. Jim Axelrod. Clintwood, VA: Resource and Information Center, Council of the Southern Mountains, 1973. Reprinted in *Colonialism in Modern America: The Appalachian Case,* ed. Helen Matthews Lewis, Linda Johnson, and Don Askins. Boone, NC: Appalachian Consortium Press, 1978, pp. 113–40.

Lewis, Helen Matthews, and Suzanna O'Donnell, comps. and eds. *Ivanhoe, Virginia, Ivanhoe History Project.* Vol. 1, *Remembering Our Past, Building Our Future.* Vol. 2, *Telling Our Stories, Sharing Our Lives.* Ivanhoe, VA: Ivanhoe Civic League, 1990.

Lewis, Helen Matthews, and George Reynolds. "From the Gold Mines to the Coal Mines and the Other Way Round." Keynote address presented at the Appalachian Studies Conference. Unicoi, GA, 1996.

Lewis, Helen Matthews, Linda Selfridge, Juliet Merrifield, Sue Thrasher, Lillie Perry, and Carol Honeycutt. *Picking Up the Pieces: Women In and Out of Work in the Rural South.* New Market, TN: Highlander Research and Education Center, 1986.

Rutherford, Frances Patton, and Helen Matthews Lewis. "McDowell County, West Virginia Enterprise Community: A Report on the Learning Team's Assessment of EC Progress." Knoxville: University of Tennessee Community Partnership Center, 1998.

Interviews with Helen Matthews Lewis

Beaver, Patricia. "You've Got to Be Converted: An Interview with Helen Lewis." *Appalachian Journal* 15, no. 3 (1988): 238–64. Reprinted in *Interviewing Appalachia,* ed. J. W. Williamson and Edwin T. Arnold. Knoxville: University of Tennessee Press, 1994.

Briscoe, Lori, Erica S. Collins, Amanda Deal, Ron Hancock, and Kristyn McGraw. "Unruly Woman: An Interview with Helen Lewis." *Appalachian Journal* 27, no. 2 (2000): 164–89.

de los Reyes, Eileen, and Patricia A. Gozemba. "No Ordinary Teacher: Helen Lewis of Highlander." In *Pockets of Hope: How Students and Teachers Change the World,* ed. Eileen de los Reyes and Patricia A. Gozemba. Westport, CT: Bergin and Garvey, 2002.

Jones, Libby Falk. "'I Stay a Little Bit Angry': Portrait of Helen Lewis, Activist Teacher." *Appalachian Heritage* 34, no. 3 (2006): 52–60.

Kirkland, Taylor. "Interview with Helen Lewis." Black Mountain, NC: Radical Roots Project, 2009.

Noble, Suzanne. Interview for dissertation at Fielding Institute, 1997.

Ross, Jamie. *Appalachia: A History of Mountains and People.* Riverdale, MD: Agee Films, 2004.

Stanton, Timothy K., Dwight E. Giles Jr., and Nadinne I. Cruz. *Service Learning: A Movement's Pioneers Reflect on Its Origins, Practice, and Future.* San Francisco: Jossey-Bass, 1999.

Sorenson, Georgia Jones. "Dr. Helen Lewis, Anthropologist and Community Activist." In *Emergent Leadership.* College Park, MD: University of Maryland, Center for Political Leadership and Participation, 1992.

Williamson, J. W. "Appalshop and the History of Appalachia: Interview with Helen Lewis and Herb E. Smith." *Appalachian Journal* 11, no. 4 (1984). Reprinted in *Interviewing Appalachia,* ed. J. W. Williamson and Edwin T. Arnold. Knoxville: University of Tennessee Press, 1994.

Further Reading

Adams, Frank. *Unearthing Seeds of Fire: The Idea of Highlander.* Winston-Salem, NC: John F. Blair Publishers, 1975.

Appalachian Journal 5, no. 1, special issue, *A Guide to Appalachian Studies* (1977). Stephen Fisher, guest ed.

Appalachian Journal 9, nos. 2–3, special issue, *Assessing Appalachian Studies* (1982). Thomas A. McGowan, guest ed.

Appalachian Land Ownership Task Force. *Who Owns Appalachia? Land Ownership Patterns and Its Impact.* Lexington: University Press of Kentucky, 1983.

Barnet, Richard J., and Ronald E. Muller. *Global Reach: The Power of the Multinational Corporations.* London: Jonathan Cape, 1975.

Biles, Roger. *The South and the New Deal.* Lexington: University Press of Kentucky, 1994.

Blee, Kathleen M., and Dwight B. Billings. *The Road to Poverty: The Making of Wealth and Hardship in Appalachia.* Cambridge: Cambridge University Press, 2000.

Borg, Marcus, and John Dominic Crossan. *The Last Week: A Day-by-Day Account of Jesus's Final Week in Jerusalem.* New York: HarperCollins, 2007.

Brattain, Michelle. *The Politics of Whiteness: Race, Workers and Culture in the Modern South.* Athens: University of Georgia Press, 2001.

Brisbin, Richard. *A Strike Like No Other: Law and Resistance during the Pittston Coal Strike of 1989–90.* Baltimore: Johns Hopkins University Press, 2002.

Brown, James. *Beech Creek: A Study of a Kentucky Mountain Neighborhood.* Berea, KY: Berea College Press. 1988.

Burawoy, M. "2004 American Sociological Association Presidential Address: For Public Sociology." *American Sociological Review* 70, no. 1 (2005): 4–28.

Cash, Jean W. *Flannery O'Connor: A Life.* Knoxville: University of Tennessee Press, 2002.

Caudill, Harry. *Night Comes to the Cumberlands: A Biography of a Depressed Area.* New York: Little, Brown and Co., 1962.

Chancey, Andrew S. "Clarence Jordan (1912–1969)." *New Georgia Encyclopedia,* http://www.georgiaencyclopedia.org.

Chomsky, Noam. *American Power and the New Mandarins: Historical and Political Essays.* New York: Pantheon Books, 1969.

Clavel, Pierre. *Opposition Planning in Wales and Appalachia.* Philadelphia: Temple University Press, 1983.

Coe, Whitney Kimball, Jennifer Cohen-Jordan, Amanda T. Hedrick, Emily Schaad, and Anna Rachel Terman, with Patricia D. Beaver. "'Looking into My Culture': An Interview with Jack Wright." *Appalachian Journal* 35, no.4 (2008): 334–56.

Couto, Richard A. "Nomination of Helen Matthews Lewis for the Wonder Woman Foundation Award." 1983. Helen Matthews Lewis Papers.

Couto, Richard A., with Stephanie C. Eken. *To Give Their Gifts: Health, Community, and Democracy.* Nashville: Vanderbilt University Press, 2002.

de los Reyes, Eileen, and Patricia A. Gozemba, eds. *Pockets of Hope: How Students and Teachers Change the World.* Westport, CT: Bergin and Garvey, 2002.

Edwards, Michael, and John Gaventa, eds. *Global Citizen Action.* Boulder: Lynne Rienner, Publishers, 2001.

Eller, Ronald D. *Uneven Ground: Appalachia since 1945*. Lexington: University Press of Kentucky, 2008.

Fanon, Frantz. *A Dying Colonialism*. New York: Grove Press, 1967.

———. *The Wretched of the Earth*. New York: Grove Press, 1965.

Fisher, Stephen L. "Appalachian Studies Programs." In *The Plow Reader: Selections from an Appalachian Alternative Newsmagazine of the Late 1970s*, ed. Ann F. Richman. Abingdon, VA: Sow's Ear Press, 1996.

———, ed. *Fighting Back in Appalachia: Traditions of Resistance and Change*. Philadelphia: Temple University Press, 1993.

Fleischmann, Arnold, and Carol Pierannunzi. *Politics in Georgia*. Athens: University of Georgia Press, 1997.

Ford, Thomas, ed. *The Southern Appalachian Region: A Survey*. Lexington: University of Kentucky Press, 1962.

Freire, Paulo. *Pedagogy of the Oppressed*. New York: Seabury Press, 1970.

Gaventa, John. *Power and Powerlessness: Quiescence and Rebellion in an Appalachian Valley*. Urbana: University of Illinois Press, 1980.

Glen, John M. *Highlander, No Ordinary School, 1932–62*. Lexington: University Press of Kentucky, 1988.

Hechter, Michael. *Internal Colonialism: The Celtic Fringe in British National Development, 1536–1966*. Berkeley: University of California Press, 1999.

Henderson, Harold Paulk. *The Politics of Change in Georgia: A Political Biography of Ellis Arnall*. Athens: University of Georgia Press, 1991.

Highlander Research and Education Center. *Highlander: An Approach to Education Presented through a Collection of Writings*. New Market, TN: Highlander Center, 1989.

Horton, Aimee Isgrig. *Highlander Folk School: A History of Its Major Programs, 1932–1961*. Brooklyn, NY: Carlson Publishing, 1989.

Horton, Myles, and Paulo Freire. *We Make the Road by Walking: Conversations on Education and Social Change*. Ed. Brenda Bell, John Gaventa, and John Peters. Philadelphia: Temple University Press, 1990.

Horton, Myles, with Judith Kohl and Herbert Kohl. *The Long Haul, an Autobiography*. New York: Doubleday, 1990.

House, Silas, and Jason Howard. *Something's Rising: Appalachians Fighting Mountaintop Removal*. Lexington: University Press of Kentucky, 2009.

Jalee, Pierre. *Pillage of the Third World*. New York: Monthly Review Press, 1965.

Johannsen, Kristin, Bobbie Ann Mason, and Mary Ann Taylor-Hall, eds. *Missing Mountains: We Went to the Mountain Top but It Wasn't There*. Nicholasville, KY: Wind Publications, 2005.

Jordan, Clarence. *The Substance of Faith and Other Cotton Patch Sermons by Clarence Jordan*. Ed. Dallas Lee. New York: Association Press, 1972.

Keefe, Susan E. *Participatory Development in Appalachia: Cultural Identity, Community, and Sustainability*. Knoxville: University of Tennessee Press, 2009.

Kennedy, Brent. *The Melungeons: The Resurrection of a Proud People.* Macon, GA: Mercer University Press, 1997.

Kiffmeyer, Thomas. *Reformers to Radicals: The Appalachian Volunteers and the War on Poverty.* Lexington: University Press of Kentucky, 2008.

Kilgore, Frank, and Stacy Fowler Horton. *The Clinch River: A World Class Treasure.* St. Paul, VA: Mountain Heritage, 2006–7.

K'Meyer, Tracy E. *Interracialism and Christian Community in the Postwar South: The Story of Koinoinia Farm.* Charlottesville: University Press of Virginia, 1997.

Lewis, Ronald L. *Transforming the Appalachian Countryside: Railroads, Deforestation, and Social Change in West Virginia, 1880–1920.* Morganton: West Virginia University, 1998.

Lippmann, Walter. *Public Opinion.* New York: Harcourt, Brace and Co., 1922.

Memmi, Albert. *The Colonizer and the Colonized.* New York: Orion Press, 1965.

Merrifield, Juliet. "Putting the Scientists in Their Place: Participatory Research in Environmental and Occupational Health." New Market, TN: Highlander Research and Education Center, 1989.

Park, Peter, Mary Brydon-Miller, Budd Hall, and Ted Jackson. *Voices of Change: Participatory Research in the United States and Canada.* Toronto: OISE Press, 1993.

Pearsall, Marian. *Little Smoky Ridge: The Natural History of a Southern Appalachian Neighborhood.* Tuscaloosa: University of Alabama Press, 1959.

Reece, Erik. *Lost Mountain: A Year in the Vanishing Wilderness.* New York: Riverhead Books, 2006.

Robbins, Bruce. "Against Literary Imperialism: Storming the Barricades of the Canon." *Monthly Review* (September 2009): 29–37.

Schumacher, E. F. *Small Is Beautiful: Economics as if People Mattered.* New York: Harper and Row, 1973.

Seitz, Virginia R. *Women, Development, and Communities for Empowerment in Appalachia.* Albany: State University of New York, 1995.

Shapiro, Henry. *Appalachia on Our Mind: The Southern Mountains and Mountaineers in the American Consciousness, 1870–1920.* Chapel Hill: University of North Carolina Press, 1978.

Shnayerson, Michael. *Coal River.* New York: Farrar, Straus and Giroux, 2008.

Valentine, Charles. *Culture and Poverty.* Chicago: University of Chicago Press, 1968.

Walls, David S., and John B. Stephenson. *Appalachia in the Sixties: A Decade of Reawakening.* Lexington: University Press of Kentucky, 1972.

Ward, Harry. *Our Economic Morality and the Ethic of Jesus.* New York: Macmillan, 1929.

Weller, Jack. *Yesterday's People: Life in Contemporary Appalachia.* Lexington: University Press of Kentucky, 1965.

Williams, David S. *From Mounds to Megachurches: Georgia's Religious Heritage.* Athens: University of Georgia Press, 2008.

Williamson, J. W. *Hillbillyland: What the Movies Did to the Mountains and What the Mountains Did to the Movies.* Chapel Hill: University of North Carolina Press, 1995.

You Got to Move: Stories of Change in the South. Video. Prod. and dir. Lucy Massie Phenix, with dir. and ed. Veronica Selver. Cumberland Mountain Educational Cooperative, 1985.

Contributing Activists and Scholars

Mary Thom Adams served as the development director at Highlander from 1990 through 1999. Following her years there, she worked as a consultant, primarily in Knoxville, Tennessee, but also for many nonprofits throughout the South and in Appalachia. She currently serves as the director of development for Ijams Nature Center, a 275-acre wildlife sanctuary and environmental learning center, and continues to work with many organizations in the Knoxville area.

Monica Appleby served as the director of the New Enterprises Fund (NEF), a community development financial institution based in the New River Valley of Appalachia, before she moved to ElderSpirit Community (ESC) in Abingdon, Virginia. Both NEF and ESC were "start-ups" and typical of Monica's life and work in the region since 1959. Appleby is the author, with Helen Matthews Lewis, of *Mountain Sisters: From Convent to Community in Appalachia* (2003).

Patricia D. Beaver is the director of the Center for Appalachian Studies and a professor of anthropology at Appalachian State University. She has conducted research in China and southern Appalachia and, with Helen Lewis, developed a study-abroad program in Wales. She is the author of numerous books and articles on Appalachia, China, and Wales, and her current interests focus on ethnic diversity in the southern Appalachians, particularly African American communities, New River headwaters history and culture change, and collaborative research.

Beth Bingman is currently the managing director of Appalshop. Her earlier work at the Center for Literacy Studies at the University of Tennessee included research, evaluation, curriculum development, and design of professional development. She has published monographs, chapters, and articles on adult education and Appalachian activism and coauthored *Life at the Margins: Literacy, Language, and Technology in Everyday Life* (1997).

Richard A. Couto is Distinguished Senior Scholar in the Ethical and Creative Leadership concentration of the Interdisciplinary PhD Program of Union Institute and University. As the director of the Center for Health Services at Vanderbilt University, he worked together with Helen Matthews Lewis on community health issues, the most critical formative element of his professional life. He writes on key Appalachian and public issues. Most recently, he edited a two-volume reference handbook, *Political and Civic Leadership* (2010).

Stephen L. Fisher is a professor emeritus at Emory and Henry College. He is the editor of *Fighting Back in Appalachia: Traditions of Resistance and Change* (1993), is the coeditor of *Transforming Places: Lessons from Appalachia* (2012), and has written extensively on a variety of Appalachian issues. He has been active in a number of Appalachian resistance efforts and has worked to build links between the academic community and activists in the region.

Hywel Francis has served as Labour Member of Parliament for Aberavon, Wales, since 2001. He is a Welsh speaker and is the author of books and articles on Welsh labor, adult education, and community development. Francis is professor emeritus at Swansea University, where he founded the South Wales Miners' Library (1973), the Valleys Initiative for Adult Education (1987), and the Community University of the Valleys (1993).

John Gaventa is the director of the Coady International Institute and the vice president for international development at St. Francis Xavier University in Antigonish, Nova Scotia. He has served as the director of Highlander Center; a professor at the University of Tennessee; a fellow at the Institute of Development Studies, University of Sussex; and the chair of Oxfam Great Britain. A political sociologist and civil society practitioner, he writes on local and international development, participatory learning, and global citizenship.

Patricia A. Gozemba, professor emeritus of English and women's studies at Salem State University in Massachusetts, met Helen when she was researching and writing about how students and teachers change the world. She wrote an essay about Helen entitled "No Ordinary Teacher," excerpted here. More recently, she coauthored *Courting Equality: A Documentary History of America's First Legal Same-Sex Marriages* (2007), with Karen Kahn and photographer Marilyn Humphries.

Judith Jennings is the executive director of the Kentucky Foundation for Women, a private philanthropy supporting feminist art for social justice. She has written on the abolition of the British slave trade and gender, art, and radicalism in the eighteenth century. She taught at Union College in Barbourville, Kentucky; worked at Appalshop; and founded the Women's Center at the University of Louisville. She researched and coproduced *Stranger with a Camera,* an Appalshop documentary directed by Elizabeth Barret.

Amelia Kirby is an activist, cultural worker, and small business owner in Whitesburg, Kentucky. She worked for eight years as a media producer at the Appalshop community arts center, where she cofounded and codirected the Holler to the Hood and Thousand Kites projects. Since 2008, she has co-owned and managed Summit City, a coffee shop, bar, gallery, and live-music venue in her rural coalfields community of eastern Kentucky.

Erica Kohl-Arenas is an assistant professor at the New School's Milano School of International Affairs, Management, and Urban Policy. Originally inspired by her relationship with Helen and the Highlander Center, she worked as a popular educator and community development practitioner in a variety of settings. She is currently working on a manuscript for her book on the history of philanthropic investment in addressing migrant poverty across California's Central Valley.

Bill J. Leonard is a professor of church history and religion at Wake Forest University. He is the author or editor of eighteen books, including *Christianity in Appalachia: Profiles in Regional Pluralism* (1999), to which Helen Matthews Lewis was a contributor. For several years, he and Helen taught in the summer program of the Appalachian Ministries Educational Resource Center based in Berea, Kentucky. His latest book is *The Challenge of Being Baptist* (2010).

Juliet Merrifield has worked as an adult educator and researcher for more than thirty years. She was the principal of the Friends Centre, an independent adult-education center in Brighton, England, and earlier served as the director of the Learning from Experience Trust in London and the founding director of the Center for Literacy Studies at the University of Tennessee. She worked with Helen Matthews Lewis at the Highlander Research and Education Center in Tennessee.

William R. Schumann is an assistant professor of anthropology at the University of Pittsburgh in Bradford, Pennsylvania, and has served as lead teacher in Appalachian State University's Summer Study Abroad in Wales since 2003. While a graduate student in 2001, he served as an intern with the National Assembly for Wales. He is the author of *Toward an Anthropology of Government: Democratic Transformations and Nation Building in Wales* (2009), as well as articles on Wales and Appalachia.

Herb E. Smith has been an Appalshop filmmaker since 1969, when he began making documentaries as a Whitesburg High student. When Helen was teaching at Wise, he was one of the Appalshoppers she invited to audit her Appalachian studies class at Clinch Valley College. There, he and other young people learned about the history and culture of their homeland. Smith has more documentaries in the works.

Sue Thrasher is a senior staff member of Five Colleges, Incorporated, in Amherst, Massachusetts. She is a former staff and board member of the Highlander Research and Education Center, where she worked with Helen Matthews Lewis. She was a cofounder and the executive director of the Institute for Southern Studies and *Southern Exposure* magazine and is an author of the collaborative volume *Deep in Our Hearts: Nine White Women in the Freedom Movement* (2000).

Maxine Waller was in the Southern Appalachian Leadership Training Program (SALT) at Highlander, when Helen wanted to do a case study of community economic development. Maxine offered to help Helen, if Helen would help her write a history of Ivanhoe, and they became a dynamic duo. Maxine is now the Volunteers for Communities program manager for the Southeast

Rural Community Assistance Project, serving rural residents from Delaware to Florida. She has four wonderful grandchildren.

Jack Wright is an actor, documentary filmmaker, and musician whose work has been featured on National Public Radio, PBS, and June Appal Recordings and in Hollywood films. He is a founding member of Appalshop, which began as part of the War on Poverty in 1969. His recent projects include producing *Music of Coal: Mining Songs from the Appalachian Coalfields,* a two-CD anthology. In 2002 and 2003, he taught at Berea College as the National Endowment for the Humanities scholar of Appalachian studies.

Index

Page numbers in italics refer to photographs or their captions.

CPSIA information can be obtained at www.ICGtesting.com
Printed in the USA
BVOW08s0531210114

342071BV00013B/8/P